M000240172

More Than a Cup of Coffee and Tea

More Than a Cup of Coffee and Tea

A Generation of Lutheran-Muslim Relationships

David D. Grafton, EDITOR

FOREWORDS BY
Elizabeth K. Eaton AND
Sayyid M. Syeed

PICKWICK *Publications* · Eugene, Oregon

MORE THAN A CUP OF COFFEE AND TEA
A Generation of Lutheran-Muslim Relationships

Copyright © 2021 Wipf and Stock Publishers. All rights reserved. Except for brief quotations in critical publications or reviews, no part of this book may be reproduced in any manner without prior written permission from the publisher. Write: Permissions, Wipf and Stock Publishers, 199 W. 8th Ave., Suite 3, Eugene, OR 97401.

Pickwick Publications
An Imprint of Wipf and Stock Publishers
199 W. 8th Ave., Suite 3
Eugene, OR 97401

www.wipfandstock.com

PAPERBACK ISBN: 978-1-7252-9043-3
HARDCOVER ISBN: 978-1-7252-9044-0
EBOOK ISBN: 978-1-7252-9045-7

Cataloguing-in-Publication data:

Names: Grafton, David D., editor. | Eaton, Elizabeth K., foreword. | Syeed, Sayyid M., foreword.

Title: More than a cup of coffee and tea : a generation of Lutheran-Muslim relationships / edited by David D. Grafton ; forewords by Elizabeth K. Eaton and Sayyid M. Syeed.

Description: Eugene, OR : Pickwick Publications, 2021 | Includes bibliographical references and index.

Identifiers: ISBN 978-1-7252-9043-3 (paperback) | ISBN 978-1-7252-9044-0 (hardcover) | ISBN 978-1-7252-9045-7 (ebook)

Subjects: LCSH: Islam—Relations—Lutheran Church. | Lutheran Church—Relations—Islam. | Islam—Relations—Christianity. | Christianity and other religions—Islam.

Classification: BP172.5.A6 M58 2021 (print) | BP172.5.A6 M58 (ebook)

06/17/21

Contents

Foreword by Bishop Elizabeth K. Eaton | vii

Foreword by Sayyid M. Syeed | xi

Acknowledgments | xvii

List of Contributors | xix

Introduction | 1
—DAVID D. GRAFTON

Section 1: **Reflections on American Lutherans and Islam**

1 Beyond Apologetics: The *God and Jesus* Project | 13
—MARK SWANSON

2 Step-by-Step: A Theological Rendering of
a Consultative Panel | 31
—MICHAEL REID TRICE

3 In Inter-Religious Context: The Promise of ELCA
Lutheran-Muslim Relations | 47
—KATHRYN MARY LOHRE

4 Reconsidering Christian Responses to Islamophobia | 63
—Todd H. Green

Section 2: **Lutheran–Muslim Relationships in Context**

5 Accompaniment, Trinity-Style: Lutherans and Muslims in
Cedar-Riverside | 79
—Jane Buckley-Farlee

6 Claremont School of Theology and the Christian-Muslim
Consultant Group: Lutheran-Muslim Community Connections
in Southern California | 91
—Thomas K. Johnson

7 Re-Envisioning: A Center of Christian-Muslim Engagement
for Peace and Justice | 101
—Sara Trumm

8 Interfaith Relations and the Work of Lutherans in Palestine | 111
—Mark B. Brown

9 Christian-Muslim "Communion" in Indonesia: Challenges
and Opportunities | 123
—Fernando Sihotang

10 Senegal: Land of Hospitality, Peace, and Mutual Understanding | 141
—Peter Hanson

11 "There Is No God Save Allah": Reflections on Theological Phobias
and Habits of Hostility | 153
—J. Paul Rajashekar

*Appendix: Further Resources on Islam and Muslims in North
America and Christian–Muslim Relations* | 169

Bibliography | 177

Index | 187

Foreword

ELIZABETH A. EATON

Coming to Expect the Unimaginable

ON OCTOBER 31, 2016, the five hundredth anniversary of the Reformation was launched by a joint Lutheran-Catholic service of prayer in Sweden. Pope Francis and the leaders of the Lutheran World Federation processed down the aisle of the cathedral, all of them wearing red stoles. It took my breath away. A mere fifty years of dialogue, propelled by Vatican II, had indelibly transformed the previous four hundred fifty years of division. Luther himself never could have imagined it, and certainly most of us never expected to see this in our lifetimes. *Yet there we were.*

One year later, on Reformation Day 2017, the Evangelical Lutheran Church in America (ELCA) held a national event to commemorate the five hundredth anniversary. Once again, triumphalism gave way to reconciliation. Our public witness focused on how we are seeking to be responsible to our Lutheran legacy and responsive to our context for mission and ministry. We lifted up stories of how we, together with our Catholic, Jewish, Muslim, and historic Black church partners, are tending to that which has harmed or is harmful, seeking reconciliation and renewal. Our self-understanding as Lutherans is not defined over and against others, but in relationship *with* them.

So it was that Lutheran-Muslim relations took center stage that day. Pastor Mandy France and her physician-turned-friend Dr. Ayaz Virji told their story of building bridges of mutual understanding through town hall events across the rural Midwest. Amid rising Islamophobia, they introduced people to Islam, correcting misperceptions or mistruths. They unpacked what it means to follow Jesus' command to "love thy neighbor." They demonstrated what it means to live by faith, not in fear. They embodied what it means "to come to [our neighbor's] defense, speak well of them, and interpret everything they do in the best possible light" (Luther's explanation of the eighth commandment, *Small Catechism*). Despite death threats and vandalism, they persist in this courageous work to this day.

Five hundred years later, real-life relationships are the antidote to Luther's troubling posture toward the Ottoman Turks—Muslims he never met. In many examples throughout this book, we can see clearly how the Lutheran tradition is continually re-formed for the sake of the free course of the gospel in the world. We find ourselves considering what we are willing to risk, in love, for the sake of our neighbor. Luther himself never could have anticipated this, and perhaps some of us never could have expected these relationships to be so important in our lives. *Yet here we are.*

Our Lutheran-Muslim relations have transformed not only how we see our past, but how we see the future, together. This book invites us to see this rapid transformation up close. In the span of a single generation, deep and abiding Lutheran-Muslim relations exist today, not only through our global partnerships but in our local communities. This is supported in the synergy between two kinds of Lutheran-Muslim relations. There is the formal work of "relations" bound by the formalities of official protocol and the informal relationships between neighbors, unbounded by the messiness of daily life.

The ELCA has taken bold steps over the past two decades with our ecumenical partners and through the Lutheran World Federation to nourish healthy Lutheran-Muslim relations of both kinds. Policies, statements, resolutions, resources, dialogues, and coalitions have supported important efforts to educate ourselves about Islam, to seek mutual understanding with Muslims, and to cooperate for the common good. Importantly, since 9/11, this has included strategic work to address anti-Muslim bigotry, violence, and rhetoric in our church and in society. Yet none of that would matter without the kind of life-changing, real-life relationships that open our minds and, more importantly, our hearts. Together with my dear colleague, Dr. Sayyid Syeed, president and founding director of the Islamic Society of North America, we are working to build church-to-mosque partnerships in local communities to develop and support these kinds of transformational exchanges that make all the difference.

In 2020 and beyond, Lutherans continue to mark the five hundredth anniversary of major milestones in the ministry of Martin Luther. Luther's treatise *The Freedom of a Christian*, published in 1520, was one of the most popular texts of its time. Today, it continues to give us guidance about what is most integral to Lutheran self-understanding and witness, and so I have invited the church to study and reflect on it together. In one of his signature both/and statements, Luther encapsulates the whole of Christian life: "The Christian individual is a completely free lord of all, subject to none. The Christian individual is a completely dutiful servant of all, subject to all." Or, to use more contemporary language befitting our context: we are freed in Christ to love and serve our neighbors in our multi-religious neighborhoods. While Luther himself never could have anticipated this, we have come to expect great joy in our companionship for the journey. *There we go, by the grace of God.*

The Rev. Elizabeth A. Eaton

Presiding Bishop, Evangelical Lutheran Church in America

Foreword

Sayyid M. Syeed

I came with my family to the U.S. with a high level of expectation. We wanted to create a new abode of peace for ourselves and establish a vibrant community in this new world. This confidence came from the fact that I was not the only Muslim student coming to the U.S. There were around half a million Muslim students coming from all over the Muslim world for the first time in large numbers. The European powers had colonized the Muslim world for decades. In fact, out of fifty-seven Muslim-majority countries that are members of the Organization of Islamic Cooperation, only three were not occupied by Western nations: Saudi Arabia, Afghanistan, and Turkey. Afghanistan, however, lost this distinction when the Soviets occupied it in 1979. Because the U.S. had no colonial history in the Muslim world, the relationship was of a different nature. We felt empowered and equal, even as students.

In the 1960s, we had Muslim students in almost all the major American universities. They organized themselves into Muslim student associations and societies on their campuses, performed their *juma* (Friday) prayers, and held Ramadan and Eid events and other social functions. It was in 1963, the iconic year of MLK's March on Washington, that about one hundred Muslim student leaders from various campuses across the U.S. and Canada met at the University of Illinois, Urbana-Champaign campus, and established the Muslim Students Association of the United States and Canada (MSA). In that sense, 1963 began the nation's march toward a more inclusive society, bringing different races closer through desegregation under MLK's leadership. This was the year when America was opening up to a new religion, to become an equal partner in a more religiously inclusive society, accommodating the emergence of the Muslim community. We shared not only coffee and tea with a very hospitable and religious society, but also, in the absence of mosques, many churches opened their doors for us to organize our Friday, the two annual Eid congregational prayers, and even Sunday schools for our children.

In 1980, I was elected MSA national president. We were on a fast track to grow and build our mosques and schools. Many of the students who had finished their highest degrees—PhDs and medical specializations—settled in the U.S., partly because they were overqualified for their fields in their own countries and partly because the seeds of democracy had not sprouted in the Muslim lands liberated from stifling European occupation. Rather, it was merely a change of masters, as they were taken over by indigenous dictators and bullies like Saddam Hussein in Iraq, Nasser in Egypt, the Shah in Iran, and Gaddafi in Libya. Such dictators did not want the Muslim American experts back in their homelands, especially the ones they knew had tasted democracy. What was called "brain drain" from the Muslim world became the building blocks for a forward-looking Muslim American community.

During my leadership of the MSA, I realized that the Muslim community was no longer a student community, but rather a community of professionals, physicians, engineers, lawyers, and more. It was at that time that we changed the MSA constitution to make it a broad faith-based organization to advance the growth and development of a Muslim American community. We graduated to the Islamic Society of North America (ISNA), while the MSA remains central to college and university students.

At every stage, we have appreciated the participation in interfaith dialogues, partnerships, and projects. It helped us overcome the hesitation of our own people in going out and interacting with people of other faiths and traditions. It also helped to transform the worldview of some our neighbors and colleagues. We were blessed in that many reforms arising in other communities were creating new ways of looking at our faith and at us. For example, the Vatican, which had used all its power and resources to foist Crusades against Islam and to declare the Prophet Muhammad (peace be upon him) an "imposter," could come to terms with its own past. In 1965–66, the thousands of bishops who converged for the Second Vatican Council or Vatican II, passed the *Nostra Aetate* ("in our times") to reassess the Catholic position toward other faiths, particularly about Islam and our Prophet. They recognized that our spiritual tradition comes from the same source—the Abrahamic lineage—as the Jews and Christians. This was a total reversal, and these reforms made the American Catholic Church more open to cooperation and toward sponsoring programs and dialogue with us.

Interfaith Initiatives

In 2020, we are celebrating the fifty-seventh anniversary of ISNA. For more than half a century, we experienced what it means to live and grow as Muslims in a democracy. No other Islamic organization or Muslim country has lived that many decades in a democratic pluralist environment. Our Prophet Muhammad had to immigrate from his birth city, Mecca, where the people persecuted his followers for practicing the pluralistic religion. He had to immigrate to Medina, where the people welcomed him and appreciated his teachings. The year of the Prophet's immigration to Mecca is the beginning of the Muslim calendar, and this year is 1441 A.H.—After *Hijrah* (immigration).

Our religious events around the year like Ramadan and Hajj are calculated according to the lunar calendar. Our calendar is an all-round reminder of the immigration of the Prophet. Upon arriving in Medina to much public sentiment and applause, he could have declared himself king or dictator. Instead of taking over as a dictator, however, he invited representatives from various faith communities and tribes to collectively draft a document of understanding—the *Charter of Medina*—spelling out the rights and duties of the various entities: Jews; immigrant Muslims from Mecca and other places, the *muhajirs* (immigrants); and indigenous Muslims in Medina, the *ansar* (hosts). It was only a generation after the Prophet that the monarchy took over his legacy of *khilafat* (caliphate, regency). Muslims celebrate the great event of the Prophet's immigration, but the memory of a constitution has not been as much in the news.

For Muslim American immigrants, immigration reinforced a commitment to the document of the U.S. Constitution, because this document determined our American citizenship, rights, and roles. We appreciated the religious freedom that the Constitution guaranteed in an environment of pluralist tolerance around us. The challenge for us was the lack of familiarity with Islam and Muslims among our neighbors. It became critical for us to reach out to people of other faiths and traditions. While establishing communities around the country, our immediate task was to build institutions—Islamic centers, mosques, and schools—to practice our faith and traditions and transmit them to future generations. It took time to have adequate facilities of our own. What impressed us about our host society was their openness to welcome us in their own religious places to hold our programs.

We started producing authentic Islamic literature to introduce our faith and traditions and to explain how closely we are connected with other Abrahamic faiths. While building Islamic centers, we confronted problems about zoning, when there were people who adamantly opposed our building centers, and bitter tensions erupted in many cities. But the mainstream congregations stood by us and supported us, which helped us secure the necessary building permits, and of course offered a neighborly welcome and cooperation like shared parking. Such openness was totally beyond our expectations. The memories of degrading colonial occupation and the long history of the Crusades and religious wars had alienated the Muslim and Christian communities for centuries. The stereotypes of each other had resulted in strange kind of images of each other. We came to realize that American Christians had gone through a sea change over the centuries. While Catholics and Protestants had fought against each other in Europe, they had established a pluralist society in America. It was here that various Christian denominations had learned to live in peace and tolerance. The tests came when America itself went through difficult experiences, like the 9/11 tragedy. We made unambiguous statements denouncing those who were perpetrating terrorism in the name of Islam. President George W. Bush established "The National Commission on Terrorist Attacks Upon the United States," also known as the "9/11 Commission," which after a year of investigation, released a report about the destruction of the Twin Towers. I used to go to different meetings and conferences with two books in my hand. One was the *9/11 Commission Report*, which had conclusively established that Muslim Americans had known nothing about the conspiracy of the nineteen terrorists of 9/11. The other book I carried was the biography of Dr. Fazlur Rahman Khan, the Muslim American who is identified as the father of modern architecture and the "Einstein of Structural Engineering," who designed the one-hundred-ten-story, 1,450-foot Sears Tower (now Willis Tower) in Chicago—then the nation's tallest skyscraper—as a true representative of Muslim American contributions to America.

Our partnerships with various national faith groups and organizations became very vibrant. We started working on American issues like gun control, health insurance, and human rights here and overseas. This led to the blossoming of an environment of trust and cordiality with our colleagues from other faiths and traditions.

Of all the denominations, the Evangelical Lutheran Church in America (ECLA) has been most forthcoming. And foremost among them are Presiding Bishop Elizabeth Eaton and the soul of their interfaith outreach, Kathryn Lohre, assistant to the presiding bishop and executive for Ecumenical and Inter-Religious Relations. They represent the compassion and humility mentioned in the Qur'an (3:113–115) as the defining qualities of the true Christian:

> Yet all are not alike among the People of the Book: there are upright people who recite the messages of God in the watches of the night and prostrate themselves in worship. They believe in God and in the Last Day and enjoin what is right and forbid what is wrong, and hasten to excel each other in doing good. These are among the righteous. Whatever good they do shall not go unappreciated. God fully knows those who are pious.

As a firm believer in the Qur'an as a divine word, I have made it my life goal to look for such heroes. In trying times in the recent history of Muslim Americans, I have discovered these two people as a fulfillment of Qur'anic prophecy, not only on the personal level but also on organizational and national levels. They have offered enlightened support and understanding on the complex issues facing us all in the shaping of our nation and the world. However, there are some, masquerading as "faith activists," who are unhappy with this cordiality and use all opportunities to promote Islamophobia based on the statements and violent actions of a few misdirected overseas Muslims. Our close allies continue to work with trust and confidence in us in the corridors of power and areas of public good.

In 2010, a little-known Florida pastor proclaimed that he was going to burn the Qur'an as an expression of his misguided belief that Islam was a violent religion and that Muslims could not be trusted. We had reached a stage where we had established our credentials and built partnerships at every level in American society. But the hate that this pastor wanted to generate was worrisome not only to us but also to our allies in religious and political circles. I recall the letters of support that I received from all the mainstream religious leaders against the pastor's venomous statements. The ardent supporters included national representatives of the United States Conference of Catholic Bishops, the American Baptist Churches USA, the National Council of Churches of Christ (USA), and the presiding bishop of the Evangelical Lutheran Church in America. More than thirty Christian and Jewish organizations not only attended a press conference we held in response to these events in the National Press Building in Washington, but the event also denounced the Florida pastor. The attending representatives announced that neither his words nor his actions reflected their faith and were against the American values of freedom of religion. But the most important decision they made was to establish a campaign to fight against such Islamophobia. They rightly named this campaign "Shoulder to Shoulder: Standing with American Muslims; Upholding American Values." Shoulder to Shoulder became a reality and is financially supported and administratively run by supporting American Jewish and Christian organizations. This is a most resourceful and respected campaign, resulting out of our interfaith dialogues. It is the best example of taking multi-religious interaction beyond coffee and tea.

Sayyid M. Syeed

President of the Islamic Society of North America

Acknowledgments

IT IS ALWAYS A risk to try to capture a snapshot of current events. Any attempt at examining things as they are will soon become outdated, perhaps even obsolete. It is also risky to look back and try to make connections to the present. There is the danger that we might be held captive to a previous vision that is no longer viable or even desired, or that we might try to make connections between the present and a past that is not even there. Nevertheless, looking backwards is critically necessary if want to know how we have arrived and what choices remain in the future.

I am exceedingly grateful that the Christian contributors in this volume agreed to participate in this project. The contributors were excited to tell their stories, which in the end is what this is about: telling stories of encounter, engagement, and relationships. I am also exceedingly grateful to Presiding Bishop Elizabeth Eaton and her dialogue partner Dr. Sayyid M. Syeed, who both agreed to pen forewords to this project. The simple fact that they have put their names down together here is one small indication of where we are now and, hopefully, of the opportunities that will present themselves in the future.

Finally, many thanks to Pastor Buckley-Farlee for the title of this book—*More Than a Cup of Coffee and Tea*—which is taken directly from her experience, as reflected in her chapter.

August 2020
Hartford, Connecticut

Contributors

Mark Brown—Senior Advisor for Advocacy and Fundraising, The Lutheran World Federation World Service. Brown, a pastor of the ELCA, served as an ALC/ELCA missionary in the Middle East during much of the 1980s and as the assistant director for International Affairs and Human Rights at the ELCA Washington, D.C., office during the 1990s. He served in Jerusalem from 2004 to 2018 as the representative of the Lutheran World Federation. He supervised and administered the LWF World Service program in Palestine and Israel. In 2018, he returned to the United States to continue his work with the LWF as Senior Advisor for Advocacy and Fundraising related to the Middle East and to the LWF's Jerusalem Program, which includes Augusta Victoria Hospital.

Jane Buckley–Farlee—Often called "Cedar-Riverside's pastor," Buckley-Farlee is the senior pastor of Trinity Lutheran Congregation, Minneapolis, Minnesota. She is author of the blog *Seeing God in Little Mogadishu*.

David D. Grafton—Professor of Islamic Studies and Christian-Muslim Relations, Hartford Seminary. A pastor of the ELCA, Grafton is a theological educator who focuses on Christian-Muslim relations. He provides workshops on Muslim-Christian relations; is the author of several books, most recently, *An American Biblical Orientalism* (Lexington Books/Fortress Academic, 2019); and has been a section editor of the series *Christian-Muslim Relations: A Bibliographical History 1500–1900* (Brill, 2014–2020).

Todd H. Green—Associate Professor of Religion, Luther College. Green is a former advisor on Islamophobia in Europe at the U.S. State Department in Washington, DC. As a public scholar, Green has been interviewed by a variety of media outlets on Islamophobia, including CNN, NPR, The Washington Post, Al Jazeera, Reuters, and The Intercept. He is the author of two books on Islamophobia: *The Fear of Islam: An Introduction to Islamophobia in the West* (Fortress Press, 2019) and *Presumed Guilty: Why We Shouldn't Ask Muslims to Condemn Terrorism* (Fortress Press, 2018).

Peter Hanson—Lead Pastor of Christ the King/Cristo Rey Lutheran Church, New Brighton, Minnesota. For nearly a decade, Hanson served with ELCA-Global Mission, accompanying both the Senegal Lutheran Development Services and the Lutheran Church of Senegal in the areas of leadership development and pastoral formation. He holds a DMin in Global and Ecumenical Studies from the Episcopal Divinity School, with a thesis entitled "Variations on a Theme: Lutheran Accompaniment and God's Mission in Senegal."

Thomas K. Johnson—Director, Center for Lutheran Studies at Claremont School of Theology. Johnson is also co-founder and coordinator of Inland Valley Interfaith Working Group for Peace in the Middle East, a board member of the Christian Muslim-Consultative Group, and a co-author of the *Standing Together* project. A retired Lutheran pastor of thirty-seven years, he is also the author of four books, including *Celebrating the Seasons of Baptismal Living* (2001), and a frequent contributor to the *Lutheran Quarterly*, *Lutheran Magazine*, *Lutheran Partners*, and *Episcopal Review*. He has taught chess at the local elementary school afterschool program for the past twenty-five years.

Kathryn Mary Lohre—Assistant to the Presiding Bishop of the ELCA, Executive for Ecumenical and Inter-Religious Relations. From 2012 to 2013, Lohre served as president of the National Council of Churches of Christ (USA)—the first Lutheran and youngest woman to serve—and edited the book *For Such a Time as This: Young Adults on the Future of the Church* (2013). Formerly, she served as assistant director of the Pluralism Project at Harvard University, Diana Eck's research project on religious diversity in the United States. She was a consulting editor for *Engaging Others, Knowing Ourselves: A Lutheran Calling in a Multi-Religious World* (2016). She is currently co-chair of the executive committee of the *Shoulder to*

Shoulder Campaign: Standing with American Muslims; Upholding American Values, a U.S.-based, inter-religious coalition to end anti-Muslim bigotry.

J. Paul Rajashekar—Former Luther D. Reed Professor of Systematic Theology and former academic dean at the United Lutheran Seminary, Philadelphia. Rajashekar also served at Gurukul Lutheran Theological Seminary, Chennai, and as professor at the United Theological College, Bangalore, India. He later served the Lutheran World Federation, Geneva, Switzerland, as executive secretary for Church and People of Other Faiths in the department of theology. He is currently a member of the Consultative Panel for Lutheran-Muslim Relations of the ELCA.

Fernando Sihotang—Coordinator for Human Rights and Advocacy at the Lutheran World Federation National Committee in Indonesia (KNLWF). In 2018, Fernando wrote a thesis on Indonesia's anti-blasphemy law for his master's studies in human rights at the University of Erlangen-Nürnberg. Apart from his human rights advocacy activities, he also has been active in the campaign for promoting interfaith dialogue, together with young religious leaders in Indonesia.

Mark Swanson—Harold S. Vogelaar Professor of Christian-Muslim Studies and Interfaith Relations, Associate Director of A Center of Christian-Muslim Engagement for Peace and Justice of the Lutheran School of Theology at Chicago. Swanson came from Luther Seminary, where he taught Islamic studies, Christian-Muslim relations, Arabic language, and early church history. Before that, he served fourteen years on the faculty of the Evangelical Theological Seminary in Cairo, Egypt. He is a member of the Consultative Panel for Lutheran-Muslim Relations of the ELCA.

Michael Reid Trice—Director, Center for Religious Wisdom and World Affairs, Spehar-Halligan Associate Professor of Constructive Theology and Theological Ethics at the School of Theology and Ministry at Seattle University. Trice served as the associate executive for the ecumenical and interreligious efforts of the office of the presiding bishop for the ELCA (2004–2011). He continues to serve on interreligious and faith and order tables at the National Council of Churches of Christ (USA).

Sara Trumm—Director, A Center of Christian-Muslim Engagement for Peace and Justice of the Lutheran School of Theology at Chicago. Trumm received a BA from Augsburg College and an MA from Luther Seminary and served at the Henry Martyn Institute in Hyderabad, India. She is a community ambassador through Interfaith Youth Core and is a qualified administrator for the Intercultural Development Inventory.

Introduction

DAVID D. GRAFTON

IN THE DAYS SHORTLY after September 11, many Americans incredulously repeated, "Why do they hate us?" The discovery that nineteen terrorists from the Middle East had perpetrated such atrocities against innocents and the nation, while publicly using Islam as a justification for their actions, created a visceral reaction against the religion of Islam and its adherents for many Americans. The United States government responded to the attacks domestically by passing the Patriot Act and enforcing surveillance and limitations not only on Muslims in America, but on all men of Middle Eastern heritage (including Christians). Abroad, the U.S. created a coalition of partners and swiftly executed a global "war on terror," which still stands as a policy objective today. During this time, Americans sought out credible information on Islam. Sales of books on Islam, Muslims, and the life of the Prophet Muhammad skyrocketed. Non-Muslim Americans wanted simple answers to their questions about Islam, the most prominent being, "Why does Islam sanction violence?" Panels of "experts" convened nightly on major networks and cable TV shows to provide their answers. However, it soon became clear that credible answers meant very different things to different audiences. The answer from some talking heads was that violence is inherent to the faith, while others (including Muslims) attempted to clarify that the actions of 9/11 were not sanctioned by the faith and were in fact were very un-Islamic. These debates about the essence of Islam began to reveal a deep divide in American cultural and political perspectives.

Christian communities across the country began to invite their own speakers and experts to hold forums on Islam. Such events were not without their controversy, as members of churches displayed the same diversity of views and opinions on Islam as the media "experts." Pastors and priests reached out to any Muslim representative they could find to come and "explain" Islam. As Sara Trumm notes in this volume, the number of "Islam 101" workshops skyrocketed. There was a genuine interest in finding out more about Muslims and Islam.

Surprising to many, among Catholics, Lutherans, Presbyterians, and the Reformed Church, there were a good number of pastors or leaders in the church who had significant knowledge of Islam in its various forms and already had relationships with Muslim communities. Since the late 70s and early 80s, there had been a growing movement of Christian-Muslim dialogue within Catholic and mainstream Protestant denominations that was driven primarily by the experience of Christian missionaries living in Muslim majority countries. Again, as one of our contributors in this volume remarks, there was a growing acceptance, though certainly not by all missionaries or mission agencies, that proselytism among Muslims did not have any great impact. And, after many years of working among Muslims in places like India, Egypt, Nigeria, Senegal, Syria, Tanzania, Turkey, the Arabian Gulf, and even in seemingly unlikely places such as Guyana and Trinidad, some Western missionaries were realizing that there were in fact many things Western Christians might find interesting about Islam as a religion, or about the practiced faith of particular Muslims, in these very different places—that is, if care was taken to listen to what Muslims were saying. Certainly there was (and continues to be) a debate about whether dialogue with Muslims was for the purpose of mutual understanding or whether it was simply another method of evangelization. Nevertheless, genuine interest in developing relationships with Muslims *as* Muslims, as co-theists, became an important shift in thinking about Islam for many. Thus, at the start of the twenty-first century, there were actually a wide variety of human and educational resources available among American Christian denominations related to learning about and engaging in dialogue with Muslims. As Michael Trice notes in his chapter, it was the Roman Catholic Vatican II Council that began the movement toward interreligious dialogue. During the 70s and 80s, the Roman Catholic Church, through its Pontifical Council for Interreligious Dialogue, led the way in this effort with Muslims. Ecumenical offices around the world began to develop their own programs on Christian-Muslim dialogue, including the World Council of Churches, the Lutheran World Federation, and the U.S. National Council of Churches. American Lutherans began developing various models for engagement with Muslims in the Middle East throughout the 1970s, primarily in Beirut, Jerusalem, and Cairo.[1]

In 1986, the Division for World Mission and Inter-Church Cooperation (DWMIC) of the American Lutheran Church released *God and Jesus: Theological Reflections for Christian-Muslim Dialog.* The booklet was a compilation of essays submitted by (primarily) Lutheran scholars on differing aspects of Christian reflection on Islam. The initiative was the brain child of Mark W. Thomsen, then director of DWMIC and later the first director for the Division of Global Mission (DGM) of the Evangelical Lutheran Church in America (ELCA), who organized the denomination's "Focus on Islam" initiative. The church-wide enterprise had been based on Thomsen's own experiences as a Lutheran missionary in Nigeria. The intent of the initiative was to explore Lutheran expressions of faith in relation to Muslims, which recognized potential commonalities as well as Christian uniqueness. The project concluded that Christians and Muslims have the same God but view this God "differently."

As Mark Swanson notes in the first chapter, the *God and Jesus* project was an early attempt to develop a relationship with Islam that today might be considered out of date. While Lutherans have always been very "Jesus-centered" with a focus on how Christ is particular, unique, and necessary for salvation, there has also been an openness to an understanding that God universally loves all creation and is for all people. Historically, Muslims, Christians, and Jews have had a unique relationship. We all profess belief in the God of Abraham, even if we have each come to understand that identity differently. Thus, dialogue with the Abrahamic faiths proceeded differently than with other world religions or indigenous faith traditions. The *God and Jesus* project intriguingly proposed a concept of Jesus as "the Risen Prophet." However, as Swanson reminds us, the whole project developed with monolithic concepts of Islam as a category and system, as if Muslims were the same throughout the world. The project was not a dialogue. It did not include any Muslims, especially any American Muslims. It was a project that promoted Christians thinking about Muslims, rather than with Muslims.

---

1. Grafton, *Piety, Politics, and Power*, 187–217.

However, after 9/11, many Americans realized that Muslims were not only "over there" but they were "here," and that they had been here for a long time. For some, this was alarming. For others, it was an important step in the self-understanding of the rich cultural and religious pluralism of the United States. African-American Muslims had been brought to the continent as slaves even before the United States was a nation. Syrian Muslims had come to work in the automobile factories for Henry Ford in Detroit shortly after the turn of the twentieth century. Many Indian and Pakistani Muslim professionals came in the 1960s to study and then stayed to build new lives for themselves and their families. Throughout the history of North America, there have been economic immigrants and religious or political refugees who came seeking a better life from numerous places such as Guyana, Ethiopia, Lebanon, Iran, Iraq, and Somalia. Surprising to many Protestant communities in suburban or rural areas across the United States, there was a diverse patchwork of Muslim communities scattered throughout the country, sometimes in the most unlikely of places, including Ross, North Dakota (the site of the very first public mosque, built in 1929), or Michigan City, Indiana.

In her contribution to this volume, Sara Trumm notes that by the beginning of the twenty-first century, there were actually many Lutherans in the ELCA who had participated in the "Focus on Islam" program, whether as missionaries abroad, graduates of Luther Seminary's short-lived master's in Islamic studies, or students from ELCA colleges and universities who benefited from newly developed classes on Islam or who had Muslim friends and classmates. Numerous pastors and lay leaders around the country had begun to develop positive relations between local Muslim communities and their congregations or synods. In the direct aftermath of 9/11, there were individuals ready to respond to the neverending requests for information about Islam. However, there were never enough volunteers to respond to the demand from anxious congregations and angry communities. Since then, in the last twenty years, a great deal of work has been done, with many programs developed, interfaith panels held, mosque visits taken, iftars enjoyed, and joint social service projects begun. And yet, as Todd Green notes in his chapter, Islamophobia is still on the rise, even among Lutherans. According to the Southern Poverty Law Center, hate crimes directed at Muslims or Muslim institutions have risen annually.[2]

---

2. Beydoun, *American Islamophobia*, 34.

As the war on terror appeared to be winding down, as foreign terrorist organizations from Muslim majority nation states seemed less threatening to Americans at home, anxieties shifted toward more domestic concerns: the impact of the Great Recession, immigration debates, and the ever-present American sin of racism. As early as the middle of the second decade of the 2000s, a black president was accused of being a Muslim and un-American, fear of an "Islamic takeover" led to anti-Sharia legislation being passed in various states (without an awareness of what Sharia actually represents for American Muslims), and local municipalities were turning down legal applications from Muslim communities to build places of worship, schools, and Islamic centers.[3] The roots of a deeply divided American public that had been latent for some time began to reveal themselves during the acrimonious debates of the Republican presidential primaries. Thus, by the time the presidential race began in 2016, there were open calls for banning Muslims from entering the country, which was ultimately promulgated with Executive Order 13769 in 2017. Such rancor in the public was reflected in a January 2017 Pew Research Center survey that found that almost half of all American adults believed that Muslims in the U.S. are "anti-American" and was fanned by social media and cable network channels.[4]

It is now the case that a younger generation of non-Muslim Americans have a new lens to view and experience the public face of Islam. Gen Zs and, to some extent, Millennials do not view Islam through the emotional lens of 9/11. That is an experience that has been taught to them. Depending on how the events have been shared by their parents or media outlets, they may have very different understandings of Islam. Rather, their primary experience has been through the national discourse on immigration, Islamophobia, and the rise of white nationalism, which has stoked anger against Muslims, who are predominantly people of color. Thus, given the dramatic division in American society, there is a bifurcated perspective on whether Muslims are seen as part of the cultural and religious pluralism of the American landscape or whether they are believed to be foreign elements that are anti-American.

2021 marks thirty-five years since *God and Jesus: Theological Reflections for Christian-Muslim Dialog*. This was the first step in an American Lutheran shift toward public dialogue with Muslims. The initiative led by Thomsen of the American Lutheran Church (ALC) provided resources and

3. Peters, "Courting Anarchy," 357.

4. Pew Research Center, "U.S. Muslims Concerned."

energy for the church to begin thinking anew about its relationships with Muslims, rather than simply talking about a monolithic religion in other parts of the world. *More Than a Cup of Coffee and Tea* seeks to examine "Where are we now?" How have North American Lutherans developed their thinking about Muslims? How have Lutheran relations with Muslims and Muslim communities taken shape since 1986? Where are Lutherans engaged directly with Muslims in North America and around the world—not only from the perspective of mission for evangelization but for the purpose of dialogue and partnership for the common good and in matters of peace and justice? What grounds Lutheran commitments to be in relationship with Muslims, and what have we learned both about our own faith and that of our Muslim relatives, friends, co-workers, and acquaintances? To be sure, not all Lutheran approaches or perspectives are alike. This book, however, focuses on the trajectory of the ELCA, its predecessor bodies, and partner churches around the world.

This volume hopes to accomplish three things. First, it documents where we have been in the last generation of Christian-Muslim encounter, relationships, and dialogue. Second, it provides an opportunity to learn and reflect from the wide variety of experiences Lutherans have had with Muslim communities for a generation or more. Finally, it is intended to provide an impetus for others who have not yet begun this journey of dialogue with Muslims to engage. There are many who have begun this venture and there are many more who can and will. The record here demonstrates the many ways to explore and engage in positive dialogue or to address interfaith relationships, specifically with Muslims. The contexts vary greatly, and the obstacles are not always easy, as Fernando Sihotang reminds us in his Indonesian context. However, in the end, we hope that this work will encourage further Lutheran reflection on interfaith issues and encourage positive encounters and activities for a new generation.

A comment should be made here about what we mean by dialogue and interfaith. Too often, "dialogue" brings to mind a formal theological meeting between official representatives of various traditions. Certainly, this is one form of dialogue that is noted, for example, in Kathryn Lohre's chapter on the official work of the ELCA. However, there are many other kinds of dialogue. In fact, most of the dialogue reflected in this book is not that type of dialogue. Most people engage in wide varieties of dialogue even if they don't call it that. The most meaningful forms of interfaith dialogue occur among people who simply share family traditions or foods that are prepared during religious holidays, or describe their worship practices, such as prayer or fasting. As Thom Johnson and Mark Brown note in their chapters, sometimes Muslims and Christians come together to provide various forms of programs or social services and then reflect on why their faith calls them to share in actions of peace and justice. Christians and Muslims engage in many different kinds of dialogue; they just might not be aware that they are doing it![5] The most common interaction between Muslims and Christians is simply what the Roman Catholic Church has dubbed a "dialogue of life." In the midst of our daily activities and routines, we may engage with people of other religions, while we make a myriad of decisions about life, schedules, commitments, volunteer activities, family, or work responsibilities.[6]

As Michael Trice notes, it has become common to prefer the term interreligious over interfaith when describing many of the activities in this volume. However, we are using interfaith, primarily to highlight the individual and intimate beliefs of adherents, rather than using the term "religious," which often carries the connotation of adherence to a particular religion or doctrine.[7]

In any interfaith encounter, the issue of truth claims inevitably comes up. It is often believed that interfaith dialogue is simply a polite way to reach a least common denominator of agreement so that no one is offended, and that it is best to avoid making statements about what we really believe. As is seen throughout the chapters in this book, this is certainly not the intent here. True interfaith dialogue relies on people of faith sharing and expressing their true beliefs. This type of dialogue helps us to see commonalities, but also differences.

What is important to note is that good interfaith dialogue pays attention to how we talk about our faith, and how we genuinely listen to the beliefs of others. The most recent 2019 ELCA *A Declaration of Inter-Religious Commitment: A Policy Statement of the Evangelical Lutheran Church in America* recognizes the tension between the Christian call to proclaim the Gospel, the "Great Commission," and the call to the Christian vocation of serving the neighbor, that is, the "Great Commandment." While proselytism has no place in the space of genuine interfaith dialogue, sharing what we believe about

---

5. For a variety of different kinds of "dialogue" see LaHurd et al., eds., *Engaging Others*, 48–81, and Smith, *Muslims, Christians*, 63–82.

6. See Paul VI, *Declaration*.

7. Mosher, *Toward Our Mutual Flourishing*, 2–3.

God in Christ Jesus, that is, the Gospel, is part of the role of growing in deep interfaith relationships for Christians. Good interfaith dialogue pays attention to how we share and how we genuinely hear our Muslim friends when they share their religious convictions about the most gracious and compassionate God and The Prophet Muhammad. Thus, while this work does not prejudge the particular faith perspectives of the contributors, it does take the following assumption from the ELCA's statement:

> As we strive to show forth God's vision, we are called to work toward justice and peace for all people and creation, that is, the common good. Religious diversity, when accompanied by mutual understanding and cooperation, enriches the whole. Through inter-religious relationships, we receive the gifts of our neighbors and experience more fully the exquisite realization that all are made in the image of God. A deep appreciation of the similarities and differences among religions and worldviews enhances working together for the common good. At the same time, cooperation can enhance both mutual understanding and the self-understanding of each participant. Seeking mutual understanding and the common good are active steps we can take toward God's vision of life abundant for all.[8]

This book is organized into two sections. The first will provide an overview of the history of the "Focus on Islam" through official ELCA programs and strategies. Mark Swanson provides the important background of this "Focus on Islam." He examines the work of the authors of the *God and Jesus* document prior to the establishment of the ELCA. Michael Trice and Kathryn Lohre provide an overview of the Consultative Panel on Lutheran-Muslim Relations, from its founding to its present and potential future work, and of the ELCA official programs and strategies through the office of Ecumenical and Inter-Religious Relations. Lastly, Todd Green addresses how white American congregations and ministries might better understand and respond to the growing challenges of Islamophobia in American society.

The second section will provide an overview of some of the various contexts in which Lutherans have been and are currently engaging with Muslims, both domestically and internationally. Jane Buckley-Farlee reflects on her experience in the "Little Mogadishu" section of Minneapolis. Thom Johnson looks back on many years of work as a pastor, professor,

---

8. ELCA, *Declaration of Inter-Religious Commitment*, 7.

and activist in Southern California. Sara Trumm provides insight into the strategic decisions being made at the Center of Christian-Muslim Engagement for Peace and Justice in Chicago at the Lutheran School of Theology at Chicago. The final four chapters provide insight into relations in very different international contexts. Mark Brown explores the important work of the Lutheran Federation with Muslim Palestinians in Jerusalem and the Palestinian territories. Fernando Sihotang provides unique insights into his human rights work with Muslims in Indonesia, while Peter Hanson shares his reflections about relations in Senegal. Each of these three chapters point to very different cultural patterns and unique histories of Christian-Muslim relationships. To be sure, this volume could have included many more examples of Lutheran-Muslim encounters: Egypt, Lebanon, Trinidad, Philadelphia, or Dearborn.[9]

Finally, Paul Rajashekar draws on a lifetime experience of living and engaging with Muslims in India where he grew up, in Europe as part of the World Council of Churches, and then while teaching at the Lutheran Seminary in Philadelphia. Like Todd Green's chapter in the first section, Rajashekar challenges us to overcome any forms of religious or theological "self-righteousness" in a dangerous time of growing intolerance toward others. A Further Resources section has also been compiled to serve individuals and groups as opportunities for learning about and developing relationships with Muslim communities in their areas.

The compilation of stories in this volume seeks to provide an opportunity for us to reflect on the humanity, spirituality, and gifts of our Muslim neighbors in all their diversity. It calls us to take the initial step toward hospitality, as well as being open to receiving hospitality through a simple but important sharing of a cup of coffee or tea. And yet, our hope is that we move beyond the initial encounter to something more, something deeper. It is our conviction that the past generation of Christian-Muslim encounters has sown seeds of deep relationships, from which many more will take root. May we be so blessed.

---

9. For an overview of ALC and LCA work in Egypt and Lebanon, see Grafton, *Piety, Politics, and Power,* 182–236.

Section 1: **Reflections on American Lutherans and Islam**

CHAPTER 1

Beyond Apologetics

The *God and Jesus* Project

MARK SWANSON

God and Jesus: The Project

IN DECEMBER 1986, THE Division for World Mission and Inter-Church Cooperation (DWMIC) of the American Lutheran Church (ALC) issued a ninety-four-page document, a simple thermally-bound letter-sized book with a one-piece pink paper cover, with the title *God and Jesus: Theological Reflections for Christian-Muslim Dialog*.[1] The document was the fruit of a project led by the Rev. Dr. Mark W. Thomsen (1931–2014), then director of the DWMIC of the ALC and later the first director of the Global Mission unit of the Evangelical Lutheran Church in America (ELCA).[2] Its aim, Thomsen immediately tells his readers, was to address questions asked by missionaries and others (*GJ* 1):

1. How can one witness to the trinitarian faith in such a way that the biblical witness is faithfully proclaimed within a Muslim context?

2. What is the purpose of Christian witness and mission among Muslims?

3. How does one effectively witness to the Christian faith among Muslims?

1. American Lutheran Church, *God and Jesus*. To reduce the number of footnotes, I will give references to this book in the body of the text, in the form *GJ* and the page number, in parentheses.

2. See Grafton, ed., *Mark W. Thomsen*.

Thomsen and the DWMIC designed a process for addressing such questions; a task force consisting of experts in relevant fields was assembled and began to meet in 1984. From the beginning, its work was to take place within the framework of a set of missiological principles that guided the work of the DWMIC (and that echo Thomsen's characteristic theological terminology): "1) contextualization of mission, 2) the finality of Jesus Christ, 3) the nature of the finality of Jesus Christ,[3] and 4) the universality of God's presence, revelation, and activity in the cosmos" (*GJ* 3–4). Meetings were held, and papers were written and discussed. A draft of the developed document was shared with a variety of people involved in Christian-Muslim relations;[4] some of their responses were incorporated into a final draft. The resulting book, consisting of an introduction and seven chapters, was then offered "to missionaries of The American Lutheran Church working within a Muslim context and anyone else who might benefit from such a document" (*GJ* 1).

A contemporary reader might be tempted to put the document aside after reading a few pages. There are ways in which the project today seems quaintly out of date. The seven specialists and chapter-authors turn out to be a group of white male theology professors in their 50s, all of them Christians, most of them with roots in Midwestern Scandinavian- or German-background Lutheranism.[5] The project is aimed at helping overseas missionaries to "witness to the Christian faith among Muslims," with the hope that some might come to faith in the crucified and risen Jesus (*GJ* 93–94). Despite this ambitious goal, there is in general a lack of evidence of engagement with actual flesh-and-blood Muslims (with one important exception among the authors, as will be noted later). Abstraction is rampant; we hear about address to "Islam" or about the beliefs of "the Muslim." There is no sign that any Muslim human being ever participated in the meetings of the task force. Indeed, one senses that when some of the team

3. This principle could be glossed as the paradoxical nature of the finality of the vulnerable and crucified Jesus Christ. See Thomsen, *Christ Crucified*.

4. I (Mark Swanson) was one of the people consulted. At the time, I was teaching in Egypt as a missionary of the Lutheran Church in America (LCA), one of the bodies that joined with the ALC in the formation of the ELCA.

5. See the list of participants in *GJ* 2–3. One exception to the characterization of the task force as "in their 50s" was the Rev. Dr. Bruce Schein, then of Trinity Lutheran Seminary in Columbus, Ohio, who began with the *God and Jesus* task force but then had to withdraw because of health issues. He was only in his 40s when he died in 1985. On Schein's role in developing the LCA's "Conversation with Islam" in the Middle East, see Grafton, *Piety, Politics, and Power*, 202–8.

members thought about Muslims, they thought solely about people *on the other side of the world*, in "Muslim areas" or "a Muslim region" (*GJ* 19, 27). The existence of a developing African-American Muslim community in Midwestern cities such as Minneapolis, or the growth of Muslim communities among immigrants from South Asia and the Middle East following the passage of the Hart-Celler Immigration and Nationality Act of 1965, was not yet on many of these scholars' radar. Nor was the presence of Muslim intellectuals at great American universities.

So, it is tempting to toss the document aside, perhaps with a sigh, and congratulate ourselves on how far we have come since 1986. We in (what is now) the ELCA have learned to tend constructive and fruitful relationships with Muslim individuals and institutions, and we strive for mutuality in these relationships (although, for example, it was only in 2019 that the Lutheran School of Theology at Chicago, where I teach, and the American Islamic College created a truly *shared* course).[6] We have gained in sophistication in the ways we talk about bearing witness to the Gospel in a religiously plural world (as in *A Declaration of Inter-Religious Commitment*).[7] At the very least, in our denominational work, we have learned how to create a task force that is somewhat representative of the diversity within the denomination.

It turns out, however, that *God and Jesus* is a much richer document than might at first be thought. I believe that reading it is still instructive after thirty-five years. And so I turn to a very selective presentation of the work.

God and Jesus: The Book

1. *The Apologetic Move*

In his introduction, Mark Thomsen quickly introduces readers to the theological symbol that the entire volume is devoted to exploring (*GJ* 4–5):

> In the very early discussion of the task force, it was decided to explore the possibility of using the theological symbol of the crucified and raised prophet as a means of witnessing to the biblical

6. The Lutheran School of Theology at Chicago was a leader among ELCA institutions in offering courses—since the late 1980s—co-taught by a Christian and a Muslim professor. (By way of contrast, when I worked towards an Islamic Studies degree at Hartford Seminary in 1983–1984, my professors were five Christians.) But genuine mutuality is something for which we are still striving.

7. The *Declaration* was adopted by the ELCA Churchwide Assembly in 2019.

faith and clarifying how Christians and Muslims believe in one God differently.[8] . . . As the task force developed its work, it found that it was possible to witness to the apostolic understanding of the finality of Jesus with the theological symbol of the raised prophet.

So here is the project's suggestion: that it might be possible to maintain the finality of Christ with faithfulness to Scripture and to speak in a way that might be comprehensible and clarifying in Christian-Muslim conversation, by speaking of Christ as "the raised prophet."[9]

A few observations may be made. In the first place, rather than simply a theological symbol, what we have here is an apologetic move, that is, a way of speaking designed to explain the Christian faith to someone outside the faith. First, *a promising area for a conversation is identified*—here, the centrality of prophets and messengers to the Islamic understanding of how God deals with human beings, reminding and guiding them with warnings and good news. Next, *common ground is claimed*: Jesus is a prophet in both Christianity and Islam. And then, one can *build on this common ground*: Jesus is the *crucified and raised* prophet.

The apologetic move just described is by no means simply a trial balloon or a piece of spaghetti thrown against the wall to see if it sticks. Rather, the task force seeks to give a theological justification for each of its steps and does so in a methodical way. Is the project faithful to Scripture (or, specifically, to the missiological principles of DWMIC)? Is it, Christianly speaking, faithful to speak of Jesus as a prophet, or enough to speak of Jesus as the crucified and raised prophet?

Finally, I note that there may have been within the task force some resistance to the characterization of the project as apologetic. This is strange, given Christian apologetics' roots in the *apologia* of 1 Peter 3:15, the defense, or reasoned explanation, that one is to offer to anyone "who demands from you an accounting for the hope that is in you," which then is to be done "with gentleness and reverence" (see GJ 69–70). However, I recall discussions in the 80s and 90s in which apologetics was associated with a kind of aggressive proselytism, and Thomsen surely wanted to steer clear of that. If at the very end of the book he can speak, in a homiletic register, about the desire that Muslims "find faith, hope, and love in God's incredible

8. From the outset, the project assumes that "Christians and Muslims believe in one God," even if "differently." An argument supporting this assumption will be presented below.

9. Or the *risen* prophet, which will supply the title of one of the essays.

prophetic embodiment in Jesus" (*GJ* 93), in the introduction his hopes for the project are more modestly stated (*GJ* 5):

> The validity of this document does not depend upon its value in convincing Muslims to be Christians, but in possibly clarifying for Muslims and Christians how we believe in God differently.

I think we should not avoid describing the project as an apologetic one, in the sense explained above, as providing a defense or reasoned explanation of some aspect of one's faith through identifying, within the interlocutor's world of discourse, some common ground upon which one can build one's case. Just so, the *God and Jesus* project can be instructive about the possibilities and limitations of such an approach—both of which (the possibilities and the limitations) may have something to say to us, the theological heirs of the *God and Jesus* task force.

2. The Framing

Of the seven essays that form the heart of the book, three of them serve as a kind of frame around the main work of apology: Carl E. Braaten's "Theological Perspectives on the Christian Mission among Muslims" (Ch. 1, *GJ* 8–19); Paul V. Martinson's "Christian-Muslim Problematics" (Ch. 2, *GJ* 20–30); and Mark Thomsen's "The Mission and Witness of the Church within a Muslim Community" (Ch. 7, *GJ* 80–94). These essays remind Christians in unflinching terms of the finality of Christ, the necessity and nature of the missionary enterprise, the sharp contrasts to be drawn between Christianity and Islam, and at the very end of the book, the hope that Muslims might come to faith in Christ. These essays reassure readers that the project will not veer into historical relativism or into John Hick's "Copernican revolution" (*GJ* 9). Braaten insists that we cannot join those who interpret the "no other name" of Acts 4:12 as "part of the husk of the New Testament message, not the kernel itself" (*GJ* 9). Thomsen drums on the words final and ultimate to describe the nature of the revelation of God in Jesus Christ, "God's ultimate and final self-identification among us" (*GJ* 80–82, here 82).

Martinson's essay moves the book into the area of Christian-Muslim interaction, but the core of the essay considers interaction of a rarified sort, at the level of theological concepts presented as binary choices. With respect to God, are reality and operation, or "the language of unity and the language of relation," exclusive or mutually inclusive? Does God relate

himself as a prophet," one among the prophets who were rejected by their own people or martyred in Jerusalem (*GJ* 53). While there are a number of passages in the Gospels where Jesus is considered to be *a* prophet very like the Old Testament prophets, there are also passages where Jesus is spoken of as *the* prophet, specifically the eschatological prophet "like Moses" (see John 6:14, 7:40; Luke 24:19, Acts 3:22-23, 7:37; *GJ* 53). Hutton concludes that this designation of Jesus "was among the earliest and most representative identifications of Jesus by his contemporaries. Indeed, it may bring us close to the self-understanding of Jesus of Nazareth" (*GJ* 54).

Hutton points out that for the church in the Hellenistic world, the title prophet gave way to other christological titles. However (*GJ* 54),

> . . . to affirm that Jesus was "the prophet from Nazareth of Galilee" (Matt. 21:11) is not to diminish his christological significance—as though "prophet" were a christological "lowest common de-nominator." As the prophet who announces and inaugurates God's eschatological reign, Jesus is imbued with crucial and decisive significance. The church's Christology is implicit in his self-under-standing as the prophet of the kingdom.

So the New Testament specialist joins the Old Testament specialist in sign-ing off on the project's apologetic move. But Hutton also points to the next step in the vetting process with this observation: "Jesus of Nazareth *was* 'the eschatological prophet.' Jesus *is* 'the risen prophet' in the church's proclama-tion" (*GJ* 55). With that, the baton is passed to the specialist in historical and systematic theology.

4. *Systematic Testing*

Robert W. Jenson immediately gives his assent to "the Risen Prophet" (also the title of his essay, *GJ* 57–67) as an adequate christological title, the salvific meaning of which could conceivably be spun out in an Islamic context with-out reference to the specific vocabularies that developed in the Hellenistic world of the first Christian centuries (*GJ* 57). Jenson's attempt to imagine how this might be done—which he warns is not "a direct message to Islam" but rather "theology for the Christian church, as it lives and indeed proclaims its gospel in Islam's world"—is summarized as follows (*GJ* 61):

> God has established one living prophet whose death is neverthe-less behind and not before him and who therefore is permanent

among the prophets. His prophecy has its final form, yet its finality in no way infringes God's freedom, for its content is precisely
God's freedom from this world's judgments, and its liveliness is
established by the definitive act of God's freedom—also for Islam—his raising of the dead. Therefore there is a criterion of right
prophecy: agreement with his. There are reliable expectations of
our position under God's prophets. Moreover, these expectations
may be of good, because the prophet with whom all prophecy co-
heres is for us unto death. *That prophecy is thus true and good is the
gospel's good news, in Islamic context.*

Jenson concludes this section by addressing the worry that seems to hang
over the project: "Is this the whole gospel?" (That is, is this *enough*?) He
responds: "Yes, in this specific context" (*GJ* 61).

Having argued that "the risen prophet" can serve adequately as a
christological title, one that can carry the necessary soteriological weight so
as to proclaim "the gospel's good news, in Islamic context" (*GJ* 61), Jenson
turns to the identification of God as Triune. Jenson is perfectly aware of the
Islamic tradition's rejection of Christian trinitarianism; but he judges that it
might "be possible to make the essential trinitarian move, for Islamic context, without contradicting any necessary tenet of Islam, save only its existing dissent from the gospel claim itself, that Jesus is crucified and risen" (*GJ*
65). This move could be expressed in sentences such as (*GJ* 64):

The word God speaks to us by his prophets, cohering and guaranteed by the Risen Prophet, and the Spirit by which prophecy is
informed, are the word [sic] God speaks to himself to be the one
personal living God and the Spirit that is that life.

Here too, Jenson anticipates the question, is this *enough*? He writes (*GJ* 64):

In the mere logic of the case, no more need be said: apart from specific historically encountered problems, the foregoing paragraph
would be a complete doctrine of Triunity for Islamic context.

5. Sparking Creativity

The moves just described could be taken simply as the systematician's
signoff, following that of the biblical scholars. Permission has been granted to
missionaries and others engaged in Christian-Muslim encounter to ponder
and test the title "the Risen Prophet" as a way of bearing witness to Jesus

that might enable conversation, avoid old dead ends (to which the immediate confession of Christ as "God" or "Son of God" might lead), and at least clarify where essential differences between the faiths are to be found.

However, there is more going on in this essay. Jenson makes at least two brilliant moves that more than repay the effort taken to read the book. Those who have experienced the bracing creativity of Jenson's theological work will not be surprised by this;[13] but here it is important to realize that this creativity is sparked by an encounter with Islamic sources—at second hand, it must be admitted, but transmitted by a sensitive interpreter of the Islamic tradition, Dr. Willem A. Bijlefeld, the project's specialist in Christian-Muslim relations. A careful reading of Jenson's essay shows it to be full of allusions to lectures on "listening to the Qur'an" that Bijlefeld had honed with Muslim audiences in various parts of the world and that he had shared in many workshops with Christians, including the LCA's "Seminar on Christianity and Islam in Egypt." (This seminar was held six times between 1979 and 1987. It was developed and led by the Rev. Dr. Harold S. Vogelaar, with the assistance of interns and colleagues, like myself, and attended by seminary professors and church leaders from around the world.) Bijlefeld undoubtedly had shared his material with the DWMIC-ALC task force.

Bijlefeld had spent a career listening to Muslims, and Jenson listened to Bijlefeld. Echoes of Bijlefeld abound in Jenson's essay. Jenson notes the qur'anic distinction between *nabi* (prophet; some of the prophets have been killed) and *rasul* (messenger; in general in the Qur'an, God saves the messengers from the plots of those who would kill them)—a distinction about which Bijlefeld wrote an important essay;[14] but now Jenson can use the distinction to draw a contrast with the vindication of the *rasul* Jesus, not through divine deliverance but through death and resurrection (*GJ* 59).

A paragraph about trinitarian "sorts of moves" in Islamic tradition is full of echoes of Bijlefeld's lectures (*GJ* 65–66):

> First, the prophetic message is indeed said to be uncreated.[15] Sec-
> ond, it is essential to Muslim prayer that God can be entreated

---

13. Entire books and special issues of journals are being dedicated to Jenson's theology, but let me mention here a memorial essay that bears personal witness to Jenson's theological creativity, McCormack's "In Memoriam."

14. Bijlefeld, "A Prophet and More Than a Prophet?"

15. A reference to the ninth-century debate over whether the Qur'an was created or uncreated—a suggestive parallel to the christological debates of the fourth century.

mercifully to intercede with himself.[16] Third, it is noteworthy that in the great confession of "God the compassionate, the merciful," both adjectives are from the same root; the distinction is between a quality of nature and a quality of action; we might translate, "God the merciful in himself and the merciful in action."[17] Thus God's nature and action are distinguished, but then the action is made to define the nature—which is exactly a trinitarian sort of move. And finally, in the Qur'an, the only limit to God's freedom is his own mercy self-imposed as restraint.[18]

Perhaps Jenson's most significant learning was about the qur'anic concept of *shirk*, the "association" of the creature in that which properly belongs only to the Creator, and the Qur'an's great sin.[19] Jenson saw that any proposal of the *God and Jesus* project would need to have the capacity to respond to the Islamic suspicion that Christians, with their christological and trinitarian discourse, were committing *shirk*. But here, Jenson boldly asserts that the qur'anic concept of *shirk* is in fact perfect for explaining what was at stake in the Christian tradition's christological debates (*GJ* 62):

> The historic doctrine of Triunity was created precisely to overcome Christian lapses into the *shirk* that characterized ancient Western paganism. It was Athanasius's chief accusation against the Arians: " . . . like the Greeks you lump creature and Creator together" (*To Serapion*, I:30).

The Nicene insistence was that Christ is not a creature to be associated or assimilated as closely as possible to God (*shirk*!), but "very god from very god." The Christian description of God may be very different from the Islamic one, and Muslims may well find it unbelievable; but the whole point of Christian trinitarian discourse is to insist that God is *one*. "Christians . . . are as insistent as Muhammad that God is one and only" (*GJ* 61).

But now, this line of apology immediately points out the need for the reform of much Christian discourse (*GJ* 61–62):

> What most Christians actually have in mind as "the doctrine of the Trinity" is not in fact the historic teaching, but one of the

16. All intercession is God's (Q 39:43–44); there is no intercessor besides God (Q 6:51, 70; 32:4).

17. This is precisely Bijlefeld's translation of *al-Rahman al-Rahim*.

18. A reference to Q 6:12 and 54, *kataba 'ala nafsihi l-rahma*, God "has inscribed mercy upon himself." Bijlefeld regularly called attention to these verses in his presentations.

19. Q 31:13: "*shirk* is great wrong."

heresies it was intended to overcome; and about these last, Muslim objections are fully justified . . . most modern Christians . . . suppose that Trinitarianism is indeed a matter of assimilating Jesus as closely as possible to God—that is to say, that it is a piece of *shirk*. In bad conscience about this, many modern Christians slack off the christological assertions—thereby only relapsing into the real *shirk* of one of the old heresies. Perhaps the attempt to deal with Muslim criticism may help cure us of this absentmindedness.

For Jenson, it is not enough to recite orthodox formulae (*GJ* 61):

> We should remember that our inherited body of trinitarian reflection represents the historical self-assertion of the biblical identification of God within the Greek context, and its critical purification in that struggle. Ripped from this context and simply recited in the very different Islamic context, inherited trinitarian slogans, for example, about "preexistence" or "three persons," may very well in fact work out as *shirk*.

Here we see some possible results of dialogue—even of a truncated dialogue at a remove (that is, as transmitted by Bijlefeld and without a Muslim response). New language has been forged, as a Christian theologian has adopted a qur'anic concept in order to make a Christian theological argument. Furthermore, the acknowledgement has been made that Islamic critiques of Christian discourse may well be true, and in any event provide a salutary impetus to reflection and delving deeply in the Christian tradition, with the aim of recovering and reforming one's own faith. It is therefore good for Christians to listen to people from outside the Christian fold; they might learn something important from it.[20]

Jenson does not stop here. In addition to what he sees as the necessary apologetic and reformatory aspects of any attempt to think through Christian trinitarianism in an Islamic context, one must take seriously the core function of this trinitarianism: to identify God. And this leads directly to the question, do Christians and Muslims worship the same God (*GJ* 62)?

In the thirty-five years since the *God and Jesus* project, this question has been addressed repeatedly, not just in scholarly writing[21] but in very public acts of anti-Islamic invective on the one hand ("my God was bigger

20. This result foreshadows the title of the work of another task force (this time of the ELCA), LaHurd et al., eds., *Engaging Others*.

21. E.g., Miroslav Volf, *Allah: A Christian Response*. Various lectures by Dr. Volf on this topic can be found on YouTube.

than his")[22] or of solidarity with Muslims on the other ("same God").[23] Long before these public controversies, however, Jenson had made a crisp contribution to the discussion. Rather than embarking upon the usual "on the one hand . . . but on the other" sort of answer, he reworks the question: when Muslims embrace Christian faith, should they be asked to renounce their previous faith (*GJ* 66)?

> The church is the community of the baptized, of those who have renounced "the devil and all his ways." The "ways" denoted were—and where applicable, are—the pagan religions. Jews made and make no such renunciation if they are baptized. At various times, Muslims who have come to Baptism have been required to renounce their previous faith.[24] Our question may be formulated: was this requirement correct?

And this reformulation of the "same God" question allows for a clear answer: "If the preceding section is true, the requirement was not correct." A Muslim who seeks baptism is not thereby *beginning* to worship the true God. "In our judgment the church's relation to Islam must in this respect be like its relation to Judaism" (*GJ* 66).

With Jenson's essay, the *God and Jesus* project offered results that were ahead of its time and that pointed hopefully to the future. What kinds of creative theologizing might take place in dialogue involving Christians and Muslims, in a format where mutual questioning and learning might take place and new vocabularies forged?

22. In 2003, the U.S. Deputy Undersecretary of Defense for Intelligence, Lieutenant-General William G. Boykin, is reported to have told audiences of evangelical Christians that, with respect to a Muslim fighter he encountered in Somalia, "my God was a real God, and his was an idol" ("US Is 'Battling Satan'").

23. The story of former Wheaton College professor Larycia Hawkins, who wore a *hijab* during Advent 2015 in solidarity with Muslim students and who quoted Pope Francis as saying "we worship the same God," is now explored in a video documentary, Hawkins, et al., *Same God*.

24. I am assuming that Jenson learned from Bijlefeld about the Byzantine "abjuration formula" that converts from Islam were required to recite (including the anathematization of "the God of Muhammad") and about the controversy that this formula evoked towards the end of the reign of the emperor Manuel I Komnenos (1118–80). An essay on this topic appeared in the proceedings of a conference held to honor Bijlefeld upon his retirement, Sahas's "*Holosphyros*."

6. *Offering Correctives and Admonitions*

Willem A. Bijlefeld, who for many years was professor of Islamic studies at Hartford Seminary and editor of the journal *The Muslim World*, was one of the most important scholars of Christian-Muslim relations of his generation. He brought a wealth of expertise to the *God and Jesus* task force, as well as a hint of theological diversity (as a Reformed clergyperson and Dutch citizen, he was the sole member of the task force who was not an ALC or LCA Lutheran). How Robert Jenson benefitted from his scholarship and teaching has been noted above. Following Jenson's chapter, Bijlefeld has one of his own, entitled "Christian Witness in an Islamic Context" (*GJ* 68-79). It begins as follows (*GJ* 68):

> Worldwide relations between Muslims and Christians have been so diverse throughout the centuries that any generalization about them is a more or less serious distortion of history. The numerous instances of close and most meaningful personal contact between Muslims and Christians in many parts of the world tell a radically different story than the one documented in the record of an often very bitter exchange of theological arguments; the undeniable burden of the latter should not be allowed to overshadow the gratitude for the joy, encouragement, fulfillment, and enrichment discovered in countless relations of friendship and trust between Muslims and Christians in past and present.

As I re-read these lines in the year 2020, I am immediately struck by the difference in tone between Bijlefeld's essay and much of the rest of the volume. If elsewhere in the volume we find broad generalizations about the history of Christian-Muslim relations, Bijlefeld reminds us that such generalizations are seldom true. If for much of the volume its Christian contributors tend to see Muslims as "over there" in "Muslim areas," Bijlefeld reminds us of "countless relations of friendship and trust between Muslims and Christians in past and present"—that is, in communities where they have lived, and continue to live, together.

It is my impression that throughout his essay, Bijlefeld is offering gentle correctives to the *God and Jesus* project, as well as admonitions as to how the work of Christian-Muslim relations might go forward. Examples are not hard to find:

- The *God and Jesus* project did not have any Muslims among its participants. Bijlefeld reminds readers of "the urgent, difficult, and delicate task of rethinking these [theological] issues imaginatively and restating them meaningfully *from within and with a view to* the ongoing dialog with the world of Islam" (*GJ* 69). The emphasis is Bijlefeld's; the words *"from within . . . the ongoing dialog"* subtly note the limitations of the (mostly pre-dialogical) *God and Jesus* project and point a way forward.

- For most of the *God and Jesus* volume, apart from Bijlefeld's essay, no contemporary Muslim human being is named; we do, as pointed out above, find abstractions such as "Islam" or "the Muslim." Bijlefeld names and quotes from a variety of contemporary Muslim intellectuals: Seyyed Hossein Nasr, Fazlur Rahman, Isma'il al-Faruqi, Frithjof Schuon, Smail Balić, and Abdoldjavad Falaturi. In addition to showing the liveliness of contemporary Islamic thought (also in its engagement with Christianity), Bijlefeld points to the reality of diverse opinions among Muslims on various issues, e.g., how to assess Christian faith in a triune God (*GJ* 71) or whether a "historical understanding" of the Qur'an is something to be pursued (*GJ* 76). Bijlefeld transports us from a world of abstractions to a world of lively debate among real (and learned and exceedingly smart) people.

- Apart from Bijlefeld's essay, *God and Jesus* is mostly silent on the existence and witness of Christians who have co-existed with Muslims for centuries and who have struggled with the question of how to bear Christian witness in their communities. No mention is made, for example, of the twelve-century-long history of Arabic-language Christian apologetic theology.[25] Bijlefeld acknowledges this lacuna; speaking of Muslims' objections to various Christian teachings, he writes (*GJ* 74):

> Only Christian theologians living and working in a Muslim environment are in a position to probe fully both the answers and the questions. Many have done so in the past, and the theological heritage of churches that for centuries have ministered in an Islamic context needs the careful and grateful attention also of Christians in other parts of the world.

25. In the 1980s, a to-this-day-unsurpassed comprehensive survey of this Arabic Christian material existed in Graf's *Geschichte der christlichen arabischen Literatur.* However, few outside a very small guild of scholars paid attention to this or to works of Christian-Muslim significance in other languages of the Christian East. This changed over the course of the next quarter-century. See now the reference work *Christian-Muslim Relations* (Thomas, ed.); Vol. Sixteen has just been published (June 2020). The first five volumes of this reference, covering the years 600–1500, survey Christian works in Latin, Greek, Syriac, Coptic, Georgian, Armenian, Arabic, and Ethiopic.

All these correctives are offered more or less in passing. The heart of Bijlefeld's essay consists of four main points, which have the character of admonitions. The first is an admonition to take Muslims' objections to christological and trinitarian discourse seriously. These objections should not be dismissed as misunderstandings, although repeated attempts have been made to do just that (*GJ* 70-71). Rather, they probe a history of Christian discourse (and Bijlefeld gives several illustrations from the *God and Jesus* volume) that itself is in need of clarification, as it often "obscures, likely unintentionally, our confession of the one God" (*GJ* 72), in support of which he can now quote from Robert Jenson's essay (*GJ* 69, 72).

A second admonition is to be on guard against a one-sided emphasis on christological titles. A title like "the risen prophet" may seem like nothing more than a gimmick in actual Christian-Muslim conversation, "*unless* consciously and consistently the effort is made to spell out what the message is that the early Christian community saw embodied in Jesus' life and ministry, in his suffering and in his death, and in his being raised from the dead" (*GJ* 75).

In the third place, Bijlefeld observes that a fundamental issue that needs to be faced is "the meaning of history and God's relation to it" (*GJ* 76). For Christian theologians, such as the contributors to the *God and Jesus* project, the being and identity of God, the nature of prophethood, and the revelatory capacity of scripture, are all made manifest in history. It is important to realize that Muslims may conceive of the relationship between God, prophethood, and revelation on the one hand, and history on the other, differently.[26] It does not help the conversation or contribute to mutual understanding if Christians perceive the Islamic distinctiveness on this point as somehow a failing or a reluctance to concede the obvious.[27]

Finally, Bijlefeld stresses, with help from Mark Thomsen's essay, the urgency that faith in "the risen prophet" address "the burning issues of the societies of which we are a part" (*GJ* 78). For the Christian-Muslim dialogue (*GJ* 79),

> . . . the most important "common ground" in many situations
> and relations is to be found not in (assumed) areas of theological emergence and in analogous affirmations, but rather in the

26. Bijlefeld quotes Abdoldjavad Falaturi: ". . . there is no reason to conceive of revelation as something temporal or historical" (*GJ,* 76). The quotation is from Falatūri's "Experience of Time," 65.

27. I am probably going beyond Bijlefeld's careful formulations at this point.

commonality of wrestling with the kind of questions that beset all of us as human beings. And seeking to articulate the relevance of our faith to the basic issues of everyday life is one of the most significant ways in which we can fulfill our calling "to be witnesses," in the fullest and most comprehensive meaning of those words.

God and Jesus: The Legacy

Did the *God and Jesus* project bear any lasting fruit? The volume does not seem to have had wide circulation; it was printed in limited quantities before the dawn of the internet era. To this day, I cannot find any pdf copy of it online, and WorldCat reports just six copies held by libraries: five in libraries of seminaries of the ELCA and one at Oxford University.

It may be that the project bore fruit in the lives and ministries of individuals—missionaries, perhaps, or the participants in the project themselves. I am tempted to think that the project's director, Mark Thomsen, may have learned some significant things from it. Over the following decade (until 1996), he headed up the global mission divisions of the ALC and of its successor body, the ELCA. Especially as director of the global mission unit of the ELCA, he saw to it that Christian-Muslim encounter was placed at the center of the unit's work.[28] He sought out occasions for genuine dialogue, supported the training of the next generation of scholars in Christian-Muslim relations, and played a role in the establishment of Christian-Muslim study centers at the ELCA theological seminaries in St. Paul and Chicago.[29] In many ways, the correctives and admonitions that I have identified in Willem Bijlefeld's essay came to be embodied in Thomsen's later career.

Be that as it may, the project remains remarkable for the theological creativity that it enabled: the use of the qur'anic notion of *shirk* to describe and to critique Christian trinitarianism, and the reformulation and clarification of the "do Christians and Muslims worship the same God" problem. With these, the project moved beyond one seeking apologetic tools

28. On Thomsen's "Focus on Islam," see Grafton, *Piety, Politics, and Power*, 228–32.

29. I (Mark Swanson) am the direct beneficiary of all of this. Thomsen supported my doctoral work (at the Pontifical Institute for Arabic and Islamic Studies in Rome) in Christian-Muslim studies and Arabic Christian theology, and eventually I came to teach at Luther Seminary in St. Paul and then at the Lutheran School of Theology at Chicago. This essay is an opportunity for me to honor Mark Thomsen, as well as my teachers Robert Jenson and Willem Bijlefeld.

to facilitate Christian witness "within a Muslim context," and offered a foretaste, an appetizer, of what might come from a Christian theology that was truly open to interreligious dialogue. The full meal is probably still in preparation; but already in 1986, North American Lutherans were given a taste of what might be possible.

Step–by–Step

A Theological Rendering of a Consultative Panel

MICHAEL REID TRICE

THE BIG IDEAS IN history are a matter of retrospect. Yet, in the present, we experience how events unfold step-by-step; if we're fortunate, then they unfold with intent and purpose, albeit with the future uncertain. In time, historical context, theological and ecclesiological insight, and organizational opportunity are all forces that have a role to play on our topic. What follows is my rendering of how some of those forces led to and through or otherwise influenced the creation of the Consultative Panel on Lutheran-Muslim Relations in the Evangelical Lutheran Church in America (ELCA), and its potential future. That rendering begins in Chicago.

The Department for Ecumenical and Inter–Religious Relations

On May 14, 2004, I stepped off a plane into a pollinated Midwestern spring Chicago day, following a turbulent flight that ended four years of student and professional life in Munich, Germany. Before that time, I was seeking a graduate degree and serving as part of a legal team in North Carolina that endeavored to represent mostly African-American men who were found guilty of the capital crime of murder and who were sentenced to receive the death penalty in North Carolina Central Prison. Most of these men were Muslim. At midnight on October 13, 2001, just a month after 9/11, one of these men, who had also become a friend—David Junior Ward—was executed by the state of North Carolina. David's death ended a long stretch of years with a forward-facing view of structural racism within the U.S. judicial system, so that, a short time after David's execution, when the opportunity presented itself to complete my doctoral work abroad, I jumped at it. I was young and disaffected and at the time had no thought of coming back to life in the States.

Four years later, at O'Hare International Airport, people jostled past one another. I collected an oversized trunk and dragged both myself and it into a cab, handing an airline napkin to the driver that contained the scribbled address of the Lutheran School of Theology at Chicago. Three months prior, I'd been asked to serve as the new associate executive for the Department for Ecumenical Affairs in the ELCA churchwide office and felt an immediate vocational response. I fully agree that religion can have a positive role to play for the common good of society; and as a Lutheran Christian steeped in an ecumenical education, it seemed a terrific opportunity to roll up sleeves with other more experienced colleagues.

The Department for Ecumenical Affairs, located proximal to the presiding bishop's office, was only years prior immersed in the work of establishing full communion relationships with the Reformed Church in America, the Presbyterian Church (U.S.A.), the Moravian Church, and the Episcopal Church. Numerous additional dialogues were taking place at that time, including with the Disciples of Christ, United Methodists, the Pan-Methodist African Methodist Episcopal and African Methodist Episcopal Zion churches. Within two hours of arriving at LSTC, I crossed the street to the front doors of the seminary and greeted Mark Thomsen.

Mark wore his vocation on his sleeve, which poured out into the offices of pastor, educator, administrator, and more. Mark was likewise the celebrated former executive director of the Division of Global Mission (DGM) for the ELCA and former director of the Division of World Mission and Inter-Church Cooperation for the American Lutheran Church (DWMIC), and had lived abroad and traveled the world in work and study. My meeting with him was not a coincidence. Referring to the new position, Mark said frankly, "You must focus on relationships with the Muslim community." He said it three times at least, with an urgency in his eyes that frames the memory in my mind today.

Mark was right, more than I realized at the time—and not only due to unresolved xenophobia within the genetics of the American experience and its founding documents, including the unresolved genocides of indigenous peoples and people of African descent who were enslaved and brought to the country against their will. Local histories and lore, rendered iconic in the numerous national heroes cast in statuary across the country, revealed a stain of white supremacy that would emerge as unencumbered racism at the highest levels of the executive branch in the U.S. government. Mark was principally right because he recognized an ecclesiological and moral necessity and the breath of the Spirit at the core of Luther's social ethics, or what theologian George Forell called "faith active in love," that is meant to be a barometer within the beating heart of Christian vocation.[1] Indeed, through the dedication of lay and ordained leaders in the U.S. and around the world, some of whom became professors in our Lutheran seminaries and universities after years of dedicated service in a global missional context, these leaders were all participants in a Lutheran theological and missional charism wrapped in ecclesial *accompaniment*, which later shaped this term's current branding purchase within the ELCA. Yes: care for others and care for neighbors included care for Muslims in the U.S. and around the world where Lutherans served. This kind of unalloyed turn to the neighbor was core to Luther's moral theological aptitude. As Luther reminds us in his explanation of the eighth commandment, "We should fear and love God that we may not deceitfully belie, betray, slander, or defame our neighbor, but defend him, [think and] speak well of him, and put the best construction on everything." In 2004, in view of the emerging geopolitical wreckage of the peace process in the Middle East and in growing alarm at the chronic national bias toward Muslims post-9/11, Mark saw a need at the churchwide offices of the ELCA. Two days after my meeting with Mark, I started my work, and in the months and years that passed, I recall the requests of university and college chaplains, seminary faculty, pastors in local communities, globally based synod friends throughout the ELCA, and colleagues in the ELCA churchwide offices, who all confirmed Mark's comments that afternoon: "Focus on relationships with the Muslim community."[2]

1. For Luther's understanding of Islam, read Francisco's "Luther's Knowledge of and Attitude Toward Islam."

2. One of the instructive works for Mark at the time included Ramadan's *Western Muslims and the Future of Islam*. In particular, Ramadan notes an approach for interreligious dialogue with Muslim colleagues (200–213).

The ELCA Department for Ecumenical Affairs was tasked first by the ELCA presiding bishop to create a formal relationship with the Muslim community. But, with all the global expertise in the ELCA Division of Global Mission, why was Ecumenical Affairs tapped with this responsibility, in practical terms? This is a question with a tangle of historical antecedents.

First, in 2004 there existed—even in the churchwide office—a healthy suspicion that ecumenical work was the terrain of ecclesio-cratic Lutherans who were at heart evangelical Catholics, attending to national and international dialogues that were disconnected from the practical lives and needs of everyday Lutheran Christians. However inaccurate this perception was, the balance of reality is most often seated in perception. One perception persisted, that the allure of esoteric theological dialogue was at odds with the practical pieties and the daily congregational realities of the church.

I met only dedicated ecumenists in my eight years at the office, including volunteers throughout the ELCA who selflessly served as the ecclesial ligature of the ecumenical and growing interreligious movements in their towns, cities, synods, and regions. These were people who bootstrapped their way to regional and national events in support of the aims of the church, who received only limited funds from synods, and who were and are some of the more dedicated and under-heralded ecclesial servants I know.

Lessons from the Lutheran–Jewish Consultative Panel

Months before I arrived, in the winter of 2004, *Guidelines for Christian-Muslim Relations* was drafted by a task force that included luminaries like Charles Amjad-Ali, Carol LaHurd, Michael Shelley, Mark Swanson, Harold Vogelaar, Nelly van Doorn-Harder, and Mark Thomsen. The project was convened by Benyam Kassahun. Existentially wise and ecclesially-minded questions of the task force at that time included how such guidelines could be translated into a resource for congregations in North America. For instance, could it help to build connections between Lutheran Christians and Muslim communities for the good of civil society; or assist in heightening awareness of the large number of Muslim immigrants and the work of Lutheran Immigration and Refugee Service; or increase a local response of solidarity to unforeseen future emergencies within a post-9/11 America; or amplify the role of Muslim communities in civic organizations in the U.S.; or more? In brief, work had already been well underway.

These efforts required greater appreciation and acceptance. In 2004, I perceived an unnecessary hurdle between the DGM and Ecumenical Affairs. It was a hurdle evident, for instance, when the close of a communique on Lutheran-Jewish Relations in the ELCA at that time concluded that "conversations with other faiths" would be coordinated through the auspices of the National Council of Churches of Christ, with no mention of the Christian-Muslim relations work being led through the DGM or of the task force that had already been working. There was no lack of good will or competency, and most often the reasons for organizational misalignment are ironed out in time. It is nevertheless important to note how Lutherans from unique directions were well on the road with Muslim neighbors already.

Within a year, I recall being in the office the day the secretary of the ELCA, in coordination with the executive for Ecumenical Affairs, decided that "Inter-Religious" would bear a hyphen, as it does to this day, a product of its time in the musings of ecumenists now tasked with a broader charge. The Department for Ecumenical Affairs in 2004 was heavily invested in five vectors of its work, these being: 1) advancing key ecumenical relationships toward full communion, in which full communion is a relationship that emerges between ecclesial bodies based on a common confession of the Christian faith and a mutual recognition of baptism and the Eucharist; 2) curating a relationship with the Jewish community following the 1994 *Declaration of ELCA to the Jewish Community* and the *Guidelines for Lutheran-Jewish Relations* that was adopted by the ELCA Church Council at its meeting on November 16, 1998; 3) cultivating national and international dialogues with the Catholic, Orthodox, United Methodist, Mennonite, Disciples of Christ, African Methodist Episcopal, and African Methodist Episcopal Zion church bodies, 4) assisting Presiding Bishop Mark Hanson, who in 2003 was the newly minted president of the Lutheran World Federation, and 5) tending to the ecumenical and interreligious relationships within conciliar ecumenism, which included the new Christian Churches Together in the USA, Churches Uniting in Christ, the National Council of Churches, Church World Service, the Lutheran World Federation, and the World Council of Churches. Like the Catholic Pontifical Council for Christian Unity's Commission for Religious Relations with the Jews, by correlation the ELCA Department for Ecumenical Affairs (which as I noted above did not include the term

Fearing serious changes to the polity and practice of the ELCA and any consequential results in reordering ministry, constitutional amendments, and liturgical revision, the Word Alone Network of Lutherans emerged. Sensing that the ELCA would insist on certain invariable practices for the realization of full communion, including the theological assertion that the historic episcopate is essential to the unity of the church, a fissure formed that preceded other ruptures. In addition, a fear of Muslims—Islamophobia—often expressed as an irritability with Islam, trailed some of these conversations. Often enough, phone calls from within the U.S. would reach me, with an inquiry about why the ELCA required furthering these relationships with Muslims in the country.

Formal interreligious dialogue proceeded from an ecumenical commitment to bilateral and multilateral dialogues (i.e., Lutheran-Jewish, Lutheran-Muslim), and national campaigns (such as the Shoulder to Shoulder campaign). This said, the creation of a Consultative Panel on Lutheran-Muslim Relations was constructed atop the successful experience of the Consultative Panel on Lutheran-Jewish Relations, and—upon viewing the 1994 *Declaration of ELCA to the Jewish Community* or the 1999 *Guidelines for Lutheran-Jewish Relations*—what the Lutheran-Jewish consultative panel had going for it was a conscious recognition of the power of an apology.[8] In these early years, both the Lutheran World Federation and the ELCA refuted Luther's anti-Judaic diatribes and quashed any future theological justification for anti-Semitism. In my estimation, what the *Declaration* achieved was a pledge, in the form of an apology, that would look backward and forward along the thin line between past and future. The labors of the consultative panel excelled at recognizing how an institutional apology requires an organization do at least three things well.

First, it must interrogate its own historical amnesia about how a malformation of its theology of grace informed the ruin of other human beings, families, and a whole community across centuries. Theology, like any language system, can be utilized to justify abhorrent actions in the name of a sanctifying righteousness. For instance, the Dutch Reformed Church

---

8. The ELCA Church Council's *Declaration of ELCA to the Jewish Community* does not actually apologize for the activities of Lutherans and the Lutheran heritage over the centuries, but it does refer to anti-Judaism as a "contagion," and grace as sufficient for reaching "our deepest shames and address[ing] the most tragic truths" of anti-Semitism is a "contradiction" to the Gospel. The statement's strength is this: "We pledge this church to oppose the deadly working of such bigotry, both within our own circles and in the society around us."

provided what amounted to a theological justification for apartheid that required the intercession of the World Alliance of Reformed Churches in 1982. The centuries-long impact of anti-Semitism and anti-Judaism for Lutherans was an exceptionally long arc, and any generative connection to Luther's theology had to be severed. This would include an eventual repudiation of the Reformer's anti-Judaic diatribes. Future relationships with the Jewish community would draw from the value of this pledge of Lutheran Christians who undertook a reforming self-awareness.

Second, the present bears a moral responsibility to the past. This reality allows for a discerning discourse on the capacity of institutions to seek and receive the forgiveness of their forebears and to explore how the present bears responsibility to those long dead. The 2019 *Declaration of the ELCA to People of African Descent* is another example of the parallaxes of apology so essential to the orbit of a shared future.

Third, the resiliency of grace and hope cannot be undervalued. The descendants of these communities do, after all, continue. Relationships can and do emerge with deeper awareness; a reconfigured connection to one's core theology may be reached with greater vitality and health; and religious adherents—in this case, Jewish and Lutheran Christian communities—are able to seek alliances of safe and creative spaces for collaboration toward shared aims in the future.

Transgressors in the past can become watchtowers for the future. This is what the Lutheran-Muslim consultative panel inherited from the Lutheran-Jewish consultative panel. In many ways, the name "consultative" is too descriptively narrow. Theologians, pastors, practitioners, and administrators comprised these panels. The Lutheran-Muslim consultative panel inherited a recognition—even an internal awareness—that hate will surge and resurge, most often masked as legitimate and viable civic discourse. Our only recourse is to be vigilant—and vigilance is not a point in time on that thin temporal arc I noted earlier. Rather, drawing on insights from the apology above, vigilance runs from a recognition of moral responsibility to the past and then turns toward the open future, without ceasing to see that the difference between loving the neighbor and harm done to others is in the will of a people to remember and to live the impact of that memory daily, with diligence.[9]

9. This view is evident in numerous ELCA documents before and since, including the ELCA social message *Human Rights* (2017); ELCA social statement *Freed in Christ: Race, Ethnicity and Culture* (1993); and the founding ELCA social statement *Church in Society: A Lutheran Perspective* (1991).

The Beginnings of the Lutheran–Muslim Consultative Panel

The Lutheran-Muslim consultative panel and a long hoped-for groundswell of local to national efforts at increased, organized dialogue with Muslims, gained in momentum following the release of *A Common Word between Us and You* document in October 2007. With an original 138 signatories, *A Common Word* was a brave and well-orchestrated open letter from Muslim to Christian leadership around the world.[10] The letter arrived via email on Thursday, October 11, in the afternoon, and too late for a response of any significance within the current news cycle. At that time, news cycles peeked on Thursday afternoons; thereafter, the window for a possible readership would shift to the following Monday. With exuberance, a colleague and I sat down on the eleventh floor of the churchwide office and began penning a response. It would need to be straightforward in acknowledgment, appreciative, earnest, and forward-thinking; it required symbolic value. By the time we were on the phone with Bishop Mark Hanson, we were ready to present him with options for a response. Bishop Hanson listened and then shaped the message with a clarity that I remember thinking demonstrated the seriousness from what we'd learned about discrimination against Jews and how we would continue to stand alongside Muslims in the country and the world. One of the highlights of my time in the ELCA was inscribed in the effort underneath the words of that statement from Bishop Hanson, presiding bishop and president of the Lutheran World Federation: "I acknowledge this letter," he noted, " . . . [and] accept it in the belief that Jews, Muslims, and Christians are called to one another as to a holy site, where God's living revelation in the world is received in reverence among the faithful and not in fear of our neighbors."[11] The statement was released on Friday morning. We sent it everywhere for a whole week. The Lutheran-Muslim consultative panel began in earnest less than a year later.

In a post-9/11 context, Lutheran scholars and practitioners—including especially those serving as pastors and lay professionals in ELCA congregations—knew that anti-Muslim bias had saturated our society. Systems of bias get underneath the skin of human intention. Once bias is chronic, like an auto-immune disorder in the human body, an unattended apology is always only a temporary salve. I was in Washington, D.C., at the Lutheran

---

10. *Common Word.*

11. Hanson, "Response."

office on Capitol Hill to witness this bias, when the United States House Committee on Homeland Security chairman, Rep. Peter King of New York, used his position in 2011 to hold hearings on the radicalization of Muslims in North America. It was evident again in the 2017 so-called "Muslim ban" by the Trump administration in its attempt to ban entry into the United States from select Muslim-majority countries.[12] These tremors of structural bias were evident in 2010 when the Shoulder to Shoulder campaign began, at the height of anti-Muslim rhetoric and hate in the United States. I recall being on the phone in a conference call when Jewish, Muslim, and Christian leaders decided on the name for this new organization. "We have to demonstrate the unity of our plurality," someone said. "We must stand shoulder to shoulder in this." That was the moment, in a conference call between Jewish, Muslim, and Christian colleagues seeking a coalition in faith. The campaign continues today with new leadership, but a shared spirit.

In 2008, the tasks of the Lutheran-Muslim consultative panel included the creation of viable resources for use in congregational contexts; advising the ELCA regarding both the conditions of Muslim-Lutheran relations and the possibilities for emerging opportunities with Muslim communities at the local to national contexts; seeking ways to cultivate deeper dialogue between these communities; and, in all things, developing a strategic sensibility for future endeavors.[13] The panel in 2008 included Nelly van Doorn Harder, Mark Swanson, J. Paul Rajashekar, Kathy Gerking, Patricia Hurd, myself and Said Ailabouni from the ELCA staff. The panel did develop resources built on established and emerging relationships—in particular, with national Muslim organizations such as the Islamic Society of North America, under the leadership of Dr. Sayyid M. Syeed, who at that time served as the national director of ISNA's Office for Interfaith and Community Alliances in Washington, D.C., and ISNA's general secretary prior to that. We also developed relationships with leadership in organizations such as the Council on American-Islamic Relations. At the local and national levels, it took some time to determine the parity of dialogue partners with Muslim colleagues, given the various ethnic composition of many of these communities.

The consultative panel was also affiliated with the creation of *Windows for Understanding: Jewish—Muslim—Lutheran Relations*, which was

---

12. Bash, "Peter King"; ACLU, "Timeline of the Muslim Ban."

13. See https://www.elca.org/Faith/Ecumenical-and-Inter-Religious-Relations/Inter-Religious-Relations/Online-Resources.

an effort to meet the needs of congregations and to equip them with information that could be useful in their local towns, municipalities, and regions. That resource included a glossary of terms and phrases, in the hopes that it might be more appreciated.

A curious aspect of this document is its first premise in the introduction, that Lutheran Christians reside "in a rich pluralistic world." Pluralism is taken up briefly by one of the writers and was also used in the 2004 *Guidelines for Christian-Muslim Relations*, in its assertion that, "Lutheran Christians are well-equipped to serve enhanced Muslim-Christian relations for a number of reasons, including . . . our legacy from Luther of *simul iustus et peccator* . . . . These elements in our tradition free us to live with the ambiguities inherent in human existence, including the ambiguities of dealing with religious pluralism."[14]

The supposition in this statement is that the both-and (*simul-et*) of righteousness before God is as evident in our approach to dialogue as to daily life, and that, amid the pluralities of difference, grace is a constant. The Lutheran Christian vocation allows therefore for substantial difference and even contradiction, both within our own selves and in how we see God's grace active in the world. This pastoral and theological chain of our DNA helps assists us in ecumenical and interreligious dialogue. At our best, we show up as pastoral theologians who are seeking to understand, undeterred by difficult topics, recognizing the power of mutal discernment, encountering others without fearing difference, and with the premise that grace is big enough for all of it. This is a Lutheran charism. For all the work that the consultative panel either created or collaborated upon, from the *Engaging Others, Knowing Ourselves* resource to 2016 onward, this emphasis upon the Lutheran Christian approach of both-and is more than operational; it is as genetically situated as ever an enculturated theology could be.

The Future of the Lutheran–Muslim Consultative Panel

The general composition of the consultative panel was of strong insight and leadership. However, one would be hard-pressed not to see how the current emergence of ideological strains in this country that no longer believed pluralism was a virtue of public life would impact the panel's perspectives. Much of those early years for the Lutheran-Muslim consultative panel were

14. ELCA Consultative Panel on Lutheran-Muslim Relations, *Guidelines*, l. 29–33.

still conscripted along the lines of a bilateral model, as a campaign of like-minded progressives. Clearly, its weakness was that progressives knew what one another thought; more conservative perspectives were absent. Since then, racial justice proponents and anti-fascist advocates have arisen. Likewise, the LGBTQIA+, Black Lives Matter, #MeToo, and POC movements may yet also transcend any religious particularity. This means, referring back to the 2004 *Guidelines*, that pluralism is not something to be "dealt" with, as the privileged statement seemed to suggest. Rather, pluralism—in all its varietals of color, context, religion, sexuality, race, and gender—is a worldview that will require the future of interreligious dialogue to be relevant and not too fixed on binaries.

From an institutional perspective, with its history of relying upon a representative principle for any dialogue, pluralism may look ambiguous and issue-based. But as a worldview, pluralism invites a creative and constructive theological imagination about the value of religious traditions and spiritual pathways that today transcends the institutional privilege of a consultative panel as it was then conceived. The #MeToo or LGBTQIA+ movements seek a depth of allies within culture, rather than a granting of permission to exist from any institution.

I started with the ELCA churchwide office in 2004 and served until 2011, continuing today to serve on the Faith and Order table of the National Council of Churches and on interreligious dialogue tables. Since that time, I've assisted as secretary of the Parliament of the World's Religions, worked alongside partners including Church World Service, and for the past nine years served as an associate professor of constructive theology at Seattle University in the Pacific Northwest. Today, I am also the director of the Center for Religious Wisdom and World Affairs at SU and serve in capacities within the Northwest Washington Synod under the inspiring leadership of Bishop Shelley Bryan Wee. In some ways, I am far removed from Higgins Road. I believe in its leadership, and I live by the expressions of the church with a love for helping form the next generation of ordained and lay leaders in our ministries. Two years ago, with ecumenical and interreligious colleagues, I founded *Religica*, an online platform—a theological laboratory—connected to my work as faculty for testing the ligature of deeper meaning from religious traditions and spiritual pathways. *Religica* begins with the premise that, in a postmodern context, the localized human story is the seat of value, and the wisdom of our traditions arrives through the individual and collective telling of those stories today. My students and colleagues convince me of the need for theological discovery that is congruent with the both-and genetic trace noted above. Even having said all this, I wonder what the composition of any reconfiguration for a Lutheran-Muslim consultative panel might be. Looking back briefly again, I'll identify some aspects of that context and conclude with five questions.

When you consider those early aforementioned and evolving stressors in the historical context of the churchwide operation, and the tensions within American society about the role of Muslim communities within civic life in the early years of the twenty-first century, ecclesial communities were thoughtful on how to go about building or enhancing relationships. At the same time, those in and around the role of religion in North America, who were colleagues to the ELCA Department for Ecumenical Affairs, were discussing a shift in American consciousness that included a curious form of emerging neo-conservativism, evident in the earliest expressions of the Word Alone movement, though not only there. There were analogues in the experience of ecumenical partners, including in emerging young Catholic clergy who were suspicious of Vatican II. What felt like an odd retrenchment, in fact represented a turn taking place within American society. We were witnessing the impact of the continued erosion of moral and ecclesial authority at the same time as the United States experienced a corollary ambivalence of faith in the civic structures that guide everyday life. By the time of the 2009 ELCA Churchwide Assembly's approval of its social statement *Human Sexuality: Gift and Trust,* the challenge was not one of moral theology, but rather, at core, a crisis of perception from within a shared theological anthropology—that is, what is permitted of the human being and who has the authority to determine it.

In the years since, up to around 2018, the arrival of far right and far left populist forces and of neo-conservative and post-liberal progressives reveals in sharp display a crisis of confidence in the authority of traditional structures to serve the existential and political needs of everyday life. The arrival of national populism, cloaked in nostalgia for a more unalloyed age of patriotism, on the right, and the left's incapacity to prove its case as a matter of common sense in the public square, devolved recently into balkanized narratives and counter-narratives, ill-equipped and suspicious of communicating amid difference in our current national climate. Distrust of expertise and the arrival of a cancel culture first began with suspicion and continued to ideological derision in the U.S. societal context. What is unfolding today through extreme movements on left or right—Antifa, NFAC, Boogaloo,

Proud Boys, to name a few—is the arrival of extreme entrenched ideologies first begun in suspicion, but now framed by a furrowed cloister of suppositions and anticipated outcomes, to which the ELCA (and our ecumenical and interreligious partners) will have to respond in these newest culture wars on who has the authority to lead a nation forward.

Having noted these stressors, I would suggest that any future iteration of a Lutheran-Muslim consultative panel for the ELCA consider in earnest five questions.

1. Where is the Lutheran theological imagination?

Since the 1991 ELCA policy statement *A Declaration of Ecumenical Commitment* called for a "separate, official statement" that ultimately arrived in the 2019 ELCA *Declaration of Inter-Religious Commitment*, does the church have a shared awareness of pluralism as gift rather than a danger? Do we have a Lutheran language in our congregations that arises from a collective theological and ecclesiological imagination that recognizes pluralism as gift?

2. What is needed right now?

It seems such a fundamental question that it hardly bears elucidation; and yet, since the beginning of the consultative panels, our national and global contexts have changed, and a pandemic is also revealing stark inequalities and underlying modalities that are steeped in assumed supremacy of "whiteness" as a source of power and privilege. We also have challenges of a changing climate that reveals disparities on a global scale. Are we at a point where the pain-points that are strewn within societies require an approach that includes, yet transcends, a bilateral approach to Lutheran-Christian-Muslim consultation? Alternatively, are we learning that, precisely due to these challenges, bilateral conversations are essential for addressing particular challenge points to these partners? Locate the needs, and calibrate the future of any panel toward meeting those needs.

3. How do we frame an integrated response of the consultative panel to the whole church?

Pope Francis, in his 2015 encyclical *Laudato Si*, refers to the "integrated ecology" of any ecclesial effort today; this means that consultation is for the whole church, at all times, everywhere. Is robust consultation seeing an integrated response from all quarters of the Lutheran-Muslim experience,

Bishop Eaton's leadership in Lutheran-Muslim relations and to recognize the fruits of Lutheran-Muslim pilot projects in several ELCA synods. In attendance were ISNA leaders, local Christian-Muslim dialogue partici-pants, and a host of ecumenical and inter-religious partners representing national organizations and initiatives.

That morning, I had called Jim Winkler, the general secretary and president of the National Council of Churches. I knew he was one of the national partners coming from D.C. to the ISNA banquet in Chicago, so I asked him to bring me a few hard copies of the *Post*. During my conclud-ing remarks that evening, I held up the front page to emphasize that we had come far enough in our work together as Lutherans and Muslims that the world was taking notice. Our mutual accountability had become a matter of public interest, and perhaps our partnership was timelier than we had even planned.

I had known from Mandy that the *Post* article was soon to be published, and we had been working with our synod bishops on the presentations for the banquet for several weeks. The fact that the article and the award came together on July 1 was a beautiful coincidence. But coincidences are not always happenstance. Decades of ecumenical and inter-religious work have laid the foundation for where we are in Lutheran-Muslim relations at the outset of 2020. This chapter will explore the significant developments in Lutheran-Muslim relations over the past two decades in the broader con-text of ELCA ecumenical and inter-religious relations.

Ecumenical Foundations

When the ELCA was formed by merger in 1988, it inherited the significant ecumenical undertakings of its predecessor bodies. Decades of participa-tion in conciliar life, various forms of ecumenical cooperation, and formal bilateral dialogues meant the new church was on the verge of significant developments. The possibility of "full communion" was in sight.[2]

2. Full communion describes a relationship intended to advance common mission in the Gospel on the basis of mutual recognition, while providing for the exchange-ability of clergy on the basis of mutual reconciliation of ministries. As a result of the Lutheran-Reformed dialogue in the U.S., the ELCA first entered into full communion in 1997 with the Presbyterian Church (U.S.A.), the Reformed Church in America, and the United Church of Christ. In 1999, the ELCA Churchwide Assembly voted to enter into full communion with the Moravian Church (Northern and Southern Provinces) and the Episcopal Church. Most recently, in 2009, the ELCA Churchwide Assembly voted to

The predecessor bodies had taken different approaches to ecumenism based on their respective polities. In order to maintain the momentum, the new church would need a coalesced ecumenical vision and strategy. At the first ELCA Churchwide Assembly in 1989, a statement on ecumenism was presented, which sought to answer the question: "Why do we engage in ecumenical relations?" The assembly sent it back to the ecumenical committee for further work. A new text was developed, one which also answered the question: "How?"

In 1991, the ELCA Churchwide Assembly adopted a policy statement, *A Declaration of Ecumenical Commitment*. It presents a trajectory of "goals and stages" of ecumenical relationship where the goal is visible Christian unity, and the stages begin with "cooperation" and culminate in "full communion."[3] The policy offers clear parameters and creative flexibility. As a result, the ELCA has come to be recognized by its partners for its theological depth and practical innovation in ecumenism.

As one would expect, *A Declaration of Ecumenical Commitment* focuses almost exclusively on relationships with other Christians. Yet in merely two lines, it set the stage for nearly three decades' worth of significant developments in ELCA inter-religious relations. Acknowledging the "distinct responsibility for the church to enter into conversations and reach greater understanding with people of other faiths," the policy calls for a "separate, official statement" in the future.[4] In these few words, the declaration accomplished two significant tasks: it claimed the ongoing vocation of the church in inter-religious relations, and it articulated the necessity of giving that vocation further definition.

At the time of these developments, the religious landscape of the United States had been changing rapidly. As a result of the 1965 Immigration and Nationality Act, the world's religions and global Christianity had become part of American religious demography. By the time the ELCA was born, it was already widely understood that the ministry of the church would be carried out in a broader multi-religious context. Building on the work of its predecessor bodies in the U.S. and the global work of Lutheran World Federation, ELCA ministries of various sorts were engaged in inter-religious relations from the beginning, including the efforts of the national church and its synodical and congregational expressions, but also in the

---

enter into full communion with the United Methodist Church.

3. ELCA, *Declaration of Ecumenical Commitment*, 8–9.

4. ELCA, *Declaration of Ecumenical Commitment*, 13.

context of global mission. As in ecumenism, the ELCA hit the ground run-
ning in inter-religious relations, especially in Lutheran-Jewish and then in
Lutheran-Muslim relations.

All of this deeply informed the development of *A Declaration of
Inter-Religious Commitment*, adopted in 2019. Unlike its ecumenical
counterpart, this policy statement could not be conceived as a roadmap
to a single goal of visible unity. Instead, it would need to be imagined as
a framework for understanding and engaging the Christian vocation in
a multi-religious world. The ELCA's longstanding Lutheran-Jewish, and
subsequently Lutheran-Muslim, relations gave clear shape to the two
central dimensions of this calling: seeking mutual understanding and
cooperation for the common good.

ELCA Lutheran–Jewish Relations

The primary inter-religious work in the early years of the ELCA was in
Lutheran-Jewish relations. These were overseen by the Consultative Panel
on Lutheran-Jewish Relations. Formed in 1991, the panel was tasked with
maintaining relations with Jewish leaders, developing educational and
dialogical resources for the church, and advising the presiding bishop and
church leaders on matters of Jewish-Christian relations.

On the basis of the actions and statement on "Luther, Lutheranism,
and the Jews" of the Lutheran World Federation a decade prior, the ELCA
Church Council adopted in 1994 a *Declaration of ELCA to the Jewish
Community*,[5] repudiating Luther's anti-Judaic writings, opposing anti-Semitism, and reaching out in right relationship to the Jewish community. This
second declaration of the ELCA became the initial foundation for ELCA
inter-religious relations, giving "special attention . . . to the distinctiveness
of Judaism" as called for in the ecumenical declaration.[6]

Over the years, the consultative panel has developed several congregational resources and guidelines for Christian-Jewish relations.[7] Panelists
have also represented the ELCA in national Jewish-Christian dialogues co-
convened by the National Council of Churches and the National Council of

---

5. ELCA Church Council, *Declaration of ELCA to the Jewish Community*.

6. ELCA, *Declaration of Ecumenical Commitment*, 13.

7. A series of pamphlets entitled *Talking Points: Topics in Christian-Jewish Relations*
and the book and DVD *Covenantal Conversations: Christians in Dialogue with Jews and
Judaism* have been particularly useful.

Synagogues. The panel played a vital role in the ELCA's first bilateral inter-religious dialogue with the Union for Reform Judaism. In 2005, then-URJ president Rabbi Eric Yoffie was the first inter-religious guest to address the ELCA Churchwide Assembly. Recently, these relations have been renewed, with a focus on shared advocacy on issues of common concern, such as immigration reform and climate justice.

Just as ELCA ecumenical relations helped clarify the distinct need for work in inter-religious relations, so Jewish-Lutheran relations have helped the ELCA to recognize in more recent years the distinct need for relations with Muslims.

ELCA Lutheran–Muslim Relations

If we go back to Luther and his troubling invectives against the Jews, we will also encounter his disturbing remarks about Muslims, made in the context of the Ottoman Turkish advances in Europe. Both Lutheran-Jewish and Lutheran-Muslim relations in contemporary context require a deep theological, sociological, and historical corrective.

Luther's contempt for the Jews was uniquely vile, and his direct encouragement of violence in thought, word, and deed—and its appropriation by Nazi Germany—demands our repudiation. In the case of the Turks, Luther was a bit more nuanced. While addressing difficult theological and pastoral questions about warfare and the call for a crusade, he sought reliable information about Islamic teachings. His agenda was to give people information that would authoritatively convince them that Christianity was superior. In so doing, he acknowledged his appreciation for the piety of Muslims and insisted that Muslim Turks could lead virtuous lives. Despite his dubious intentions, there are aspects of his thought that are a useful basis for our relations with Muslims today.

Current work toward *A Declaration of the ELCA to the Muslim Community* was begun in 2020. This work will need to address the complicated history between Luther and Islam, as well as our contemporary context in which anti-Muslim bigotry, discrimination, and violence have risen sharply, especially in the U.S., since September 11, 2001. It will also require that we reckon with the Islamophobic attitudes held by many within the ELCA. Once adopted, this declaration will be shared as a contribution to the Lutheran World Federation for its more complicated task of issuing a global statement on the topic. This will be a reversal from the LWF-ELCA process on a

Declaration of ELCA to the Jewish Community, but for good reason, given the vast contextual differences in Christian-Muslim relations.

The Initial Efforts

The tipping point toward establishing formal Christian-Muslim relations in the U.S. was the tragedy of September 11, 2001. As Muslims were coming under significant scrutiny and even attack, many Christian churches longed to build bridges of understanding and solidarity. Organic conversations between Christians and Muslims were eventually formalized with leadership from the Islamic Society of North America and the National Council of Churches, becoming the National Muslim-Christian Initiative in 2008.[8] This Christian-Muslim dialogue, in which the ELCA actively participates, has continued to meet annually, with a recent focus on religious bigotry and racism.

In 2007, the emerging dialogical efforts in the US were accelerated by the global initiative *A Common Word between Us and You*. This was an open letter signed by 138 Muslim leaders and addressed to Christian leaders worldwide. It called for unity and peace on the basis of the Christian and Muslim shared commitments for love of God and love of neighbor. The ELCA joined in ecumenical responses and also offered its own. Then-presiding bishop and LWF president Mark Hanson wrote that he accepted the letter, "in the belief that Jews, Muslims, and Christians are called to one another as to a holy site, where God's revelation in the world is received in reverence among the faithful and not in fear of our neighbors."[9]

The following year, a group of ELCA scholars, pastors, and practitioners were convened to explore how the church could enhance its own Muslim relations, becoming the Consultative Panel on Lutheran-Muslim Relations. Drawing upon the wisdom and experience of the Lutheran-Jewish panel, this new body set out to develop resources to educate ELCA members and ecumenical partners on Islam, to nurture dialogue and engagement, and to advise the leadership of the church on its relations. Some of the resources developed by the panel directly mirrored those of the Lutheran-Jewish panel, for example, *Talking Points: Topics in Christian-Muslim Relations*. But it was more than just the models and templates that were instructive. The shared commitments and Lutheran-Jewish relations

8. For a fuller treatment of this history, see Trice, "Lutheran and Muslim Relations."

9. Hanson, "Response."

themselves propelled Lutherans into deeper engagement with Muslims—including, especially, on the issue of religious bigotry.

Addressing Anti-Muslim Bigotry

By the fall of 2010, Islamophobia in our public discourse was at an unforeseen level in light of the so-called "Ground Zero Mosque" controversy and Terry Jones threatening to burn the Qur'an in Florida. In solidarity, Jewish and Christian leaders stood shoulder to shoulder with Muslim leaders to defend them against bigotry and to uphold the values of Islam, like other religions, as consistent with American democracy. The ELCA presiding bishop and staff participated in an interfaith press conference at the National Press Club that September, in which these commitments of solidarity were declared publicly. But much more was needed than simply a pronouncement.

Out of that public expression, the Shoulder to Shoulder campaign was born. The campaign is a national coalition of religious denominations and faith-based organizations that are committed to working together to end discrimination and violence against Muslims. In 2020, its tenth anniversary year, the campaign is more urgent than ever. The coalition continues to convene press conferences and issue statements. In recent years, the campaign also had worked to educate and network local religious leaders to address root causes of anti-Muslim bigotry. Several "Faith over Fear" trainings are convened around the country each year to equip people to counter anti-Muslim bias, discrimination, and violence in their own communities and to address the broader narrative of fear and divisiveness in our country.

In addition to employing cutting-edge research and industry-leading tools, these trainings also rely heavily on the expertise and insights of those with on-the-ground experience. The ELCA has been a strong leader in this regard, with people like ELCA Pastor Mandy France, mentioned at the outset of this chapter, and Pastor Terry Kyllo—the director of a Lutheran, Episcopal, and Muslim organization in Washington state called Neighbors in Faith—helping to plan and lead the trainings. With the encouragement of Presiding Bishop Elizabeth Eaton and their synod bishops, substantial numbers of ELCA pastors, lay leaders, and seminarians have also participated in these trainings. A Center for Christian-Muslim Engagement for Peace and Justice at the Lutheran School of Theology at Chicago has been a key partner as well. We have also worked to encourage synod bishops to respond to local incidents of anti-Muslim bigotry and hate crimes, by supporting them in writing timely op-eds for local news outlets and in hosting education, dialogue, and solidarity events. We are beginning to form a corps of leaders who are equipped to provide proactive, as well as reactive, leadership in this urgent realm of work.

Since 2018, I have been serving as co-chair of the campaign. This has been an opportunity to deepen our ELCA engagement with inter-religious partners in confronting anti-Muslim bigotry in society. It has also served as a platform for the difficult work of addressing Islamophobia within our church as well. Through Shoulder to Shoulder, we have had greater capacity for educating people across the ELCA about Islam and the realities of anti-Muslim bigotry. We have also had the opportunity to build stronger relationships with Muslims.

Education and Relationship–Building

It was precisely in these broader ecumenical and interfaith spaces—the National Muslim-Christian Initiative and the Shoulder to Shoulder Campaign—that the significant bilateral relationship between the ELCA and the ISNA began to mature. On the tenth anniversary of 9/11 in 2011, Dr. Sayyid Syeed, on behalf of ISNA, was the second inter-religious guest to address the ELCA Churchwide Assembly. He described how, "during the last millennium, mountains of hate [and] discrimination have been built. Our job," he said, "is to see those mountains of hate removed." Since then, we have shared in reciprocal exchanges at each other's events. The ELCA has had a strong presence at the annual ISNA convention, including the participation of the presiding bishop on several occasions. Dr. Syeed has been present for various ELCA gatherings, including ELCA 500, the commemoration of the five-hundredth anniversary of the Reformation in Washington, D.C., on October 31, 2017.

The strengthening of this partnership has also highlighted the need for further education about Islam across the ELCA. At times, bias or, in some cases, outright anti-Muslim bigotry has been expressed in response to the presiding bishop's leadership in Christian-Muslim relations. This has fast-tracked efforts to distribute and utilize the educational and dialogical resources developed by the consultative panel across the church. The 2012 addition of a film series and study guide, *Discover Islam*, has been crucial to reaching new audiences. Endorsed by ISNA, the films cover six topics, such as "African-Americans and Islam" and "Christianity and Islam." They are packaged on a flash drive, together with an ELCA study guide jointly developed by the consultative panel and A Center for Christian-Muslim Engagement at LSTC, providing an interpretive framework from a Lutheran Christian perspective that can be used to facilitate discussion. The parent organization, Discover Islam—USA, has generously distributed the resource to any ELCA individual or group and to our ecumenical partners, at no cost, greatly facilitating our educational efforts.

As this work deepened, so too did the demands of accountability to our partners. In December 2015, in the midst of backlash against American Muslims after the San Bernadino shootings by two self-proclaimed *jihadis*, Bishop Eaton issued an open letter to the American Muslim community. It was reflective of the new depth of our relations. She wrote, "In our love for you, our Muslim neighbors, we are distressed by the ways in which you are being forced to bear the fears held by many in our nation. Therefore, we renew our commitment to find even more effective ways to protect and defend you from words and actions that assault your safety and well-being. . . . [W]e will seek to stand shoulder to shoulder with you as agents of peace, justice, understanding, welcome and reconciliation for the sake of the world God so loves."[10] The letter was posted publicly and sent to the partners of the National Muslim-Christian Initiative. From there, it was circulated through many local Islamic Centers, some of which wrote letters of gratitude in response. The presiding bishop's unequivocal leadership also encouraged other ELCA pastors and lay leaders to provide such leadership in their own contexts.

In 2016, when Dr. Syeed addressed the Churchwide Assembly for the second time, Shoulder to Shoulder's executive director Catherine Orsborn was also present. The assembly adopted the resolution *My Muslim Neighbor*, commending ELCA educational resources for use across the church, encouraging ELCA members to work to eliminate anti-Muslim bigotry, and encouraging ELCA leaders to engage in dialogue and cooperation with Muslims. In setting this mandate for the ELCA, the Churchwide Assembly was recognizing and encouraging a comprehensive strategy for deepening and expanding Christian-Muslim relations, and declaring a public commitment in the presence of our partners.

Immediately following, Bishop Eaton and Dr. Syeed met to plan and launch a yearlong series of pilot projects. Three ELCA

10. ELCA, "ELCA Presiding Bishop."

Synods—Southeastern Pennsylvania, Southwestern Washington, and Southeast Michigan— partnered with ISNA to build church-mosque relations, advocacy, and coalitions at the local level. Other synods, such as Metropolitan Chicago, deepened existing work. Bishops from these synods presented on this work at the 2017 ISNA convention banquet when Bishop Eaton received the Interfaith Unity Award.

We are also deepening Lutheran-Muslim relations through a series of international efforts in which we find ourselves at the invitation of our Muslim partners. The Forum for Promoting Peace and also the Modern Alliance of Virtue have been spaces where, together with other (primarily U.S. evangelical) Christians and Muslims from around the world, we affirm our commitments to seeking peace on the basis of shared values. This is also true of our participation in other long-standing multi-religious coalitions, including Religions for Peace, the Council for a Parliament of the World's Religions, and so on.

Towards an *Inter-Religious Declaration*

In 2012, about a year after I came on staff, I worked with Darrell Jodock and Mark Swanson, the two respective chairs of the ELCA's Consultative Panels on Lutheran-Jewish and Lutheran-Muslim Relations to organize their first-ever joint meeting. The primary purpose of this meeting, convened by the presiding bishop, was to explore together the possibility of working toward a theological framework for the ELCA's inter-religious relations. It quickly became clear that other, more preliminary steps needed to be taken. One was to assess the state of inter-religious relations across the church, in a variety of ministry contexts.

To this end, the panels jointly undertook a case studies project, calling for submissions across the church. The end result was the publication of case studies, theological framing, practical tips, and historical analysis, in the book *Engaging Others, Knowing Ourselves: A Lutheran Calling in a Multi-Religious World* from Lutheran University Press in 2016. Many of the cases are about Lutheran-Muslim relations in congregations, campus ministries, community-based work, and chaplaincy. One example is from Wexford, PA, where the central question is: Will a Lutheran church say yes to the request from a local Muslim community, or worshipping community, to use their space for worship?[11] Cases such as this are helpful for exploring

---

11. Lohre, "A Prayerful Place," 46–47.

the theological and practical dimensions of inter-religious relations, and are illustrative of the ways in which Lutherans are actively seeking to love and defend our Muslim neighbors.

A second project was to assess the pitfalls and the promise of the Lutheran theological tradition with regard to inter-religious relations. This work resulted in the pamphlet written by the Lutheran-Jewish consultative anel and published as a resource for the five-hundredth anniversary of the Reformation, *Luther and Contemporary Inter-Religious Relations.*[12] It highlights four of Luther's theological principles that can serve as a guide for our thinking and doing today.

On the basis of this groundwork, Presiding Bishop Eaton announced at the 2016 Churchwide Assembly that she had appointed a task force to undertake the development of an inter-religious policy statement. Four of the ten task force members were from the consultative panels; the others included Lutheran scholars and practitioners in inter-religious work from across the church and a Sikh professor from one of the ELCA's universities.

The task force held its first meeting that fall and had a full draft within a year. In late 2017, ecumenical and inter-religious partners participated in a preliminary review of the draft. Their ideas informed the first major round of revisions and served to strengthen our self-understanding, as well as our mutual accountability with our partners. For the first half of 2018, the draft was made public for input and feedback across the church. Over the summer of 2018, the drafting team used the responses to work toward final revisions to the document. The declaration, in its final form, reflects the realities of our long-standing inter-religious relations as a church and gives us a framework for a common articulation of our context, calling, and commitments to this vocation of mutual understanding and cooperation with our neighbors. In short, it answers the critical questions of how and why we engage in inter-religious relations. At the heart of the document are twelve commitments, which function as a concise summary of the policy. The statement also includes the scriptural, confessional, theological, and constitutional basis for the policy, and calls for additional guidelines and resources to be developed to support the church's efforts in this area.

In October 2018, the ELCA Conference of Bishops strongly encouraged the ELCA Church Council to recommend the proposed policy statement for adoption by the 2019 Churchwide Assembly. In November 2018, the ELCA

---

12. ELCA Consultative Panel on Lutheran-Jewish Relations, *Luther and Contemporary Inter-Religious Relations.*

Church Council unanimously did so. The document was presented during the Churchwide Assembly in August 2019, and hearings were held for voting members to share their questions, concerns, and experiences.

The adoption of *A Declaration of Inter-Religious Commitment* took place in the context of the ecumenical and inter-religious plenary on Thursday, August 8, 2019. Importantly, just prior to the action, the Assembly commemorated the twenty-fifth anniversary of the *Declaration of ELCA to the Jewish Community*, by partaking in a *Litany of Confession*[13] based on the text. The reaffirmation of our commitments to Jewish relations and our repudiation of anti-Semitism and religious bigotry of any form set the stage. Rabbi Jonah Pesner of the Religious Action Center of Reform Judaism and representatives from ISNA and Shoulder to Shoulder addressed the assembly immediately following. When it came time for the action, the nearly fifty ecumenical and inter-religious partners were introduced and assembled on stage. The proceedings, which included a theological debate about the limits of what we know about God, as well as the limits of what we know about our neighbor's relationship with God, resulted in the adoption of the text, unamended, by a vote of 97.48%.

Importantly, all of this took place in the presence of our partners. Throughout the proceedings, our guests stood on the stage, facing the assembly. In so doing, they served as a reminder of the real, human partnerships at the heart of *A Declaration of Inter-Religious Commitment*. As the ELCA, we have declared that we believe that our inter-religious partners help us to authentically engage our commitments. They challenge us to be accountable to ourselves and to them. They remind us that everything we do as a church is not done in isolation from, but in relationship with, others.

Today, the ELCA has a corpus of social teaching that undergirds our church's ecumenical and inter-religious relations. It includes three declarations: *A Declaration of Ecumenical Commitment*; the *Declaration of ELCA to the Jewish Community*; and *A Declaration of Inter-Religious Commitment*. (As noted earlier, *A Declaration of the ELCA to the Muslim Community* will soon be added.) Each of these stands alongside the others, as complimentary to, consistent with, and conditional on each other.

In early 2020, the Lutheran-Jewish and Lutheran-Muslim consultative panels were convened by the presiding bishop for their second-ever joint meeting, eight years after their first. (Neither panel has met in person since the Inter-Religious Task Force was appointed in 2016, though they

---

13. ELCA, *Litany of Confession*.

have continued to work by virtual means.) Their agenda was to debrief and assess the state of the work and to develop a strategy for next steps. They also consulted with and advised the presiding bishop on the structures that will best serve the ELCA in tending to the unique relations with Jews and Muslims, as well as with the broader multi-religious context in which our work and witness as the church is taking place.

Broadening Relations

The ELCA participates in several inter-religious coalitions, such as Religions for Peace, the Council for a Parliament of the World's Religions, and Interfaith Youth Core. Those bodies each have a specific mission, and we are glad to partake with others. But what about the dialogical task of seeking mutual understanding? At the same time as we were knee-deep in the inter-religious case studies project, and in the early stages of the policy statement, we began to have conversations with other ecumenical and inter-religious partners about our hopes for an expanded set of dialogue partners, representing more fully our multi-religious context. But how?

After the shootings at the Oak Creek gurdwara in Wisconsin in 2012, the ELCA was the first national church body to reach out in solidarity to the leadership of the World Sikh Council—America Region. This led to further conversations with Sikh leaders and ultimately to Tarunjit Singh Butalia, then-president of the World Sikh Council, addressing the ELCA Assembly in 2013. He was the third inter-religious guest, and the first beyond the "Abrahamic" family. For a moment, we explored the possibility of something Lutheran-Sikh—and I say "something" because we never clarified what it would be. While our rich and complex relationship as Lutherans with Jews and also with Muslims requires special consideration, we were unable to articulate a clear reason, theological or otherwise, why we would engage with Sikhs on our own, beyond our initial outreach in response to tragedy.

Naturally, other churches in the U.S. were also expressing interest in an expanded approach to inter-religious dialogue. Like us, they were wrestling with the rapidly changing landscape and the exponential growth of the interfaith movement, in which their churches were becoming increasingly active. In fact, the restructure of the National Council of Churches in 2012–2013, which I oversaw as then-president, called for an expanded set of interreligious dialogue partners at the behest of its member churches.

After careful planning and the development of strategic partnerships, the National Council of Churches has launched three new national dialogues since 2018 with Hindus, Buddhists, and Sikhs. The Hindu and Buddhist dialogues are co-convened by the NCC and The Guibord Center in Los Angeles, in partnership with the Buddhist Churches of America and the Vedanta Societies. The Sikh-Christian dialogue is co-hosted with the Sikh Council for Interfaith Relations.

As the ELCA, we are living into Commitment Seven of *A Declaration of Inter-Religious Commitment*, which says that we will "whenever possible, work with other Christians and through ecumenical and inter-religious coalitions in [our] quest for inter-religious understanding and cooperation."[14] In part, it was this recent wrestling to expand the scope of our partners that clarified our commitment to that approach. In that sense, the inter-religious declaration has already proven itself to be a document that speaks both to us and to our partners.

Questions about a broader approach have helped us to think about inter-religious relations in the context of other relations, as well. As I mentioned earlier, the ELCA now has a social teaching corpus of three declarations that serve to guide our ecumenical and inter-religious relations. We also can look at this as a corpus within a slightly larger body of social teaching on relations. The whole category of ELCA declarations currently includes a fourth document, *Declaration of the ELCA to People of African Descent*, adopted by the Church Council in July 2019, in the quadricentennial year of the transatlantic slave trade. This document apologizes to people of African descent for the church's complicity in slavery and its vestiges of racism and white supremacy, and offers confession, repentance, and repudiation of the church's silence in the face of racial injustice. It was presented publicly at the Churchwide Assembly in August 2019, and the apology was publicly accepted by the African Descent Lutheran Association, with calls for accountability. Of note, the president of that association was a member of the ELCA Inter-Religious Task Force, which drafted *A Declaration of Inter-Religious Commitment*.

We might also look at the action of the 2016 ELCA Churchwide Assembly to repudiate the doctrine of discovery, which justified the colonization of indigenous lands and peoples in this context for centuries. In our inter-religious policy statement, the colonizers' denial of religious freedom to the indigenous peoples already there is named explicitly

14. ELCA, *Declaration*, 11.

in describing our multi-religious context. The 2016 repudiation is also named explicitly together with the LWF Statement and the 1994 *Declaration of ELCA to the Jewish Community* in Commitment Eleven, calling for confession, repentance, and reconciliation with those whom we have caused offense, harm, or violence.[15]

In 2017, for the occasion of the five-hundredth anniversary of the Reformation, the Consultative Panel on Lutheran-Jewish Relations developed a *Litany of Confession* based on the 1994 *Declaration*, which was repurposed again for the twenty-fifth anniversary in 2019. In an early public usage of that litany in 2017, I was approached by a colleague from the ELCA's American Indian and Alaska Native community who was hurt by the language in the 1994 *Declaration* that reads: "In the long history of Christianity there exists no more tragic development than the treatment accorded the Jewish people on the part of Christian believers." What about the treatment accorded indigenous peoples? The language in the opening paragraph of the litany was adjusted accordingly to reflect our acknowledgement that the suffering of the Jewish people in the name of Christianity is shocking and tragic, without weighting it as more or less tragic than another development right here in our own North American context.

Lastly, I would be remiss not to mention today's growing transnational white supremacist movement and its undeniable links to the rise of anti-Semitism. The manifestos of many of the white supremacist extremists name influencers that are linked to one another in a tangled web of hatred, racism, and bigotry. Whether we are speaking of Charleston, Charlottesville, Christchurch, or Tree of Life, it doesn't take much to connect the dots from the shooters or organizers to those who are appropriating, again, the legacy of Christian anti-Jewish teachings. The 1994 *Declaration* needs to be reckoned with—by the ELCA, and with our Jewish partners—in light of these most recent manifestations of anti-Jewish hatred. There is much work to do. These three examples illustrate the simple truth that our relations led us into broader relational thinking and engagement and that we have much more to learn.

What Have We Learned?

Perhaps the single greatest learning from our Lutheran-Muslim relations, and inter-religious relations more broadly, is that by authentically

15. ELCA, *Declaration*, 11.

engaging with others, we become more deeply grounded in who we are. In dialogue with others, we are challenged to clarify what it is we believe and why. In partnership with our neighbors who share our concerns for the common good, we find opportunities to collaborate for the sake of the world. In other words, inter-religious relations both strengthen and support the Lutheran vocation.

A second, related learning is that we must be responsible to our Lutheran legacy—including the reprehensible parts—and be responsive to the rapidly changing multi-religious context in which we serve. If we do not acknowledge, wrestle with, and continually repudiate the parts of our tradition that are evil, they will not only hold us captive, but they will be used to inflict terror and trauma, as they have in the past. This difficult work will not be accomplished though any declaration of words alone, but through consistent actions that follow. Doing so is urgently demanded by our multi-religious context.

Lastly, relations are with people, not with ideas or doctrines or traditions. People are the real connective tissue between our traditions, not the other way around. Learning about our neighbors and what they believe is not enough. We must continually put ourselves in the context of authentic relationships with our neighbors of other religions and worldviews. Therein we will find that mutual expressions of commitment and, at times, criticism will serve to strengthen our inter-religious relations in ways we could have never imagined or planned.

CHAPTER 4

Reconsidering Christian Responses to Islamophobia

— TODD H. GREEN

I WOKE UP THE day after the 2016 election of Donald Trump feeling like a colossal failure. Years of work devoted to analyzing and combating Islamophobia were repudiated in the course of one evening. Or so it seemed. I had to face an uncomfortable truth. When it came to countering Islamophobia, whatever it was that I, as a professed ally of American Muslims, was doing, whatever it was that we as Christian allies were doing, wasn't working. This was either because the premises and methods of our work were flawed, or not enough of us were doing this work. Or both.

Candidate Trump successfully instrumentalized Islamophobia in his presidential bid, and he did so under our watch, at times with our consent. As Christians, we must own this. We must acknowledge the degree to which our own complicity and failure to organize a successful resistance to the politicization of anti-Muslim bigotry contributed to an Islamophobic candidate gaining the keys to 1600 Pennsylvania Avenue.

Islamophobia has gained ground since Trump's election. In addition to the anti-Muslim policies that preceded Trump's election—deportations, detentions, extraordinary renditions, registration systems, surveillance, torture, anti-Sharia laws—the Trump administration introduced additional measures targeting Muslims, most notably the "Muslim ban."[1] President Trump also continued to cast Muslims as anti-American and sympathetic to terrorism, as demonstrated in his public criticisms of Representatives Ilhan Omar and

---

1. Green, *Fear of Islam*, 273–302.

Rashida Tlaib.[2] He has retweeted and supported prominent anti-Muslim racists, including the likes of Katie Hopkins, a British media pundit who once advocated for a "final solution" for British Muslims.[3]

All of this contributed to a hostile atmosphere in which Muslims are targeted with violence in and beyond America. Anti-Muslim hate crimes rose 67 percent in 2015 and another 20 percent in 2016, the two years coinciding with the presidential campaign season and the anti-Muslim rhetoric that pervaded it.[4] White nationalist terrorists also saw in Trump a symbol of white renewal that undergirded their hostility toward Muslims. Brenton Tarrant, the man who murdered fifty-one people in a mosque in Christchurch, New Zealand, saw in Trump "a symbol of renewed white identity and common purpose."[5]

Now more than ever, Christians must prioritize the difficult and daunting work of interfaith engagement and activism on behalf of Muslims. Our congregations and clergy can no longer afford to relegate interfaith outreach to an extracurricular activity, something we get around to after we've done the "real" work of ministry. Standing in solidarity with Muslims and combating anti-Muslim hate is the real work of ministry. If interfaith outreach to Muslims, who are outcasts in our dominant American culture, is not a central component of Christian ministry, if our Muslim neighbors still wonder where we stand in regard to Islamophobia, then we are contributing to an Islamophobic social and political order and are therefore part of the problem.

The good news is that the rise and spread of Islamophobia since post-9/11, which was accelerated in the Trump era, has spurred greater interest in some Christian circles to build bridges with Muslims and to take stronger public stands against Islamophobia. The ELCA has been a leader in this regard, particularly through its formal organizational and governing structures, as well as through the efforts of determined Lutheran scholars and clergy. Building on earlier theological outreach to Muslims, including the 1986 publication *God and Jesus: Theological Reflections for Christian-Muslim Dialog*, Lutherans in recent years have strengthened efforts to develop theological reflections and resources for Lutheran-Muslim relations.[6]

2. Tracy, "They're As Different" and Siegel, "President Trump Falsely Claims."

3. Papenfuss, "Trump Promotes Far-Right Commentator."

4. FBI, *Hate Crime Statistics, 2015* and *Hate Crime Statistics, 2016*.

5. Davidson, "State of the Nation."

6. American Lutheran Church, *God and Jesus*.

This includes edited volumes such as *Engaging Others, Knowing Ourselves: A Lutheran Calling in a Multi-Religious World* (2016), congregational resources such as *My Neighbor Is Muslim* (2015), and the policy statement *A Declaration of Inter-Religious Commitment* (2019).[7]

The Rev. Elizabeth Eaton, presiding bishop of the ELCA, has taken strong public stands against anti-Muslim policies and practices. In particular, she noted that Trump's efforts to ban Muslims from entering the country have resulted in "fueling Islamophobia in our public discourse" and perpetuating religious bigotry.[8] She assured Muslims that as Christians, we must "renew our commitment to find even more effective ways to protect and defend you from words and actions that assault your safety and well-being," adding that "God calls us to resist what is divisive, discriminatory, xenophobic, racist or violent" in our capacity as allies.[9]

Even with efforts like these from the ELCA, not to mention the strong positions challenging Islamophobia from other Christian denominations, such as the United Methodist Church and the United Church of Christ, formidable challenges remain.[10] Most importantly, plenty of Christians hold prejudicial, if not hostile, views of Islam and Muslims. Some prominent evangelical Christians with powerful media and political platforms enthusiastically give their consent to anti-Muslim policies and contribute actively to the forces of Islamophobia. Franklin Graham, evangelist and son of the late Billy Graham, insists Islam is "a very wicked and evil religion."[11] Robert Jeffress, a prominent Southern Baptist minister in Dallas, argues Islam "is a religion that promotes pedophilia."[12] Jerry Falwell, Jr., president of Liberty University, believes "if more good people had concealed carry permits, then we could end those Muslims."[13]

Polling data also reveals high levels of Islamophobia among both white evangelical and non-evangelical Protestants in America. According to a 2019 poll from the Institute for Social and Policy Understanding

---

7. LaHurd et al., eds., *Engaging Others*; Lutheran Social Service of Minnesota, *My Neighbor Is Muslim*; ELCA, *Declaration*.

8. Eaton, "Trump's Travel Ban."

9. Eaton, "An Open Letter."

10. "UMC Stands Against Islamophobia"; United Church of Christ, *On Actions of Hostility*.

11. Mathias, "A Pastor Who Said."

12. "Dallas Pastor's Broad-Brush Criticism."

13. Bailey, "Jerry Falwell Jr."

(ISPU), white evangelicals are more likely than any other religious community to hold Islamophobic views, with 44 percent of white evangelicals holding negative opinions versus only 20 percent holding positive views toward Muslims. Non-evangelical Protestants do not fare much better. They are evenly split, with 31 percent each holding favorable and unfavorable views toward Muslims. By contrast, 53 percent of Jews hold favorable views toward Muslims, this despite concerted efforts in some far-right political circles to pit Jews against Muslims.[14]

The persistence of Islamophobia among Christians means we have our work cut out for us. It's time to rethink why Islamophobia has taken such a strong hold among Christians and many others, and how those of us who strive to be Christian allies can be more effective in our efforts to dismantle Islamophobia. What I will argue is that for Christian allies, problematic paradigms about Islamophobia are limiting and at times impeding the impact of interfaith engagement and activism on Islamophobia. For Christians who are committed to or at least interested in combating Islamophobia, misconceptions abound concerning what we are combating and how we should combat it. We must clarify these misconceptions so that we can develop anti-Islamophobic strategies that yield better results.

I will tackle three of the most common misunderstandings about Islamophobia that, in my experience, prevail among many Christian allies who are otherwise acting in good faith: 1) Islamophobia as driven primarily by ignorance (as opposed to racism); 2) Islamophobia as the primary responsibility of Muslims to challenge (as opposed to white and white Christian populations); 3) Islamophobia as a natural response to Islamist terrorist attacks (as opposed to a product of bad faith actors who manufacture it for financial and political gain).

Islamophobia as Ignorance

The most common misunderstanding about Islamophobia is that it is driven by ignorance. If people simply knew the truth about Islam—the Qur'an, the five pillars, what jihad really means—then Islamophobia would wither away, or at least be reduced significantly. Such an assumption has led to countless efforts to offer "Islam 101" presentations in schools, community centers, churches, and other houses of worship.

14. Mogahed and Mahmood, "American Muslim Poll 2019." Note that the poll parsed out white evangelicals from other Protestants.

It is true. Islamophobia entails ignorance. Most non-Muslim Americans know very little about Islam, either in an academic sense or as a lived religion. It's also true that a knowledge of Islamophobia helps to bolster one's spiritual immune system when it comes to resisting anti-Muslim bigotry. A 2019 ISPU poll found a strong correlation between people who have a knowledge of Islam and those who have more positive views of Muslims.[15] A Pew survey in 2019 also found that Americans with greater religious knowledge have more positive feelings toward Muslims, not to mention toward most other religious communities, than those with less knowledge of Islam.[16] Efforts to educate non-Muslim Americans about Islam therefore have merit and should remain a part of the arsenal used to challenge and defeat Islamophobia.

But there are also reasons to be cautious about equating Islamophobia with ignorance and, by extension, reducing the fight against Islamophobia to giving "Islam 101" presentations. First, the data noted above can be difficult to interpret. It is unclear from these studies whether people are less Islamophobic because they have gained a knowledge of Islam, or whether they have gained a knowledge of Islam because they are already less Islamophobic. If we take a closer look at the ISPU data, we discover that other strong predictors of lower levels of Islamophobia include holding favorable views of racial and religious minorities along with LGBTQ people. It is possible that, in some cases, non-Muslim Americans who are already committed to promoting inclusion and to combating bigotry are also the ones who are most curious to learn about a religion whose practitioners are subject to so much suspicion and hostility.

Second, efforts to educate the broader public on Islam are sometimes met with resistance, particularly from individuals who already harbor a deeply Islamophobic mindset. Ingrid Mattson, a professor of Islamic Studies in Canada and a prominent interfaith activist, notes the real frustration she has experienced since 9/11 in trying to educate various publics on Islam. This includes individuals who sit through her presentations on Islam, only to respond during the Q & A with incredulity about what they heard and with responses that reflect bigoted and uninformed assumptions. These individuals react to Mattson's presentations as if they possess a deeper knowledge of

---

15. Mogahed and Mahmood, "American Muslim Poll 2019."

16. Pew Research Center, "What Americans Know."

Islam, even though Mattson's education and experience in the study of and belief in Islam is far superior to theirs.[17]

I imagine many scholars and activists who regularly give public presentations on Islam can relate to Mattson's frustrations. I have lost count of the number of times an audience member has asked me a loaded question about "creeping Sharia," only to struggle to articulate anything about Sharia beyond the misinformation and stereotypes gleaned from an Islamophobic website. No matter how much I try to explain the complexities of Islamic law and jurisprudence, the audience member refuses to yield or rethink his or her erroneous views. Some people are not interested in critically reexamining their pseudo-knowledge about such a complicated, nuanced topic.

Finally, we are not lacking in efforts from well-trained scholars and activists to provide the public with correct information about Islam, nor are we suffering from a paucity of good books, articles, and websites devoted to this cause. We've never had more outstanding resources for educating the public about Islam and more resources accessible to non-specialists, than we have at this moment in our history. And yet Islamophobia, by most metrics, is getting worse. Why is that?

What is going on here is a fundamental misunderstanding of what drives Islamophobia. Islamophobia certainly involves ignorance, but it is not driven by ignorance. It is driven by racism. Islamophobia is the fear of and hostility toward Muslims and Islam that is rooted in racism and that results in individual and systemic acts of discrimination, exclusion, and violence targeting Muslims and those perceived as Muslim. Ignorance is still a factor, but ignorance is not so much the cause of Islamophobia as it is the byproduct of it.[18] It is racism that animates Islamophobia, and that ultimately produces the ignorance of Islam and Muslims that is so widespread and that helps to reinforce discrimination against Muslims.

Islamophobia as racism makes it difficult for increasing numbers of Christians to "download" correct information about Islam, so that our suspicions are alleviated and we become more positively oriented toward our Muslim neighbors. Islamophobia as racism distorts and damages our cognitive frameworks, so that it becomes epistemologically and theologically challenging for many of us to learn about Islam in a healthy and

17. Green, *Fear of Islam*, 331–3.

18. Ibram Kendi makes a similar point about anti-black racism. While the "popular folktale of racism" holds that ignorance produces racist ideas which then produce discrimination, Kendi argues that ignorance is not the cause of racism but the byproduct of it (Kendi, *Stamped from the Beginning*, 9).

constructive manner, or in a manner that is consistent with how Muslims understand and live out their faith. Islamophobia as racism reprograms us so that we become predisposed to "learning" about Islam and Muslims in a way that reinforces the belief that both are existential threats to our congregations, communities, and country.

"But Islam is not a race. Muslims are not a race." That's the most common retort I encounter on this point. It's true: Islam is not a race, nor are Muslims. But they are racialized. Muslims are treated as a race, as a monolithic entity collectively presumed guilty of harboring terrorist impulses. They are viewed and dealt with as a suspect population, deserving of contempt. Their religion is framed as a belief system inherently oppressive and violent and therefore as a threat to an ostensibly peaceful Western society. It's a form of racism that scholars refer to as "cultural racism," or racism that involves hostility toward a community based on real or perceived religious beliefs, cultural traditions, and ethnicity.[19] All of this opens the door for government-led surveillance, racial profiling, immigration bans, and other forms of systemic discrimination against anyone connected to Islam. Cultural racism also paves the way for many in the non-Muslim majority to give their consent to state-sponsored discrimination of Muslims.

It's also a racism that at times relies on traditional racialization categories such as skin color. That's why it's not only Muslims but those who are "read" or perceived as Muslims who are targeted with racist rhetoric and violence. The first post-9/11 retaliatory murder, for example, claimed Balbir Singh Sodhi as its victim. The killer was Frank Roque, a man who thought Sodhi was a Muslim. Sodhi was in fact a Sikh, but Roque made no distinction between Sikhs and Muslims. Individuals with a South Asian or Middle Eastern background, irrespective of their actual religion, are often subject to discrimination and violence based on their perceived religious identity, a perception driven by assumptions based on skin color and/or cultural and religious difference. We've witnessed other notable instances of this kind of racism leading to violence against non-Muslims, including the 2012 massacre at a Sikh gurdwara which involved the perpetrator, Wade Michael Page, likely mistaking Sikhs for Muslims.

Shifting our thinking from Islamophobia as ignorance to Islamophobia as racism matters in how we understand and counteract it. If we

19. Semati, "Islamophobia, Culture and Race"; Meer and Modood, "Racialisation of Muslims"; Selod and Embrick, "Racialization and Muslims"; Husain, "Moving Beyond"; and Husain, "Retrieving the Religion."

view Islamophobia primarily as ignorance, our energy will continue to be disproportionately given to teaching the public about Islam, in the hopes that if enough individuals acquire basic information about of Islam, Islamophobia will subside. But if we view Islamophobia primarily as racism, then our gaze will widen to the systemic and violent aspects of Islamophobia, and our energy will be redirected to developing strategies modeled on other successful anti-racism movements in modern American history. This includes non-violent protests, economic boycotts, and other forms of high-impact grassroots activism, all of which can involve Christian communities, as was the case in the civil rights era. We can then rethink how the task of educating the public about Islam fits into this larger anti-racist framework.

Islamophobia as the Primary Responsibility of Muslims

One doesn't need to search for long to find examples of politicians and journalists in the past decade going out of their way to call out Muslims for their failure to condemn terrorism and urging them to do better on this front. Roger Cohen, columnist for the *New York Times*, once stated in a CNN interview that we will continue to struggle in the battle against terrorism "until moderate Muslims really speak out—really say, 'This is not our religion.'"[20] Sean Hannity of *Fox News* took these same sentiments and put them in the form of a question: "Will prominent Muslim leaders denounce and take on groups like ISIS, Hamas, and condemn and also fight against the unthinkable acts of terrorism?"[21] These two journalists represent different ends of the political and ideological spectrum, but their message to Muslims translates roughly the same: It's *your* job above all else to counter terrorism.

Lost on both journalists was the simple fact that Muslims have relentlessly condemned terrorism. In fact, there are so many examples of Muslims condemning terrorism that, in 2017, University of Colorado student Heraa Hashmi was able to create a 712-page Google document that cataloged these condemnations.[22] Even prior to the creation of this database,

20. "NYT Columnist."
21. Sandmeyer and Leung, "Muslim Leaders."
22. Mahdawi, "712-Page Google Doc."

evidence abounded of Muslims speaking out against terrorism.[23] It didn't matter. For many politicians and journalists, including Cohen and Hannity, it wasn't enough. Muslims had to do better.

Implied in this message is the notion that Muslims must face the consequences of their "failure" to address terrorism. After all, neither Cohen nor Hannity take the opportunity to condemn the national security apparatus that presumes Muslims to be guilty of harboring violent or terrorist sympathies. Neither takes issue with the surveillance, profiling, and counter-terrorism programs that disproportionately target Muslims based on a guilt-by-association framework. Muslims have the obligation to say more, to do more, and if they don't, then they have no right to complain about the suspicions and discriminatory practices aimed at them by government entities and the general public in the aftermath of Islamist terrorist attacks.[24] In other words, it's not just terrorism that's their responsibility to combat; it's Islamophobia as well.

The assumption that Muslims are the ones who have a special obligation to do more, not only in the fight against terrorism but in the fight against Islamophobia, rests on the misunderstanding addressed above, that Islamophobia is driven by ignorance—either of Islam or of what Muslims "really" believe—which means that Islamophobia will not be reduced significantly until Muslims do some explaining. The burden is on them, not us.

Foisting expectations upon Muslims to do more to address misconceptions of Islam reinforces a narrative that places blame on Muslims for Islamophobia. It presupposes that Muslims really are the problem, that Islamophobia wouldn't be so bad if Muslims did a better job of explaining their religion. This is akin to asking Jews in America to do more to fight anti-Semitism by convincing the rest of us that they really aren't trying to control the world or that they really are loyal to the United States. To ask Jews to assure Christians that anti-Semitic canards are not true, places the burden on Jews to fight anti-Semitism and lets us off the hook. Such an expectation in itself is anti-Semitic.

There is plenty of merit in making sure Muslims have access to public platforms to tell their stories and to define for others what it means to be Muslim. After all, Muslim voices have often been marginalized or silenced by the political and media establishment when it comes to interpretations

---

23. See Kurzman, "Islamic Statements against Terrorism."

24. For a critique of the discourse that singles out Muslim Americans and Europeans and asks them to condemn terrorism, see Green, *Presumed Guilty*.

of Islam. It's long past time for the rest of us to pass the mic. But if all of this comes with the expectation that Muslims have the responsibility to put Christians and others in the majority population at ease or to assuage our anxieties, then what we are doing is not really passing the mic but doubling down on the racism that drives Islamophobia.

Islamophobia as systemic racism emanates from the non-Muslim majority, particularly white and white Christian Americans who benefit from a social and political order predicated on racism. This means the moral responsibility falls on people like me to combat Islamophobia. *I* need to do more, as do other white and white Christian Americans.

None of this is a commentary on whether Muslims should or shouldn't combat Islamophobia. It's more of a commentary on who bears the greater moral responsibility to do so. This greater moral responsibility lies not with Muslims but with white and white Christian Americans. We will see no significant reversal in Islamophobia until white and white Christian Americans accept this responsibility and promise to do more to challenge the racism that targets Muslims and those perceived as Muslim.

Islamophobia as a Natural Response to Terrorism

A final misunderstanding among Christian and other Muslim allies involves the widely shared belief that Islamophobia, while unfortunate and regrettable, is understandable in light of the 9/11 attacks and other Islamist terrorist activity over the past two decades. Because there are Muslims "out there" terrorizing innocent people, it makes perfect sense that non-Muslim Americans would be suspicious and fearful of Muslims. One could add that this is the sort of thinking that helps rationalize counterterrorism programs that target Muslim communities. These programs are presumably necessary because of the "bad Muslims" and the possibility that the "good Muslims" might be infected by their nefarious co-religionists. It is thought that once the bad Muslims go away—or, better yet, once they are defeated in the war on terror—there will no longer be a need for surveillance, profiling, and countering violent extremism initiatives. Until then, such programs are considered a natural response to terrorism, so natural that few prominent politicians or journalists raise significant questions about them.

The assumption that Islamophobia is a natural response to terrorism is deeply problematic on several grounds. First, it reflects yet again a guilt-by-association mentality. Muslims are *a priori* considered guilty of harboring terrorist sympathies or violent inclinations, even though only an incredibly small minority of people with a Muslim background participate in violent acts of terrorism. This presumption of guilt fuels Islamophobic attitudes and policies, but it is a presumption not made of white non-Muslims. The double standard is significant precisely because we have plenty of data indicating white nationalist terrorism is a far more significant problem in the United States than terrorism carried out by Muslim extremists. According to an Anti-Defamation League study of domestic extremist-related killings in 2018, almost all deaths came at the hands of individuals driven by white supremacy or right-wing anti-government ideologies. These two kinds of extremism were responsible for 98 percent of the deaths that year. Between 2009 and 2018, right-wing individuals were responsible for 73 percent of domestic extremist-related fatalities. Three out of four of those killings were carried out by white supremacists.[25]

Yet white Americans do not suffer from a presumption of guilt, despite the much larger problem of white nationalist and extremist violence. As a white American Christian, I don't get bombarded with requests to condemn white nationalist terrorists or white extremist violence. No one asked me to condemn Dylann Roof after his massacre of nine African American Christians in Charleston's Emanuel African Methodist Episcopal Church. No one asked me to condemn Robert Bowers after he murdered eleven people at the Tree of Life synagogue in Pittsburgh. No one asked me to condemn Patrick Crusius after he shot twenty-two people at an El Paso Walmart. Why? Because as a white Christian, I am afforded individuality. I am given the benefit of the doubt. Bigotry toward me and people like me is not a "natural" response to white nationalist or extremist violence. Such violence is deemed exceptional and out-of-the-ordinary when it involves people who look like me or share my racial or religious background. But the fact that Muslims are not afforded individuality, the fact that Muslims are not given the benefit of the doubt, the fact that Muslims are subject to systemic discrimination because of the actions of a few—all of this points not only to double standards. It points to racism.

Assuming Islamophobia is a natural response to terrorism also disregards the role of U.S. imperialism and militarism in fueling terrorist attacks. This assumption assumes that we can isolate something called "Islam" and view it as the cause of violent extremism and avoid the larger

25. Anti-Defamation League, "Murder and Extremism.'"

political factors that give rise to terrorism. High on the list of these factors is the foreign policy of the United States and its involvement and intervention in the Middle East.

Key studies on terrorism address these larger political factors. The scholar Robert Pape conducted research of these factors and found that the overwhelming majority of suicide terrorist bombings in the world—over 90 percent—have been carried out by individuals or organizations responding to real or perceived military occupation. This was the case irrespective of the perpetrator's religious identity, with many perpetrators having no religious identity.[26]

A cursory examination of statements made by Muslim extremists reveals the importance of politics, particularly the perception of military interventionism or occupation, as a motivating factor in their violent agendas. At its founding, the militant organization Hezbollah openly stated that its main purpose was "to put an end to foreign occupation." What this meant in practice was "to expel the Americans, the French and their allies from Lebanon, putting an end to any colonialist entity on our land."[27] Al-Qaeda's Osama bin Laden frequently railed against U.S. military occupation and intervention in Muslim-majority countries. In his "Letter to America" (2002), he complained: "You steal our wealth and oil at paltry prices because of your international influence and military threats . . . . Your forces occupy our countries; you spread your military bases throughout them."[28] While none of this justifies the horrific attacks on civilians and non-combatants by these and other terrorist organizations, it goes a long way in explaining some of the core political grievances that animate their agendas. This includes grievances against U.S. foreign policy and interventionism.

Finally, and most importantly, the notion that Islamophobia is an understandable response to terrorist attacks fails to account for the extraordinary efforts that go into manufacturing fear and hatred of Muslims in the United States. A $1.5 billion industry has emerged in the post-9/11 era to co-opt public discourse about Islam and to infuse it with hysteria, misinformation, and outright lies about the supposed threat posed by American Muslims.[29] This Islamophobia industry consists of far-right pundits,

26. Pape, *Dying to Win*, 4. For a summary of some of the scholarship on the political factors driving terrorism, see Green, *Presumed Guilty*, 6–12.

27. Pape, *Dying to Win*, 4.

28. "Full Transcript."

29. CAIR, "Hijacked by Hate."

politicians, bloggers, and pseudo-scholars who are making a living off of demonizing and dehumanizing Muslims. Once fringe players outside of mainstream politics, since 2010, this network of anti-Muslim hate speakers and organizations has become a pervasive influence in the American political system, from local town and city governments to state legislatures to the corridors of power in Washington, including the U.S. Congress and the White House. Key figures who have served at some point in the Trump administration have deep ties to this industry, including Mike Pompeo, John Bolton, and Kellyanne Conway.[30]

The industry's main players include Frank Gaffney, Jr., a prominent proponent of the "birther" conspiracy theory that the Muslim Brotherhood has infiltrated the highest levels of the federal government, including the State Department and the Department of Justice; Robert Spencer and Pamela Geller, the primary orchestrators of the opposition to the Park51 Center (a proposed Islamic community center) in lower Manhattan and peddlers of the belief that Islam is inherently a religion of violence and intolerance; and Brigitte Gabriel, head of the largest anti-Muslim organization in the nation—ACT! for America—and an advocate of the theory that any practicing or observant Muslim should be considered radical and therefore a threat to the country.

The influence of this industry was on full display in the 2015–2016 presidential election cycle. Ben Carson, one of the candidates for the Republican nomination, took to the airwaves and repeated core elements of the Islamophobia industry's talking points, including the belief that a Muslim could not uphold Sharia and be loyal to the United States, and the notion that Muslims are commanded to lie in order to achieve their true (and insidious) political goals.[31] It should be noted that drumming up concern for "creeping Sharia" has become embedded in the GOP platform. A questionnaire appeared on the websites of both the Trump/Pence reelection campaign and the Republican National Committee that asked the following question: "Are you concerned by the potential spread of Sharia Law?"[32]

This industry pulls out all the stops to ensure that as many of us as possible act on our worst impulses in the wake of terrorist attacks. They

---

30. Hasan, "Mike Pompeo Has Extreme Views"; Sampathkumar, "US National Security Adviser"; and Beinart, "Denationalization of American Muslims." For a broader discussion of the Islamophobia industry, see Green, *Fear of Islam*, 205–36; Lean, *Islamophobia Industry*; and Bail, *Terrified*.

31. Kessler, "Ben Carson's Claim."

32. Moran, "RNC Asked Tweeters."

play to our fears and paranoias, not to the better angels of our nature. In doing so, they distract us by projecting onto Muslims our own unresolved anxieties about white and white Christian violence, not to mention some of the horrific violence carried out by our government in the past two decades alone. This includes the never-ending war on terror, which has resulted in hundreds of thousands of civilian casualties, millions of displaced persons, and gruesome torture campaigns from Abu Ghraib to Guantanamo Bay to CIA black sites. As long as we are fixated on "violent" Muslims and the presumed threat they pose to a "peaceful" America, we need not come to terms with our own violent past and our ongoing complicity in a violent world order.

Conclusion

Islamophobia poses one of the greatest moral challenges to the United States at this particular moment in our political history. The sooner we develop a better understanding of Islamophobia—what drives it, who bears the primary moral responsibility for countering it, and who manufactures it (and for what purposes)—the sooner we can develop more effective strategies for dismantling this vicious form of bigotry. Only then will our Muslim neighbors be allowed to flourish fully in this pluralistic society and enjoy the privileges and freedoms experienced by Lutherans and many other mainline Protestants.

Section 2: **Lutheran–Muslim Relationships in Context**

Accompaniment, Trinity–Style

Lutherans and Muslims in Cedar-Riverside

JANE BUCKLEY-FARLEE

AMONG SOME OF THE earliest immigrants to Minnesota, historical records show that Muslims have been in this state since at least the 1880s. They came from Syria and Lebanon, then part of the Ottoman Empire. Two of the first mosques in the United States were in the Midwest. In Ross, North Dakota, the Ross Mosque was built in 1929, and in Cedar Rapids, Iowa, the Mother Mosque was built in 1934. Today, the Muslim community in Minnesota is diverse. In the 1990s, the Muslim population began to grow the fastest as Muslims from East Africa, Somalia, and Bosnia came here fleeing violence and war in their home countries. While it is difficult to get an accurate count of the Muslims, as of 2012, approximately 150,000 Muslims lived in Minnesota.

While the acceptance of Muslims by the dominant European and Scandinavian cultures varies throughout Minnesota, Muslims have been quite successful. Minnesota was the first state to elect a Muslim to the United States House of Representatives, Representative Keith Ellison. (Ellison now serves as the first Muslim elected as the Minnesota attorney general.) Ilhan Omar, a Somali-American, is the first woman originally from East Africa to be elected to the United States House of Representatives. Several additional Somali-Americans have been elected to local positions of leadership, including as city council members in several towns and to various school boards. Brother Ali, a locally and nationally well-known hip-hop artist, was originally from Minnesota. For a state that only a little more than a hundred fifty years ago was populated solely by Native Americans and was then home to immigrants from Sweden, Norway, Denmark, and Germany, this has been quite a change.

Cedar–Riverside

As stated above, Muslims have been welcomed in Minnesota to varying degrees. One neighborhood of Minneapolis, Cedar-Riverside, has been perhaps the most influenced by Muslims. Cedar-Riverside, on the eastern edge of Minneapolis, has been a first stop for new immigrants since the 1880s. Originally part of the Mni Sota Makoce ("Land where the waters reflect the clouds"), it was the homeland of the Dakota people. After the first immigrants came from Scandinavia and Western Europe, the following years brought immigrants from other areas around the world to Cedar-Riverside. Beginning in the 1990s, people from East Africa—Ethiopia, Eritrea, and Somalia—began coming in large numbers. Cedar-Riverside has become the home for the largest concentration of Somalis outside of Somalia. Bordered by Interstate 35 on the west, Interstate 94 on the south, and the Mississippi River on the north and east, anyone who spends time in Cedar-Riverside will understand why this .549 square mile triangle of land is affectionately known as "Little Mogadishu" by those who live, work, pray, and play here. With three mosques, a vibrant mall, and many shops on the streets, to walk the streets is to be able to imagine walking in Somalia.

Cedar-Riverside has also been the home of Trinity Lutheran Congregation since 1868. Founded by immigrants from Norway and Denmark, Trinity has seen many changes. Once home to people who looked, talked, thought, and worshiped the same way they did, Cedar-Riverside is now home to people from other parts of the world. With roots in the Lutheran Free Church, Trinity has a history of a strong commitment to Christian missions around the world. The world has now come to Trinity's neighborhood in a new way, opening the door for being Christ's presence and for living out the accompaniment model in almost everything we do, by showing up, listening, participating, and helping when appropriate.

One of the changes to impact Cedar-Riverside was Interstate 94. Just as the highway affected many communities, it changed Cedar-Riverside drastically, isolating it from other nearby neighborhoods. Neighbors and businesses that had been just a short walk down the street were separated by four to six lanes of freeway with few bridges between them. An extra intentional effort became necessary to patronize the unique restaurants, music venues, and other businesses that had formerly been owned and run by next-door neighbors. The interstate also brought change to Trinity. Trinity's building was razed to make way for the highway. Once Trinity had decided that Cedar-Riverside was their home, they voted to stay, losing many members but remaining strong to their commitment to the neighborhood. Leaving their building on Pentecost in 1966, the people of Trinity were nomads in their own neighborhood, worshipping in several spaces for twenty-three years. Trinity's nomadic years took the congregation to the Fire House (a former fire station), Riverside Presbyterian Church, the West Bank Child Care Center, the Rectory of Our Lady of Perpetual Help, and various rooms at Augsburg University. When Augsburg built their chapel in 1989, Trinity was invited to use that space for Sunday worship. This invitation to use the chapel is another occasion of our long-lasting partnership, and in a way completed a circle.

In 1869, Augsburg Seminary was founded in Marshall, Wisconsin. When it became clear that the seminary could not stay in Marshall, Trinity's pastor, Ole Paulson, was instrumental in the decision to move Augsburg Seminary to Minneapolis in 1872, where it then became a college and, most recently, a university. Since then, Trinity and Augsburg have worked together on countless initiatives, activities, and program in Cedar-Riverside. A transaction in the mid-1960s that involved Trinity, Augsburg, and Fairview Hospital made it possible for Trinity to purchase Block 185, one square block at Riverside and 20th Avenues. Except for one remaining building on the northwest corner, Block 185 was developed into housing, including townhomes and apartments. This building became Trinity's office space in 1990 and is where weekday activities and programming take place to this day.

In the early 2000s, Trinity updated its mission statement. The statement came from a practice of accompaniment before the accompaniment model of the Evangelical Lutheran Church in America (ELCA) became popular. After much discussion and editing, the mission statement read, "Nurturing Wholeness and Holiness in Cedar-Riverside." Trinity intentionally did not define whose wholeness or holiness. Our hope was not to have our neighbors become like us, but to help them be the best they could be, no matter their race, country of origin, faith, or skin color.

Trinity has found that accompaniment has not been a prescribed program or plan of action. It is a way of being in our context. For us, it has included radical hospitality, deep listening, patience, not having the answers, and letting go of preconceived notions of how something might take shape. The hope of nurturing the neighborhood is in the forefront of our being present, but the details of how this happens tend to be quite fluid. Through that fluidity, we not only are Christ's presence in this community by supporting and loving our neighbors, but we ourselves have been changed. Perhaps that is the most important piece of all.

Stories from a Safe Place

The needs in Cedar-Riverside are many. The density and poverty are palpable. Cedar-Riverside ranks eleventh out of ninety-two as the most densely populated neighborhoods in Minnesota. Twenty percent of the residents of Cedar-Riverside are under eighteen years of age. In terms of median income, the neighborhood ranks ninety out of ninety-two in the state.[1] One of the needs of the Cedar-Riverside was identified through a community listening opportunity. In the spring of 2000, a local school sponsored a gathering of middle schoolers and community leaders. At that meeting, we heard the top three needs from the children: a safe place after school, help with homework, and money for the bus. We didn't have money for the bus, but we did have a large room that was used very little. From that realization came Trinity's Safe Place Homework Help program. Since the fall of 2001, Safe Place has been going strong. An average of fifteen children from the neighborhood, all Muslim East Africans, come from each school day and meet with tutors from Augsburg University and the University of Minnesota, both of which are only a block away. They all work on homework together. Of course, a lot more than homework happens. Relationships between students and tutors form, and conversations across faiths, cultures, languages, and skin colors happen. The tutors learn as much as the children. Walls and barriers come down. Grades are improved, but, more importantly, everyone is changed. How can they not be?

---

1. *Statistical Atlas.*

Prayer in My Office

In an attempt to welcome our neighbors in our space, we have several prayer rugs available for those moments when one of the five daily prayers occurs during Homework Help time. However, we did not have a free, quiet space for the rugs or for prayer. On one Friday afternoon, our building was full. Kids and tutors were everywhere, including the hall floor and two office spaces. After spending the day working on my sermon, struggling to produce every word on a particularly challenging sermon, it was finally finished. As I then began working on the prayers for Sunday, there was a quiet knock on my door. "Could I pray in here?" "Of course, don't let me bother you," I responded. Fartun laid down her prayer rug as I turned back to my computer to finish writing our prayers. I could see her standing, bowing, and kneeling, praying, out of the corner of my eye as I tried to type my own prayers for Sunday. It suddenly dawned on me that we were doing the same thing. I stopped typing. I tried to pray but no profound words came to me. Just being in my suddenly Spirit-filled office with her was enough. And I was changed forever.

An Ash Wednesday Story

On Ash Wednesday in 2016, Trinity's pastoral intern had assisted at Augsburg University's chapel service. Hours later, having forgotten all about the cross of ashes that she had received on her forehead earlier that morning, the intern walked through the hall at Trinity where students were sitting on the floor doing homework. One of the kids looked up and asked, "What's that plus sign on your forehead?" With one simple, sincere question, the door was opened for an amazing conversation. The intern explained the meaning of Ash Wednesday, the importance of the day for Christians, and compared Lent to Ramadan. As the conversation was coming to an end, the intern also explained that the ashes remind us that everyone dies, to which one of the students replied, "Well, duh!" Another student asked, "Can you get those ashes on Amazon?" (Yes, you can!) Five young girls wearing their hijabs and one pastoral intern wearing her clerical collar had become just a bit more aware of each other's worlds and faiths. And they were changed forever.

A Conversation with a Mom

Fayo had often stopped in my office to talk. She brought her two young daughters to Homework Help. Fayo and I had built a relationship over the years. This time she was more intense than usual as she began talking about how she had been treated where she works. Every day, people said mean things to her, and sometimes they told her to go back to where she came from. We talked about the current wave of anti-Muslim rhetoric. She recalled several more comments that had been directed at her and then looked straight at me and asked if I thought these people were going to gather up all of the Muslims and burn them. She was, of course, referring to the Holocaust. I was left speechless. I tried to say it couldn't happen here, it couldn't happen now. I wanted to say that no one would allow it. But, I couldn't. It was good German Lutherans just like me who turned a blind eye to it all, not so many years ago. I was changed forever.

ICSA/Dar Al-Hijrah Mosque

Trinity has a special relationship with one of the mosques in Cedar-Riverside, The Islamic Civic Society of America (ICSA) at the Dar Al-Hijrah Mosque. In the mid-2000's, two of their leaders had come to Trinity for a conversation. In all honesty, I'm not sure exactly who came. Even so, the two of them and I had a wonderful conversation and agreed that we should get together more often and work together. After that initial meeting, we did a few things at the same neighborhood events, and we were present for press conferences and community meetings when anti-Islamic sentiments began to run high. We had begun to know and trust each other.

That all changed on January 1, 2014. A fire broke out in Cedar-Riverside. An apartment building was destroyed. Three people died, several were injured, and many were left homeless. It was a tragedy unlike any our neighborhood had seen in a long time. People gathered at the community center that day, awaiting news of loved ones and about the cause of the fire. As the fire still burned, before anyone had been able to look for a cause, news agencies were eager to make headlines by blaming anything on Islam they could think of, even suggesting that it could have been started by a bomb. While a cause was never determined, authorities believed the cause was most likely a gas leak.

Throughout the chaos, fire fighters, police officers, the Red Cross, elected officials, and community leaders seemed to have constructive roles to play. So, I put on my clergy shirt. (In Minnesota, a clergy shirt can serve as a pass into spaces that might not otherwise be accessible. People know what that piece of clothing signifies.) On that day at the community center, it did serve as a pass, but for most people my role there was not so clear. All those who were waiting were East African and Muslim, many of them new to the U.S. They had no idea who I was or what I might be doing there. And in all honesty, neither did I. Should I pray? I don't speak Somali, so what would I say? How could I listen? We didn't even practice the same religion. In spite of feeling useless, it seemed important to be there, to be present. And it was.

In the weeks that followed, there were many neighborhood meetings to plan how to care for the victims and their families. Not much was discussed in English. Yet it was important to be there, to be present, even though I did not understand much of what was being said. One day towards the end of a meeting Imam Sharif from ICSA/Dar Al-Hijrah said, "Sister, we are glad you are here." From that point, it became clearer how Trinity could help. ISCA/Dar Al-HIjrah, which was next to the destroyed building, had been damaged by smoke and water. They, too, had lost their home. Trinity and Dar Al-Hijrah having worked together before this fire was enough for us to have the beginning of trust between us. And it became clear, through sitting and listening, that Trinity would invite ICSA/Dar Al-Hijrah to use our lower level. Augsburg was renting the space and was in agreement. ICSA/Dar Al-Hijrah spent the next one and a half years using our lower level as office space and for prayers, until they could move back into their center.

In the summer of 2014, ICSA/Dar Al-Hijrah invited Trinity, Augsburg, and friends to an iftar in the space they were using in Trinity's lower level. The gathering and meal was such a success that it was decided not to wait until Ramadan the next year to gather again for food and conversation. Out of that experience came a monthly interfaith event. The goal was to build relationships by sharing a meal and discussing different topics through the lenses of our various faith backgrounds. These conversations have morphed over the years but continue through the interfaith cohort at Augsburg University.[2]

2. The Interfaith Scholars is a collaboration between Augsburg's Christensen Center, Campus Ministry, and Religions Department. Students from a variety of traditions explore the religious diversity of the Augsburg student body, the Twin Cities, and the United States.

Since 2014, ICSA has invited Trinity to iftars and other events. Trinity has invited ICSA/Dar al-Hijrah to "Fat Tuesdays" and other events. Each time, we come a bit closer. With time, it has become clearer that we have a common commitment to Cedar-Riverside and to the work of raising healthy and faithful families. All of this was possible because we listened. We did not have the answers to many of the issues raised by the fire. We weren't even aware of many of the practical challenges. It would have been inappropriate for us to give our solutions. Our role was to be present, listen, and offer what we could, without taking the lead. It was for the community of Cedar-Riverside to deal with the aftermath of the fire. It was our place to show up, listen, and accompany. With time, through many meetings spent feeling useless and wondering why we were even there, an invitation came. We were able to hear it.

With our common commitment to Cedar-Riverside and with an openness to deep interfaith work, we are now in a joint conversation about forming a non-profit and a building shaped by both faith communities. It is yet to be seen how this dream all comes together, but the dream and commitment are strong. And as we say, "This is the time and this is the place." This is the twenty-first century in Cedar-Riverside.

Urban Hub

Another initiative with roots in Cedar-Riverside is the Urban Hub. This group currently includes Augsburg University, Bethany Lutheran Church, the Council on American-Islamic Relations—Minnesota, Darul Quba, ICSA/Dar Al-Hijrah, and Trinity Lutheran Congregation. This group has come together with the hopes of creating collaboration between the faith communities in Cedar-Riverside. The Urban Hub and its actions have come from listening to the community through the lenses of the neighborhood faith leaders. As we have listened together, two main initiatives have taken shape. One is almost as simple as it sounds—serving coffee and tea after Friday prayers. This simple act of hospitality began in January 2017, after the first Muslim travel ban. In Cedar-Riverside, the fear was palpable. The Muslim East Africans, those who walk the streets, own the shops and restaurants, and pray in the mosques, were all afraid. They were afraid to be on their own streets, and it was very quiet.

And so, on a very cold Minneapolis January Friday afternoon, we stood outside of Dar Al-Hijrah with freshly made coffee and sweet Somali tea. We served the pray-ers as they came out. During his sermon that day, the imam had mentioned that we would be there. Even so, the people came out into the cold, not sure what to expect. Their past experiences had told them that groups gathered outside their doors were not always friendly. As we passed out the hot coffee and tea and said just a few words, "We're glad you're here," they began to see that we were, indeed, friends.

The Coffee and Teas continue. Since those early months after the first ban, we have limited ourselves to the warmer months. We have served drinks at two of the neighborhood mosques. The third mosque is not quite ready yet, but we are hopeful that they will welcome us in welcoming them. It was remarkable how such a small and simple act could have such a large impact. Perhaps for the first time for some of them, they were greeted warmly as friends by white Christians. At a time when their safety and security were threatened, we were able to show them a different story, that, indeed, we are glad they are here. After two years of Coffee and Teas, we know each other and linger long after the coffee and tea is gone, checking in with friends, old and new.

Our Urban Hub has become known for our Coffee and Teas. We serve at other community events, making our presence as faith communities working together a part of the neighborhood. So, the Urban Hub has broadened its activities. During Ramadan, there is a different kind of energy in the neighborhood. During Ramadan, many Muslims fast from sunrise to sunset. Each day ends with an iftar, a breaking of the fast. Iftars often happen at homes with family and friends. In recent years, community iftars have become more popular. Mosques invite their neighbors to a meal after the evening prayers. Food is shared, conversations happen, and relationships are built.

In 2019, the Urban Hub, as a collaborative of the neighborhood's faith communities, decided to plan an iftar with an emphasis on faith rather than on social and other issues. When that Ramadan May day had come, the skies had threatened rain all day. Risking a downpour, it was decided to hold the iftar outside as planned. The question was then asked, "Is it OK to ring church bells, but not to announce Muslim prayer outside?" A special permit with the town council had made this possible. For only the second time, the *adhan*, the call to prayer, was heard outside in Cedar-Riverside. A local imam was invited to chant the *adhan*. For many, it was the first time they had heard the *adhan* outside since coming to America. There were tears of joy throughout the community, and not just in the eyes of the

Muslims. It was a holy moment for many others who were present. Faith leaders spoke, and an Islamic litany was led by a neighborhood imam. The meal was shared. People were spread around the park, sitting on chairs, on the ground, standing, all enjoying a holy meal together. After the meal, the men and women gathered on the soccer field to pray. The rain had waited, and we all agreed it would happen again next Ramadan.

Accompaniment, Trinity-Style

Events, activities, and initiatives are the visible fruits of deep relationships that are built across the barriers of faith, culture, language, and skin color. As much or more so, the invisible fruits deserve mentioning. It is the invisible gifts of being able to see the world and God through a much broader lens that ultimately make the visible fruits possible. Although the invisible and visible fruits work hand in hand, if one is not open to being changed, the ways of the world cannot be changed. Given the rising tensions between faiths at home and around the world, change is sorely needed.

Among the invisible fruits have been the ways in which Trinity members have been changed. Much of it is not obvious, not visible from the outside. Much of it is about the privilege we carry with us without even realizing it. The privilege of being white has become more real. We hear too many stories of people we know and love being pulled over for driving or walking while black.

Christian privilege also rears its head from time to time. Christian privilege can be harder to see, especially as the U.S. becomes more secular, as the *nones* continue to be the fastest and largest growing faith group. We find Christian privilege in a most basic way, the calendar. At some point Christmas break became winter break. Easter break became spring break. But we all know in our bones that they are still really Christmas break and Easter break. We know that is the reason for the time off. All the store displays make this quite clear. We find it in the structures of the institutions that surround us and in legislations, old and new, that govern our lives.

In Cedar-Riverside, there is a refreshing other side to that issue. The Muslim holy month of Ramadan turns the tables just a bit. Throughout the year, there are many regularly scheduled community meetings and events. Most of those come to a halt during Ramadan. Meetings are postponed until Ramadan has ended. If a meeting does take place, it becomes obvious that this neighborhood is on a different calendar. If prayer time comes during a meeting, the meeting stops. All the Muslims find a space to pray. The rest of us non-Muslims wait. It is not a problem; it is just the way things are done. While the Muslims pray, we are left to contemplate our own lack of regular practices of prayer.

In many ways, Trinity Lutheran Congregation's practice of accompaniment in Cedar-Riverside is not about what we have done. It is more about how we have been present. It is about showing up and listening. It is about entering a space without any agenda other than helping where it is appropriate and possible. It is about being in a space that used to be ours, willing to give up all notions of our white Christian privilege. More often than not, simply showing up and listening is the most important role we play. This all takes time, and time is too often something we think we don't have. It is too easy to go in with a quick answer, a simple solution, and push for the solution, before even knowing what the real issue is, before we realize that there are many dynamics at work under the surface. Being in the minority in Cedar-Riverside is a very different place to be than most white Minnesota Lutherans are used to. At the same time, perhaps it is one of the most valuable places to be in. It is the reality in most of the world, and it will soon be a reality in our own country and cities. A hymn that has become more important to me is #887 from *Evangelical Lutheran Worship*, "This Is My Song."

Time for Conversations

There is great interest among some Christians these days in getting to know their Muslim neighbors. There is a hunger for building relationships and doing something meaningful and true to our Lutheran understanding of the radical nature of God's grace. Either everyone is covered or not. So, it is a blessing to be in this Muslim majority neighborhood. It is a blessing to be in the minority as white Christians. Trinity is grateful that we are in this place at this time. We are honored to live out a narrative far different from the one we hear most on the news and from those around us.

When enough stories have been heard, when enough news items convince us of the need for change, initiatives begin to take shape. That has been true in Minneapolis and in Minnesota. The Minneapolis Area Synod of the ELCA at its 2017 Annual Assembly passed the resolution *Engaging in Solidarity with Our Muslim Neighbors*. This resolution was written by the chair of the Social Ministry and Justice Committee of Grace University

Lutheran Church and was passed at the Central Conference of the Minneapolis Area Synod 2017 Annual Assembly. In this resolution, the Synod agreed to encourage its congregations and members to:

> "sponsor one or more educational sessions on Islam or on interrupting religious bias; reach out to build relationships in their neighborhood with a non-Christian place of worship or another religious institution, particularly any being targeted for hostile words and actions; write and endorse a statement condemning hostility in the name of religion and expressing solidarity with members of other faith traditions; initiate and engage in interreligious service projects which include spiritual reflection and discussion; engage in advocacy actions; and, establish a task force to make resources available for education on Islam and on leading skillful, effective interfaith initiatives."[3]

The synodical task force has been meeting regularly. To ensure the task force's integrity we have included Muslims from the Minneapolis/St. Paul metro area. The task force has gathered resources and created a webpage and Facebook invitation for a one-day workshop, "Allies and Friends."[4] This day of conversation, learning, and relationship building included speakers experienced in the challenging and rewarding work of building understanding and relationships between communities. Lutherans and Muslims came together and learned about Islam, Islamophobia, and the call to this work based on our Lutheran theology. There was time for conversations between Christians and Muslims.

Accompaniment, Trinity-style, is all about relationships and conversations that include deep listening and mutual respect. It's about taking the time to let the Spirit do her work and the openness to seeing the bigness of God. Ultimately, it's about being changed.

---

3. Minneapolis Area Synod, *Engaging in Solidarity*.
4. Minneapolis Area Synod, *Allies and Friends Workshop*.

CHAPTER 6

Claremont School of Theology and the Christian–Muslim Consultant Group

Lutheran–Muslim Community Connections in Southern California

THOMAS K. JOHNSON

I TEACH A COURSE on Dietrich Bonhoeffer at the Claremont School of Theology, California (CST). For the past eight years, we have organized a Bonhoeffer festival at the school, hosted by the Center for Lutheran Studies at CST, where I serve as the current director. We have had a variety of keynote speakers and each year have had an interfaith panel respond to the speakers. The panel has consisted of representatives from the Jewish, Muslim, and Christian traditions. In 2018, I invited the principal of a local Muslim school to be on the panel. She contributed to a very engaging conversation on how Bonhoeffer is an excellent example of what it means to put one's faith into practice and pursue justice and compassion for all. For the past few years, I've been invited to serve as a judge for the speech contest at this same school. I have listened to over one hundred fifty speeches on compassion and justice from Muslim children from the first grade up to eighth grade. They were inspirational and moving. One little boy talked about the importance of speaking out on behalf of those who have no voice and are being oppressed. He explained how the Lutheran theologian and pastor Dietrich Bonhoeffer was a perfect example of this, and he was his hero. The principal immediately looked my way with a big smile. I gave her a thumbs up and later told her, in jest, that the boy got one of the highest scores possible. In some respects, it was a surprising place to find common ground. Yet, to me, it typifies my experience of connections between the Lutheran Church and the Muslim community. It reflects our mutual priority for seeking peace, justice, and respect for people of all faiths.

The Christian Muslim Consultant Group

This in turn is the driving force behind such efforts as the Christian Muslim Consultant Group (CMCG) that has met monthly for the past eleven years at the Islamic Center of Southern California. The CMCG is made up of members who serve as representatives for mainline Christian denominations, the Church of Jesus Christ of Latter-Day Saints, and various Muslim leaders who represent organizations like the Council for American Islamic Relations (CAIR), the Muslim Political Action Committee (MPAC), and the local Shura Council. The purpose of this group is be a network for educational resources, creating opportunities to bring Muslim and Christian communities together for study, dialogue, and advocacy, to speak out on issues such as the "Muslim ban" and other forms of discrimination.[1] The founding chairs of the CMCG were an Episcopal priest, the late Rev. Dr. Gwynne Guibord, director of the Guibord Center, and the imam of the Islamic Center of Southern California, Jihad Turk.[2] Turk has since gone on to become president of the Bayan Islamic Graduate School, which is under the umbrella of the Claremont School of Theology.

One major contribution of the CMCG has been *Standing Together*, a six-part DVD series that brings a group from one local Muslim and one Christian congregation together to discuss the basic foundations of each tradition and learn together how one practices one's faith. The gatherings focus on Christian-Muslim similarities and differences. The series was originally put together in 2008, then made available at www.standingtogethernow. org. Over fifteen pairings between mosques and churches have taken place in Southern California since its inception. In addition, other organizations

---

1. The "Muslim ban" is a widely referred to term for the Trump Administration's 2017 Executive Order 13769, prohibiting citizens from several Muslim majority countries from legally entering the country.

2. For further information on the Guibord Center, see Grafton, Duggan, and Harris, *Christian-Muslim Relations*, 84–92.

from around the country have purchased the study guide and now are using it in their communities. Personally, it was an honor to do a presentation in the instructional video of *Standing Together* with world-renowned scholar Dr. Maher Hathout on the basics of Islam and Christianity.[3] It is clear that my Lutheran theology deeply influenced my presentation and impacted our overall dialogue as he responded to my emphasis on grace.

The members of the CMCG developed the concept for *Standing Together* because we realized that there weren't any study guides on Islam and Christianity developed by teams of Christians and Muslims working in partnership on the same materials. In this sense, *Standing Together* represents a unique collaboration that reveals the richness and vibrancy of these faith traditions and teachings. The goals of *Standing Together* are:

- *break down the dehumanizing stereotypes that keep us apart and fearful of one another.* We live in the same neighborhoods, our kids go to school together, we see each other in the supermarket. However, we often don't know each other very well, if at all, since it is rare for Christians and Muslims in the United States to socialize, formally or informally. With *Standing Together*, the members of the CMCG hope to bridge relationships in our communities together.

- *create opportunities for faithful Muslims and Christians to engage with one another about beliefs and practices.* With *Standing Together*, face-to-face interactions develop a deeper, first-hand knowledge of the ways in which our faith traditions are both similar and distinctive. Furthermore, in the process of this dialogue, participants can clarify their knowledge about their own beliefs and traditions.

- *lay the foundation for possible future projects* that enhance the well-being of all your members and communities. The members of the CMCG have found ways to partner on many projects of common interest beyond the original intent of the organization and to share fellowship with one another as our bonds of friendship deepen.

It is also important to clarify what *Standing Together* is not. *It is not an opportunity to try to convert one another.* Participants are encouraged, as they talk about their own faith traditions, to speak from their experience and knowledge, and in a way that honors the experience and knowledge of all the members of their group. They should come to the dialogue assuming

---

3. Dr. Hathout has written several books, including *In Pursuit of Justice*.

that they will disagree on some matters, but being open to hearing the perspective of the other side. They should listen for the unexpected ways in which they may be more alike than different, with the possibility of being renewed in their understanding of what makes them who they are and in the faithfulness of our Creator.[4]

Over the years, I have often found myself in a lively discussion with Islamic scholars and imams over the differences between grace and mercy. The question is whether grace suggests unconditional acceptance and love without the need to do anything to earn it; or do we become worthy of God's favor and earn mercy by acts of goodness performed. Luther strongly emphasized that grace is not attained by our merit but comes freely as an unearned gift. From a Muslim perspective, mercy is always God's to give, but also ours to earn by our merciful acts toward others. Still, it is not whether we deserve to receive it or not, but it is in God's nature to show mercy when God chooses. As I attempted to explain the Lutheran concept of "works righteousness," my colleagues often agreed that humans are in fact judged according to our deeds and our lives, so how we live matters. Nevertheless, fortunately for our sake, God is also merciful and focuses primarily on our good works at the final judgment.[5]

I have served on the CMCG on behalf of the Southwest California Synod bishop (previously Bishop Dean Nelson and currently Bishop Guy Erwin), who has been very supportive of this organization and has attended numerous gatherings. The CMCG has in the past hosted a special reception for Lutheran clergy of the synod to come and experience the call to prayer (*adhan*) and Friday sermon (*khutbah*), followed by a time of discussion. This group is well known throughout Southern California, and many of us are asked to be speakers at local events, especially iftars (the meal held at sunset when the Ramadan fast is broken). During Ramadan I attended at least five to six itfars and often have been asked to be the keynote speaker at iftar programs. When I attend the local iftars, I try my best to fast on those days, but I am certain that, ironically, I tend to gain weight during Ramadan!

For a number of years, I also organized continuing education events at Claremont School of Theology. In 2006, my dear friend Sandy

4. For further information on the guide, which includes detailed agendas and timelines for each session along with participant handouts and educational video clips, see *Standing Together*.

5. For further explorations of Christian and Muslim conversations, see Mosher and Marshall, eds., *Sin, Forgiveness, and Reconciliation*.

Olewine, pastor of the First Methodist Church of Pasadena and co-chair of the Christian Muslim Consultant Group, who had previously served as United Methodist liaison for Protestant churches in Palestine, including the ELCA, returned to the U.S. I asked her help to put together a two-day conference on peace in the Middle East. Together we arranged an impressive list of speakers, including Jihad Turk. (It is noteworthy to mention that his attendance at this event was the first time he was on the campus of CST.) As the event drew closer, we felt something was missing. Suddenly it dawned on me that within the immediate proximity of the Claremont community, there was a Jewish synagogue and a Muslim mosque, Temple Beth Israel and the Islamic Center of Claremont. I went to visit both locations and found both communities were very eager to provide a representative to be on the planning committee.

We then met together regularly, which added a more intentional component, as this subject was not just an interesting topic but one that impacted the lives of the committee. In fact, Dr. Ahmed Sobol, the representative from the Islamic Center, was born in Palestine. Cantor Paul Buch from the local temple brought an authentic investment as well. As a result, we ended up having significant participation from members of both these religious communities. This turned the event into a heartfelt conversation. Although the planning became more challenging when opposing viewpoints and positions were presented, it certainly made the event more worthwhile. The conference was quite successful in many ways: excellent attendance, a community meal that fostered bridge building, and a wonderful musical presentation that incorporated all three Abrahamic faith traditions. Afterwards, we held our final evaluation meeting, and the consensus was clear. We agreed to continue meeting and to further our efforts to provide educational and interactive opportunities for the various faith communities to be an example of how mutual respect and peacebuilding is possible. Our hope was that other communities would catch the same vision that if we could "get along" here, we could be united in our efforts to shape U.S. policy in the Middle East and be an inspiration for how peace is possible. We also decided we liked each other and wanted to keep meeting, especially when we always had food at our gatherings! (The importance of hospitality is something I learned from the Arab culture while living in Egypt).

Annual Walk for Peace

We decided our next project would be an Annual Walk for Peace. This is a "protest walk" for peace from the various houses of worship participating in our group. We begin at an Islamic school (of kindergarten to eighth grade), then walk to the local mosque nearby, then to a Christian church (which is an ELCA congregation). We end at the local Jewish temple with a light meal. This event proved to be very successful and effective, especially by allowing people to visit places they had perhaps never stepped foot in before, to be welcomed by members of that faith tradition, and to experience their hospitality firsthand. The event essentially broke down some of the stereotypes about the "other." Walking, talking, and eating together enabled us to better appreciate each other and our common goal of working for peace.[6]

The event was first planned to coincide with the September 11th anniversary. Our hope was that this would help to deter some of the animosity people felt toward Muslims, to help participants realize that not all Muslim were terrorists but were in fact neighbors and co-workers. I will always remember the second year we planned the walk. It was the same time that the fundamentalist pastor in Florida, Terry Jones, threatened to burn a Qur'an on September 11.[7] It was all over the news. The Walk for Peace gave an opportunity for people who were opposed to this pastor's actions to respond. Instead of the three hundred to four hundred we had expected to attend from the previous year, over nine hundred people showed up! We had police protection, as some anticipated that there might be a negative or even violent response. But the walk was very peaceful and a wonderful example of mutual cooperation and support. The only dilemma we encountered was that the mosque, which was providing the closing meal, ran out of food as they had prepared for only four hundred. However, they placed an order at a local pizza place owned by one of the members of the mosque. Over one hundred pizzas appeared, and there was plenty for everyone: another manna or feeding of the five thousand story all over again! In 2019, the group hosted its eleventh Annual Walk for Peace, and the closing meal was at the temple, who were also celebrating Succoth, the feast of the harvest. We had moved the walk to October because it was too hot in September, and we also change up the walk every year to include and accommodate new locations and hosts.

---

6. "Join in the Journey."
7. MacAskill, Adams, and Connolly, "Pastor Terry Jones."

A professor from the University of Southern California made a professional video of one of the walks with interviews of the participants and planning committee. It also become a professional project of doctoral students at the Claremont Graduate School, exploring the premise of why and how has this group experienced such longevity. The history of this group, along with information about the CMCG, is covered in the recent resource book *Engaging Others, Knowing Ourselves: A Lutheran Calling in a Multi-Religious World*.[8] You can see videos and photos of past walks and more about this group at its Facebook page, "Inland Valley Interfaith Working Group for Peace in the Middle East."

CMCG also has sponsored interfaith Seders, iftars, picnics, and an educational event every year. In the past, we have had Rick Steves as our guest to watch and then discuss his documentary on the Holy Land. We also have hosted touring musicians from Israel and Palestine, who not only shared their music but their stories of working for peace. We have watched many inspirational movies, such as *Encounter Point, O Little Town of Bethlehem, The Band, The Jump,* and *Occupation 101*, which all document the challenge to build peace between these communities. Although, as our rabbi likes to say, the occupation is not a religious issue; it is a political one. I have also often highlighted the work and ministry of Peace Not Walls, an ELCA advocacy and educational ministry that attempts to make people aware of the situation in Palestine and the injustice the Palestinians face every day.

The relationships that we have formed through this interfaith ministry have become significant in building a deep sense of trust, so we are able to discuss difficult issues, such as Jewish settlements, and advocacy, including boycott, divestment, and sanctions of companies involved in the Israeli occupation, child detention, and the rising violence on both sides. These are all issues that the ELCA raised at the 2019 Churchwide Assembly, and I believe our Muslim friends see this kind of support and advocacy and appreciate it.[9]

Relational Ethics in a Local Congregation

Through the Inland Valley Interfaith Working Group for Middle East Peace, I not only represented the Claremont School of Theology but also the ELCA congregation where I served as pastor for twenty-three years,

8. LaHurd et al., eds., *Engaging Others*, 53–55, 67.

9. See ELCA, *Pre-Assembly Report.*.

Prince of Peace Lutheran Church, in Covina, CA. (In 2019, I retired from parish ministry after thirty-six years, but continue to provide pulpit supply for Lutheran and non-Lutheran congregations in the area). From the perspective of a parish pastor, I was taken by the transformation of my own members through their interaction with Muslims in the Walk for Peace, the interfaith Seders, and iftars. Prince of Peace also visited several of the local mosques regularly. Dr. Ahmed Sobol extended to us an open invitation to come, so he could share more about what it means to be Muslim and to help dispel many of the myths being perpetuated by Fox News and other media sources. After one such gathering, that always included the hospitality of a meal by members of the Islamic community, one of my members who asked many questions about the treatment of women, the tendency toward violence, and Sharia law in the U.S. (many of the common talking points of Fox News, which he watched faithfully), told me that he really had a change of heart. He realized that "they were really good people," and that most of what he accepted as truth by the media was false. I have found that the primary way this kind of transformation is possible is through direct interaction, by creating opportunities to encounter the other, to see them face to face as another human being. I like to call this process "relational ethics." Sermons and educational seminars are all well and good, but personal interaction and dialogue, eating a meal together, or joining together for a common cause (like a food pantry or environmental concerns) can change one's attitudes and one's ethical framework to be more inclusive and less judgmental. Witnessing this change of heart is one of the greatest joys of doing interfaith work.

For many years, my congregation has been connected to Chino Valley Islamic Center, the local mosque. We visit them regularly to witness the call to prayer. They have also come to join us for a Sunday worship service. After each experience, we always have a time for Q&A, where members from both communities can ask basic questions, such as, "What do the bread and wine represent?" and, "Why do the women pray behind the men or in another location?" We also regularly would bring the confirmation students along with their parents to visit the mosque and to engage in questions and answers.

This intentional building of mutual integrity leads to the development of deeper relationships. It has been fascinating to watch the gradual progression of friendship to more of a family atmosphere, where I have heard members of both sides say, "If anyone says anything negative about you, just let me talk to them." In turn, this is one of the reasons why this interfaith group enjoys a remarkable longevity and grows only stronger in quality and quantity. Authentic relationships of mutual respect have developed, so that our activities and events have a sense of a family reunion, as everyone is glad to see each other again.

Claremont School of Theology

Another major development in Muslim-Lutheran relationships in Southern California has been the mission of CST. Rooted in the Methodist tradition, Claremont has become an ecumenical and interreligious academy. The Lutheran church has had a partnership with CST for the past forty years. In 2012, CST entered into an agreement with Bayan Islamic Graduate School and the Academy for Jewish Religion to allow students to cross register in courses from all three schools. This meant that I had, for the first time, Muslim and Jewish students in my two online courses, "The Role of Prophet and Pastor: Introduction to Dietrich Bonhoeffer class" and "Reformation and Emergent Movement: A Comparative Study and Practical Applications." The change in student demographics prompted me to redesign other courses to be more inclusive, as well as to explore possible parallels between the various religious traditions and theologies. Many students found the focus of being prophetic and pastoral a universal challenge, regardless of one's faith tradition. The Jewish and Muslim students were inspired by Bonhoeffer's emphasis of needing to put one's faith into action by confronting oppressive structures and to align oneself with those who are suffering.[10] In addition, the question of what customs or beliefs need to be reformed in each faith tradition was also perceived to be a universal religious trait. The inclusion of multi-faith traditions in the classroom enlivens the conversation between students. Once, a Lutheran student remarked that he felt uncomfortable with Bonhoeffer's strong Christocentric theology and practice and even seemed to apologize for it to his fellow Jewish and Muslim students. However, a Muslim student replied that he appreciated Bonhoeffer's clear position and respected those who could embrace it, while at the same time respecting other faith traditions. He essentially encouraged the Lutheran student to remain firm on what she believed and to practice it with conviction, instead of trying to water it down for his sake, so that an

10. One of the books used for this course includes Jenkins and McBride, eds., *Bonhoeffer and King*.

honest dialogue could take place. This then upholds the integrity of each other's beliefs. It was a perfect example of what can happen as you engage in interreligious dialogue and explore together what it means to practice your faith in a way that benefits the whole world.

As I continue to teach both of these courses, examples of this kind of exchange have multiplied. I have seen Lutheran pastors who were my students and CST alumni not only become more tolerant but actively involved in promoting interfaith programs within their communities. They were in fact inspired by the CST model, which gave them the tools they needed to carry on or to begin their own crucial interfaith ministry. Many have reported back to me that they too have now organized Walks for Peace, conferences on various significant issues that are interfaith in nature, and built bonds between their church community and local Islamic Centers in Southern California.

Whether it be the Prophet Muhammed or Dietrich Bonhoeffer, both are guided by the same principles: to put one's faith into action, pursue and practice peace, advocate for justice, and stand with those who are oppressed—mandates set forth by Jesus, who not only is held in high esteem, but is considered a model for godly life by both faith traditions. Not only do we share the same creator and sustainer God, we are united in our endeavor to care for those in need and demonstrate compassion and grace to all.

Re-Envisioning

A Center of Christian-Muslim Engagement for Peace and Justice

——————————————————————— Sara Trumm

When I began my work at the Global Mission Institute at Luther Seminary in 2001, just weeks before the terrorist attacks of September 11, I had not given Islam much more than a passing thought. Growing up in a rural area of Minnesota and traveling internationally with Christian hosts had never given me the opportunity to meet a Muslim, at least as far as I knew. Islam was to me an exotic, foreign religion. So, it was surprising to me and to the many congregations requesting information and speakers, that the seminary not only had rich resources on world religions in general, but an actual program in Islamic studies and graduates from that program upon which to call.

With the guidance of Dr. Mark Swanson, director of the Islamic studies program at Luther Seminary at that time, students, graduates, and other leaders in the church recognized the necessity for better understanding Islam and getting to know our Muslim neighbors in a more personal way. As Islam became the center of mostly negative attention in the nation, it became imperative to these leaders that an accurate image of Islam in all its diversity and history be shared, and that Lutheran congregations get to know Muslim neighbors, rather than avoid them. I personally responded to this call to "love my neighbor" by teaching English to Somali refugees and participating in a course about Islam in

Egypt while working at Luther Seminary. When I had finished my job at Luther Seminary, I found myself attending a seminar for Christians on Islam through the Henry Martyn Institute (HMI) in Hyderabad, India, where I then served in HMI's academic program for a year. This is a place where the Evangelical Lutheran Church in America (ELCA) and former Lutheran bodies have had long-standing relationships.

In addition to the important teaching and community engagement at HMI, I was drawn to a place that recognized the complexities of religiopolitical rule in India, past and present. Knowing the detrimental and unjust history of colonialism, much of it perpetuated by Western Christian missionaries, it was inspiring to know that the Institute was named after an Anglican missionary who had served in India when it was under British rule, Henry Martyn. However, unlike many of his colleagues at the time who were focused on converting Muslims through coercion, Martyn sought understanding and respect of Indian culture in general and of Islam in particular. Even at that time, Martyn sought the kind of mutual understanding described in the ELCA's *A Declaration of Inter-Religious Commitment,* adopted at the 2019 Churchwide Assembly. It says, "'Mutual understanding' involves moving from factual knowledge of commonalities and differences to grasping coherence and even glimpsing beauty. . . . Mutual understanding opens the possibility of friendship and accepting responsibility for each other's well-being." Also from the ELCA's *Declaration*:

> As Lutherans, we are called to move from mere coexistence to a more robust engagement. It is through authentic, mutual relationships that we can truly love our neighbors as people made in the image of God. This commitment includes confronting whenever possible the often-compounding oppressions experienced by people of various religions and worldviews on the basis of race, ethnicity, gender, and class. . . . When the alternatives are so devastating, respectful conversation, dialogue, advocacy, accompaniment, friendship, and cooperation are imperative. We are called to move beyond encountering our religiously diverse neighbors to actively engaging with them.[1]

Upon my return from India in 2008, Islam maintained its foreign flavor for me, although it was no longer nearly as exotic as I had once imagined. The general attitude toward Islam in the United States continued to be one of negativity. Dr. Swanson and I found ourselves working together

---

1. ELCA, *Declaration*, 6 and 3–4, respectively.

again, this time at A Center of Christian-Muslim Engagement for Peace and Justice (CCME) at the Lutheran School of Theology at Chicago (LSTC). CCME, along with the Harold S. Vogelaar Professor of Christian-Muslim Studies and Interfaith Relations Chair (in which Swanson was serving) had both been inaugurated in 2006. The center and chair were established due to the commitment of the ELCA and of LSTC seminary leaders, as well as a generous endowment given by donors who had been touched by the work of Dr. Harold Vogelaar and Dr. Ghulam-Haider Aasi.[2]

I am deeply grateful for the forethought and long-term relationships developed among Lutheran and Muslim leaders in Chicago, led by Voge-laar and Aasi, starting in 1984. Because of it, LSTC was well-equipped to support and educate a society embedded within a culture of fear and mis-information about the "other." This work already included well-established team-taught courses on Islam and Christian-Muslim relations and had cre-ated deep friendships within the local Muslim community, not to mention the formation of the CCME in 2006.

CCME expanded the already strong academic exposure to Islam for students, as well as venturing into additional extra-curricular Christian-Muslim experiences. Vogelaar states, "The aim always was to integrate our interfaith work into the total program of the seminary. . . . We did not want our work to be thought of as an appendage or addendum to the main curriculum."[3] The center's mission and vision statements read: "CCME was founded on the conviction that Christians, Muslims, and neighbors of other faith traditions, in their co-humanity, created by and responsible before God, are called to know, respect and learn from one another, despite or even because of our differences." CCME fosters and deepens relations between Christians and Muslims as a significant part of its larger purpose of building bridges of mutual understanding and respect and cooperation among people of all faiths. More social interactions, arts-related experi-ences, and community projects were developed alongside educational con-ferences, lectures, and written resources.

While dialogue-based programs, such as an annual sacred text confer-ence and theological lectures with presentations from Jewish, Christian, and Muslim speakers, were appreciated by many, programs which incorporated

---

2. In the late 1980s, Dr. Mark Thomsen, Dr. Roland Miller, and other Lutheran lead-ers saw to it that Christian-Muslim relations was given a special place in the advanced studies programs of both Luther Seminary and LSTC .

3. Vogelaar, "Twenty-Five Years," 410.

interfaith experience and a deeper relationship into one's daily life proved more meaningful. For example, seminary students have found themselves unexpectedly working closely with Muslims during their internship year. Many in the seminary community have been involved in refugee support through campus housing, mentorship, fundraising, and friendship. Visiting Muslim scholars come to LSTC through CCME from several months up to two years, interacting with the seminary community in academic and social settings. Other examples of events LSTC and CCME have hosted are:

- Interfaith concerts by the Salaam-Shalom Music Project, Rose Ensemble, and Sounds of Faith

- Plays, such as *Unveiled* and *Mecca Tales* by local playwright Rohina Malik and *Obstacle Course* by the Chicago theater company Silk Road Rising

- Social justice projects, such as Share-a-Meal at Interfaith House, Food Justice gardens in Hyde Park Area, property clean-up and a breast cancer awareness event with the Zakat Foundation, Hyde Park and Kenwood Interfaith Council's soup kitchen and refugee project, Winter Farmers Market with Faith in Place

- Workshops to help non-Muslim health care chaplains better serve and interact with Muslim patients and their families

- Weekly iftar meals during Ramadan with the local Turkish community

An attitude of hospitality, grounded in biblical examples, became the basis of all the programs supported by CCME. Students, local congregation members, and other participants explored how the ideals of love for neighbor and not bearing false witness drew them into deeper relationship with Muslims. Constituents found that comparing and contrasting theological concepts, as well as faith in practice, helps them to develop a new appreciation for the other and an enhancement of their own faith. Not only is it necessary to dig deeper into one's own language and practice when describing faith to someone outside of the tradition, but a discovery and new appreciation of one's own expression and faith often emerges.

Testimonials to the positive experience of these programs have come from LSTC alumni who answered a 2018 CCME survey, with such comments as:

> I've learned quite a bit about Islam—aspects that are religious and/
> or cultural. It has helped me strengthen interfaith relationships

and has given me information to use in educating others, especially in the area of avoiding stereotypical and false viewpoints.

My understanding of Islam, the Qur'an, and The Prophet Muhammad was greatly deepened and has allowed me to be a better chaplain. It has also allowed me to have much more confidence when discussing Islam.

While on campus it was a valuable resource for interfaith study and understanding. Since leaving campus I look to CCME and its values to shape my decisions around advocacy and interfaith partnership.

This survey was part of a year-long re-envisioning process in response to a number of factors at the CCME in 2017–18: the retirements of both Dr. Aasi and the center's director, Dr. Michael Shelley; LSTC's new "public church" seminary curriculum; and an increasingly polarized nation. As the re-envisioning team leader, Carol Schersten LaHurd explained, "This is an important time for re-thinking inter-religious relations. When CCME was founded in 2006, many of us were just beginning to learn about other religions and to develop strategies for friendship and dialogue. Now, twelve years later, Christians, Muslims, and others are focused also on showing solidarity for each other in the public arena and working together for the common good."[4]

Through the survey, consultations, conversations, and correspondence, a team of nine volunteer professionals and seminary leaders absorbed and explored the Christian-Muslim context for one year. Local and national Christian and Islamic theologians and lay leaders provided input and advice regarding the current needs of their communities and the role of CCME in enriching Christian-Muslim relations at this time and place. The team listened and evaluated how best to implement what we heard into the ongoing work of CCME. Experience and wisdom flowed generously, especially at the two day-long consultations that were held, as well as at the Faith over Fear training that CCME co-hosted with the Shoulder to Shoulder campaign at the Muslim Education and Cultural Center of America (MECCA) in Willowbrook, IL, in January 2019. Dr. Swanson was able to summarize the many learnings from the re-envisioning process, and that summary gave us a template for our next steps. The main points of the

---

4. Lutheran School of Theology, "Year of Re-Envisioning."

summary are listed at the end of this chapter, and I will draw upon these points throughout the remainder of the chapter.

One of the first things we acknowledged is that we can't do it all—and fortunately, we don't have to. The diversity within both faith traditions is vast. In addition to the various interpretations and practices of adherents, the rural/urban contexts, socio-economic classes, racial identities, and degree of exposure to other faith traditions all have an impact on the kinds of experiences and educational opportunities that individuals and communities have with one another. Thanks to the well-established work of CCME, many more constituents now have experience and relationships with Muslims and Islam than previously. Nevertheless, in any event, our audience may run the spectrum from a Christian who has heard only about religious extremism all the way to a Muslim theologian.

Thankfully, there are more and more individuals and organizations with whom LSTC and CCME can now partner. For example, with the help of the Shoulder to Shoulder campaign mentioned above, we stay aware of the damaging work of the Islamophobia industry and learn how to counter the hate-filled messaging in our own communities with personal, articulate, and public responses. The Inner-City Muslim Action Network (IMAN) located on the south side of Chicago, not far from LSTC, provides resources, guidance, and a strong example for how to engage the community on local issues. Through the many relationships already formed, and the additional connections made through the re-envisioning process, the Chicago area's interfaith needs can be addressed from a variety of perspectives and activities. So, considering both our limited resources and relatively unlimited assets, the team sought to answer: What is the CCME's niche?

Educating, engaging, and supporting our seminarians and other leaders in the ELCA is where the CCME's expertise and emphasis lies. Equipping Lutheran and other Christian leaders for faithful work in a multi-religious society is a primary goal. We can do this by connecting not only with our present students, but also through reaching out to alumni and other ELCA communities. The ELCA's Ecumenical and Inter-Religious Relations office and the Shoulder to Shoulder campaign enable us to provide support more broadly and nationally. It is equally necessary to continually expand and deepen our circles of engagement in the Muslim community in the Chicago area. Partnering with the American Islamic College (AIC), for instance, is a natural and historic connection that can be nurtured. Through AIC, we can seek out other Muslim communities and organizations beyond those with whom we already relate. Our attention is to be focused on tending and building upon these relationships, seeking additional Muslim collaboration on community concerns, activism, and friendship. Involving Muslim leaders to help us more deeply connect to the local context and to continue offering courses on Islam and Christian-Muslim relations regularly at LSTC is paramount to ensuring that we connect communities in an authentic way.

Hiring a new Muslim(ah) colleague at the CCME would share in our center's goals of bringing social justice and academic study together in our programming. One of the changes noted during our re-envisioning process was that there has been a cultural move from a primarily academic interfaith dialogue approach among theologians and leaders to a more multi-faith and inter-religious engagement among lay people. Engagement was already central to CCME, as indicated by the name of the center, but a recognition of this continued cultural shift also occurred in the seminary as a whole and in the Association of Theological Schools (ATS). ATS urges its schools to emphasize awareness of "the multifaith and multicultural nature of the societies in which students may serve." In the fall of 2014, LSTC launched a curriculum which "cultivates competencies for leadership in a public church that focuses on community engagement, public witness, and social transformation. Our holistic approach to theological education breaks academic disciplines out of their silos and allows creative collaboration to flourish."[5]

The team-taught Christian-Muslim courses and seminars that build on the above-named competencies and that bring students into spaces of public engagement in Chicago, as well as in Israel-Palestine, India, and other parts of the world, serve as innovative models for public church pedagogy. Already in 2019, a course that was not only team taught, but was also made up of students from AIC, McCormick Theological Seminary, and LSTC, explored leadership in our respective religious. In addition, LSTC's new Public Church Fellows program, which combines academics with community service, nonprofit partner mentorship, and spiritual reflection, has brought many students into side by side work with Muslim community partners for up to seven hours each week. One Public Church Fellow (PCF), working with IMAN, involved several of her classmates and LSTC staff in a summer festival organized by the organization and welcomed several new people to smaller, more intimate women's

5. Lutheran School of Theology, "Public Church."

gatherings for fellowship and community activism. Several PCFs have been instrumental in helping to bring refugee families to Hyde Park and supporting them, together with interfaith partners.

An additional feature of the public church curriculum of LSTC is that it encourages learning and engagement across disciplines. This is in line with another aspect of the CCME's work highlighted during the re-envisioning process: Christian-Muslim relations is best done in collaboration with other centers at LSTC, with the Association of Chicago Theological Schools, and with student groups and initiatives within our institution. These other groups have also seen an increased need to break down divisive walls in the social fabric of our country, walls that polarize communities in a myriad of social issues. Islamophobic messages continue to pervade our media and political rhetoric, and Muslim rights and bodies are targeted. Leaders in both Christian and Muslim communities recognize the urgent need to attend to changing the polarizing narratives and attitudes around us. Again, we do not do this alone. Not only are there many allies who are diligently working toward ending stereotypes and hatred toward Muslims, but we join also with those addressing similar systemic issues such as racism, xenophobia, and anti-Semitism, learning from them and joining together to build loving and inclusive communities. As religious and other kinds of discrimination continue to be all too common in the United States, being a member of groups like the Chicago Inter-Religious Rapid Response Network is crucial. The network allows us to mobilize multi-faith responses to acts of hate targeting religious communities in the Chicago area and to give support to those attacked. When a Sikh man was beaten in a hate crime in a suburb of Chicago in 2015,[6] or when Wheaton College professor Larycia Hawkins was under fire for her embodied solidarity with Muslims,[7] there was a strong group of allies to call upon to give support and to call attention to the issues publicly. The rapid response team also builds the capacity to work toward dispelling misconceptions about minority communities. Through programs like Faith over Fear training sessions, community faith leaders are equipped to better advocate against a narrative of fear and divisiveness, centered around anti-Muslim bias, discrimination, and violence. The first Faith over Fear training in January 2018 was organized by Shoulder to Shoulder and through the initiation of Rev. Terry Kyllo, an LSTC alum working for an interfaith organization in Seattle, WA. About fifteen LSTC students joined a group

6. Fornek and Schering. "Sikh Man Who Was Attacked."

7. Pashman, "Wheaton College, Professor at Impasse."

of rabbis and pastors in learning how to talk with congregation members, other community leaders, and media sources in a way that promotes understanding and positive change.

While addressing these systemic issues in the public sphere, self-examination is also necessary for real transformation to occur. The use of the Intercultural Development Inventory at LSTC is one of the tools being used to encourage and equip students, faculty, staff, and the board for greater cultural competency. Individuals are provided the format and guidance for creating a personalized plan to develop their attitudes, skills, and behaviors in various cultural contexts. The seminary as a whole is then better able to plan and evaluate its programs and curricula to improve institutional policies and create a more inclusive learning environment.

Balancing cultural similarities and differences, honoring communal and individual contexts, learning from both curricular and extra-curricular activities, addressing theological and social issues, taking the lead and supporting initiatives of others, and responding to the needs of diverse Christian and Muslim communities, are all tasks and issues to which our seminary and center are called. While we still can't do it all, a pathway forward is in place. We look forward to reaching out to the broader community for continued input, such as what we received during the re-envisioning year.

During the re-envisioning process, the CCME's previous work in Christian-Muslim relations was deeply affirmed, a more defined focus was identified, and new ideas were proposed. It became clear that maintaining a posture of responsiveness will help us be open to new and insightful approaches or attitudes. While we already have many resources at the ready, we hope to be creative and flexible when new situations arise. For example, when a newly proposed Muslim community center faces opposition (due to what is stated as zoning or traffic concerns), we want to prepare local faith leaders to facilitate public discussions and address the underlying issues with grace. When a local congregation or institution plans to host a speaker who is known to espouse Islamophobic rhetoric, we seek to gather faith leaders to oppose the hate-speech and/or encourage event leadership to rethink their choice of speaker. When resources such as a *Discover Islam* DVD series are offered to Christian communities to learn more about Islam, we hope to make the most of such an opportunity, improving accessibility and guiding healthy adult forum discussions through a study guide written by our Lutheran colleague, Dr. Carol Schersten LaHurd. When tragedy strikes a faith community, we want to give support. When polarizing governmental policies are put in place, we seek to join others and advocate for change.

The key points from Dr. Mark Swanson's summary for CCME's 2018 re-envisioning report are suggestive of a promising future for this seminary's Christian-Muslim center and for partners like it around the country:

1. The past thirteen years have led to *expanding circles of engagement, which are locally focused and grounded.*

2. This re-envisioning year underscores the continuing importance of *building and tending.*

3. CCME's commitment to maintain a *posture of responsiveness* with local and national partners is strengthened.

4. It has become even more crucial to *break down the curricular/extra-curricular barrier* in the seminary's curriculum.

5. Especially from our consultation partners, we have learned the importance of *addressing systemic issues* in American culture.[8]

We have already begun the process of updating our database and website, hoping to provide digital resources for a greater number of alumni and congregation members. Program collaboration is well underway with area institutions. The most exciting aspect of the implementation of this process is anticipating the hiring of a Muslim(ah) team member for the work ahead. In sha'Allah, we will be even better situated to serve God through Christian-Muslim engagement!

8. Sevig, "CCME Leads the Way."

Interfaith Relations and the Work of Lutherans in Palestine

MARK B. BROWN

AFTER MANY YEARS IN the Middle East, mostly in Palestine and Israel, I returned in 2018 to the United States. There's a lot I don't miss about Jerusalem—discrimination, house demolitions, walls—but those are topics mostly for other articles. What I do, in fact, miss about Jerusalem is how the faith and the religious practices and activities of my Jewish, Christian, and Muslim colleagues and neighbors had a daily impact on my life. The Muslim call to prayer five times a day, the bell towers, and the Shabbat siren, all reverberating throughout the city of Jerusalem, gently called me to be still and to remember at that moment who I am as a person of faith. I looked forward to the sound of a cannon on Salah 'Eddin Street each day during the holy month of Ramadan. The boom in the distance announced the setting of the sun and the breaking of the fast for Muslims, and it also prompted me to think about my own faith and how fasting and prayer have been particularly important to me at different points in my life.

Living in Jerusalem, one is acutely aware of and oftentimes confronted by the activities of the religious communities around one, and for me it wasn't that strange to be inspired, awed, challenged, confused, or disheartened by what I saw or heard in the course of a week. There is a lot of religion per square meter in Jerusalem, and it's not all uplifting. It's hard not to notice a fair amount of local cynicism about religion and religious people. The political situation has taken its toll as well, with religion sometimes being a force for justice and equality, but too often being a justification for oppression or violence.

My focus in this essay, however, is on a few of the exemplary Lutheran institutions in Palestine and how they are leading the way in promoting understanding between people of different faiths and in efforts to strengthen and invigorate interfaith relationships for the common good of a community.

Augusta Victoria Hospital

Augusta Victoria Hospital (AVH) is a strong and professional medical institution located in Jerusalem on the Mount of Olives, serving Palestinians from Gaza and the West Bank. The hospital, owned and managed by the Lutheran World Federation (LWF), was established in 1950 in partnership with the United Nations Relief and Works Agency (UNRWA) for Palestine Refugees, in order to provide medical services for Palestinian refugees following the 1948 conflict.

As the main facility providing treatment for oncology and nephrology to patients in the Palestinian territories, the Muslim and Christian staff at AVH are under enormous pressure. And yet, watching up close for fourteen years as the LWF representative overseeing the work of the LWF's Jerusalem Program, what left a lasting impression with me were the remarkable acts of kindness, resilience, and tolerance that I witnessed, not once in a while or every month, but virtually every day.

For many of the staff, there isn't much time to be "religious." Most are battling traffic and checkpoints for hours each day as they come to AVH from the West Bank and when they return home after a long day of work. While they are at AVH, they have a nonstop schedule of patients for whom they need to be fully present. At AVH, it isn't enough to have the science exactly on the mark, although they do that well. The hospital has the accreditation from the Joint Commission International as one of many milestones confirming the medical excellence of the institution. At AVH, you will find love for the children who, year after year, make the trek from West Bank towns and villages three times a week for kidney dialysis. There is a deep compassion for the Gaza patients with cancer who may be going up to Jerusalem for the first time in their lives, and especially for the children whose parents are usually not allowed to accompany them on their journey to Jerusalem and the tough days of testing and treatment that they face.

There is a commitment at AVH to further the LWF's diaconal work for the alleviation of suffering, the promotion of peace, the protection of human rights, and the strengthening of civil society, and to do so without regard to race, creed, gender, or national origin. There is a lot of diversity among the AVH staff in terms of political views and affiliations, financial status, level of education, and cultural traditions. I believe that one of the key factors that unites members of the AVH staff in serving the most needy and vulnerable in Palestinian society is the calling to work for justice, equality, and healing that their faith and faith communities have instilled in them. This calling is reinforced by and resonates with the many systems that the LWF and AVH have in place to hold people accountable in the work place, to promote gender justice, and to encourage professional growth.

Walid V. Nammour, the hospital's chief executive officer and a Latin Catholic Palestinian Christian, said in an email, "I have a deep sense of satisfaction with my work at AVH where the cross-boundary nature of such work calls for cooperation and collaboration among all involved. The ecumenical character of the LWF work is notable; the AVH CEO is Catholic, the AVH Chief Finance Officer is Orthodox, the previous AVH CEO was Episcopalian. In addition, at AVH, Muslims, Christians, and Jews have all agreed that we have one enemy: it is *disease*, and we all shall fight that enemy with compassion and the desire to do good."

The AVH staff of four hundred fifty is mostly Muslim, and in that way, it is a reflection of Palestinian society overall. In addition to the professional and caring environment that exists at AVH, perhaps most of all I miss the greetings of peace and the responses of *alhamdulillah* ("praise be to God") and *ashkurallah* ("I thank God") that roll off the tongues of people when you ask them how they are. And there is the prayer—or word of hope, expression of confidence, sometimes fear—that the phrase *inshallah* ("if God wills") conveys, purposefully or reflexively acknowledging the divine involvement in our most profound decisions and in our most mundane activities.

The staff rarely talked about Christian-Muslim relations at a theological level at AVH, as far as I was aware. But there were ample indications that the Christians and Muslims on the staff valued their relationships. Muslims and Christians on the AVH staff greeted each other warmly, often with handshakes and hugs, on occasions like the AVH-sponsored Christmas staff lunch and Ramadan iftar, at the graduation of a cohort of Palestinian oncology nurses, at the opening of a school inside the hospital for children who are away from home for weeks at a time while they receive cancer treatment, or at a whole host of other occasions when we celebrated together.

In November 2011, AVH was the conference venue for the Faith Based Health Care Network, founded in 2008 in Atlanta, Georgia, as a network of leaders in faith-based healthcare focusing on local expressions of practice and mutual support. The conference topic of faith and healing resonated with us at AVH, a multi-faith hospital seeking to provide excellent medical care, while also providing vital psychosocial care for patients of different faiths and backgrounds. I had the privilege of welcoming the conference participants and began by quoting from a 2010 book, *Making Health Care Whole: Integrating Spirituality into Patient Care*, by doctors Christina Puchalski and Betty Ferrell:

> Physicians, nurses, and other health care professionals commit themselves, often by oath, to caring for patients as whole persons. Because illness and injury disrupt a patient's life in ways that extend beyond the body, encompassing families, communities, and a patient's religious commitments, a commitment to caring for whole persons must entail going beyond the care of only the body.[1]

For fifty years, from 1950 to 2000, AVH offered primary and secondary healthcare. Over the last two decades, AVH transitioned to providing specialty care in the areas of oncology and nephrology. As a result of these changes, the need to treat the "whole patient," particularly oncology patients, became even more acute. Oncology patients are at critical junctures in their lives. In these vulnerable moments, patients and medical staff alike often call on their faith as a source of strength. As a faith-based organization, LWF's AVH is both a center providing excellent medical care and a center of caring and compassion for its predominantly Muslim patients. AVH staff members, informed by their own religious backgrounds as well as by the values articulated by the organization, recognize the dignity of every person and seek to provide unusual services that uphold their dignity. AVH provides services such as the patient and staff buses which provide transportation to and from the West Bank and reduce the humiliation of long waits at checkpoints, and the accommodations at a nearby hotel where Gaza cancer patients and family members stay while the patients are receiving treatment. The Gaza patients cannot risk having their treatment interrupted due to the lack of permission to travel to Jerusalem for treatment, so they often stay in Jerusalem for the duration

1. Puchalski and Ferrell, *Making Health Care Whole*, 32.

of their treatment. These extraordinary efforts illustrate the AVH commitment to meeting the needs of the whole person. The AVH care for patients reaches far beyond the confines of the stone walls of the historic building on the Mount of Olives. In February 2010, AVH began sending a mobile mammography unit to villages throughout the West Bank. Staffed by an all-female, predominantly Muslim, team of physicians, nurses, technicians, and counselors, the mobile mammography unit to this day helps to identify women with breast cancer at an early stage, so they may be referred to AVH for treatment with better outcomes.

However, it should be emphasized that our commitment as Lutherans cannot and does not stop at providing these medical services. We also seek to change the systems that hinder people from gaining access to healthcare and other basic human rights. In the words of the conference participants from the LWF's 2002 global consultation on diakonia in South Africa: "Diakonia is central to what it means to be the church. . . . [But] while diakonia begins as unconditional service to the neighbor in need, it leads inevitably to social change that restores, reforms and transforms."[2] While our faith calls us to serve our neighbor, a prophetic diakonia calls us to take the risk of speaking truth to power and challenge the systems of injustice that perpetuate cycles of poverty and violence, recognizing that human suffering is not only medical, but social, economic, emotional, and spiritual as well. The goal of providing excellent medical care inevitably leads us to care for all dimensions of human suffering by working for radical transformation of the systems that oppress the people we serve.

The Israel-Palestine conflict is a long conflict, consuming the energy and resources of Palestinians, Israelis, and the community of nations. It has cut deeply into the lives of Palestinians and Israelis and has been particularly damaging to Palestinians over the years, who have seen their land confiscated, homes demolished, families separated, citizens tortured, cities heavily damaged by bombings, demonstrators and medical workers attacked with lethal force, and so on. Institutions like AVH and the other East Jerusalem hospitals, including Makassed Islamic Charitable Hospital, Red Crescent Maternity Hospital, St. John of Jerusalem Eye Hospital, the Princess Basma Rehabilitation Centre, and St. Joseph's Hospital, are critical for strengthening Palestine, ensuring a shared Jerusalem, and opening up prospects for a just resolution of the conflict. These hospitals are at the heart of capacity building for an emerging state, they are inspiring examples of

2. Böttcher, ed., *Prophetic Diakonia*, 6.

both medical professionalism and human compassion, and they are models of Christian cooperation among Palestinians.

That is really a big understatement, actually. There is not just cooperation between Christians and Muslims at AVH, there is a sense of comradery, of neighborliness among the staff that often goes beyond what we, as Americans, would expect. Yes, we celebrated together, but we also shared some of the lowest points imaginable, offering and receiving comfort in times of unspeakable heartache and grief, mourning the loss of a beloved colleague after a long and arduous struggle with cancer, informing a family that they had only days, not weeks, left to be with their tiny child.

I don't mean to give an impression that there are never tensions and conflicts among the hospital staff members, or that some people don't act at times out of self-interest, or that religion is never a source of the stresses and strains among the staff. That just wouldn't be true. What I do want to say is that, at AVH, one gets a glimpse of the eternal, of true compassion, however fleetingly, and it is these moments that we hang on to and on which we build.

AVH plays a leadership role in the East Jerusalem Hospitals Network (EJHN), a coordinating body that unites AVH and five other hospitals in their efforts to provide effective and efficient medical services. The focus at AVH is on oncology and nephrology treatment to Palestinian children, women, and men living in the West Bank and Gaza. These hospitals and counterparts in the United States have been struggling over the last couple of years to restore U.S. funding to the East Jerusalem hospitals after cuts by the U.S. Administration.

As a Lutheran institution, AVH values the engagement it has fostered among health professionals—Palestinian Christians, Muslims, and Israeli Jews—who participate in activities centered on serving patients and developing higher levels of medical knowledge and expertise. Engagement with the Peres Center for Peace and Innovation, the Hadassah Medical Organization, the Middle East Cancer Consortium, Rambam Health Care Campus, and others has been important for AVH, especially in the years when it was transitioning from being a general hospital to a specialized center focusing on cancer treatment. More recently, the strength and strategic nature of these relationships was demonstrated when a group of Israeli medical professionals publicly called on the U.S. government to restore its support for AVH and the East Jerusalem hospitals.[3]

3. Clarfield, Glick, and Carm, "American Funding Cutback," 1624.

The Israelis who signed the document acknowledged that they themselves had "diverse political views," but that, as medical professionals, they were united in their conviction that "health cooperation is an area in which we urge decision makers to distance themselves from politically related considerations."[4] The professional dialogue over the years helped to foster friendships that have provided a context for increasing religious tolerance and mutual respect. Will continued interaction in the health sector help to end the Israeli occupation and bring justice for an oppressed people?

Mount of Olives Sports Field

The same intentionality around fostering good and vibrant relations between Christians and Muslims that exists at AVH is also present at the LWF's Vocational Training Program, and in other aspects of the LWF's Jerusalem Program. The property under the stewardship of the LWF on the Mount of Olives presents many challenges and opportunities. For decades, there had been a rocky dirt field at one corner of the LWF property. Despite its rough condition, it had been used extensively by the young people of the East Jerusalem neighborhood of At-Tur. In recent years, the LWF worked closely with the neighborhood not only to preserve this space, one of very few fields in East Jerusalem, but to transform it with high-quality artificial turf and lighting. Because of the cooperation between the LWF, the neighborhood of At-Tur, the Islamic Development Bank, the United Nations Relief and Works Agency, and the governments of Sweden and Turkey, the sports field is a treasured space that is safe and provides an inviting environment for young people and families for soccer games and community activities.

ELCJHL Schools

Like AVH, the Lutheran schools in Palestine have made Christian-Muslim relations a high priority. At the heart of the work of the Evangelical Lutheran Church in Jordan and the Holy Land (ELCJHL) are the schools and educational programs. The Lutheran schools reach approximately 2,300 students in Jerusalem, Ramallah, Bethlehem, Beit Sahour, and Beit Jala. In the 2018–2019 academic year, 65% of the students in the four K–12 Lutheran schools

---

4. Clarfield, Glick, and Carm, "American Funding Cutback," 1624.

were Muslim and 35% Christian (Greek Orthodox, Lutheran, or other). The beginnings of the robust school system that we know today go back to 1851 with the arrival in Jerusalem of four deaconess sisters from Kaiserswerth in Germany to open a school and hospital.

The schools are designed to meet the needs of the Palestinian people as a whole and reflect the diversity of Palestinian society. By embracing and empowering students and families in the region from all religions and economic and social backgrounds, the schools provide the opportunity to live and to learn in an atmosphere where each person is respected. As all are created in the image of God, Lutherans hold fast to the notion that the freedom and dignity of each person is inviolate. Students and faculty members are equipped and freed to accept each other's gifts, talents, and weaknesses, regardless of gender or religion.

A number of the ELCJHL overarching goals that guide the work of its schools and educational programs are vital to promoting healthy Christian-Muslim relations within the schools. The Lutheran identity of the schools is evident in expressing and striving toward these goals. The following five overarching goals stand out to me in relation to the church's role in society and commitment to strengthening relationships between Muslims and Christians:

- To develop wholesome, creative, and innovative students through a holistic approach to education that addresses their needs and develops their talents, competencies, inclinations, and ability to cope in an ever-changing world.

- To integrate peace education and culture, reinforce democracy, and encourage tolerance, co-existence, love, and respect toward others.

- To mold and reinforce the national and Christian Palestinian identity.

- To appreciate individual differences and assist in integrating students with special needs and/or disabilities in the school and the community.

- To reinforce and support the role of women in Palestinian society.[5]

Numerous initiatives of the ELCJHL schools naturally flow from these overarching goals. However, as a participant in the ELCJHL schools board for over a decade, I can assure the reader that many studies went into the development of the programs mentioned below, that there were various and

5. Many thanks to the ELCJHL schools for the information provided for this article. See Evangelical Lutheran Church of Jordan and the Holy Land, *Our Schools*.

sundry obstacles and challenges in the implementation of the programs, and that the creativity and persistence of the director of education, principals and teachers, volunteers, and other leaders were essential for success.

The Lutheran schools' *Leadership Program* trains and mobilizes eight or nine students in each school every year to do volunteer work within the community, as well as within school population. They are often models for volunteerism and social involvement. The West Bank communities where the Lutheran schools are located are places where Muslims and Christians are neighbors. Some West Bank cities are majority Muslim or majority Christian. Therefore, students are taught to serve their neighbors and community, regardless of religion. The Leadership Program teaches students to be committed and engaged with the entire community, Muslim and Christian, by bringing donated items to the elderly in their homes, for example, visiting city leaders in their offices, starting recycling programs in the schools, or teaching younger students about the environment.

Through the *Mediation Program*, students are empowered to become leaders and learn to promote peace between the religions. The Mediation Program is a year-long curriculum of weekly training in problem solving, communication skills, conflict resolution and leadership. The students participating in the program in each of the ELCJHL schools are trained as mediators and are expected to practice their training with fellow students during the recess of schools. The Mediation Program provides a platform for healthy interfaith dialogue. For example, in one of the schools a quarrel between two sixth grade students (a Muslim and a Christian) ensued over religious issues, and two eighth graders (a Muslim boy and a Christian girl) intervened, applying their mediation training, and managed to resolve the issue.

The *Lutheran Model United Nations* (LuthMUN) is an educational, afterschool activity that utilizes diplomacy, international relations, and other techniques of the United Nations to sharpen English language skills, public speaking, writing, critical thinking, and teamwork. These skills organically lead to positive exchanges in interfaith relationships during the LuthMUN training and beyond the classroom into the community. LuthMUN involves both Christian and Muslim students and is an opportunity for them to come together with people of different faiths, much as the representatives at the United Nations do, to hear and struggle with points of view that may be diametrically opposed to their own political beliefs and values.

The Lutheran schools' educators developed the *Joint Christian and Islamic Education Lessons* curriculum, established in 2000 at the Dar al-Kalima

School in Bethlehem for first- through eleventh-grade students. In Palestine, where Christians and Muslims have long lived side by side, it is essential that the various religious communities receive accurate education about the religion of their neighbor. Now, monthly joint lessons combine religion classes that run parallel to the ongoing separate weekly classes for Muslims and Christians, as required by the Palestinian Authority. The religions are taught together once a month in an open, safe space for inquiry and discussion. The students exchange experiences and learn about each other's faith in order to foster respect for each other and reduce harmful misconceptions. These classes go beyond the walls of the school when children share with their parents and families about their interreligious lessons.

In order to stay current with changes in religious practices, a committee of Christian and Islamic educators meet yearly to review the curriculum and possibly propose adaptations. Currently, the Lutheran schools are hoping that the Palestinian Ministry of Education will adopt the curriculum for all of its public schools. These joint lessons are key in developing respect and peace for a new generation in Palestine.

The Arab Educational Institute is a resource that the Lutheran schools use to help instill Palestinian identity by supporting youth, women, and educators in building community and voicing their cultural identity and human rights. The teachers participate in training sessions that incorporate teachers from both faiths. The institute offers information and training on how to impart peace and reject violent attitudes among the students. The institute resources allow yet another venue for dialogue between the two religions, since a person's faith often informs how that person responds to conflict and stress.

Finally, all students in the Lutheran schools have a strong understanding of Lutheran identity. In a region where Lutherans are the minority among the traditional Christian denominations of the Middle East, it is important to share with our Christian and our Muslim brothers and sisters the meaning of the Lutheran faith. This is robustly celebrated throughout the ELCJHL schools on Reformation Day. Christian Lutherans, Latin Catholic, Orthodox Christians, and Muslim students spend the day learning the history of the Reformation through activities, music, plays, and crafts. The Reformation Day celebrations in the schools give all students a chance to engage in the history of reform and to adapt the concept of reformation to our times and to the Palestinian context.

Dr. Charles D. Haddad, ELCJHL director of education and a Palestinian Lutheran, reflected in an email on the significance of these ELCJHL initiatives: "It is a feeling of great joy to see that we have successfully created a school environment where children live, interact and work closely together with total disregard to their religious backgrounds. It is as if there is no religion when it comes to collaboration, cooperation, team work, mutual respect and friendships."

Conclusion

This essay has not been an exhaustive survey of all the things that Palestinian Lutherans and Lutheran partners around the globe have done or are doing to promote interfaith understanding and cooperation in Palestine and Israel. This essay also only touches upon the efforts of these institutions to promote peace with justice and to further the values of tolerance, nonviolence, and compassion. My hope is that the reader will visit AVH, the LWF Vocational Training Program, and the ELCJHL schools and other ministries to witness these programs—perhaps with the guidance of the Peace Not Walls campaign of the Evangelical Lutheran Church in America—or invite representatives of these institutions to speak to their congregations or communities. We have much to learn about and together as Christians and Muslims.

Now that I am back in the United States, as a Christian, I am part of the majority culture, and after so many years in the Middle East, I welcome opportunities to be in solidarity with Muslims in this country. One opportunity came in the form of an invitation to speak at an iftar here in Maryland. It was a chance to reflect on the connections I had with Muslims in Jerusalem and our common commitments around fasting and prayer, spiritual reflection, and solidarity with the poor and vulnerable in society, values at the core of our Muslim and Lutheran/Christian traditions. I also reiterated the commitment of Lutherans and many other Christians in the U.S. to love our Muslim neighbors by standing shoulder to shoulder with them against Islamophobia, anti-Muslim bigotry, and any expressions of religious intolerance or racism; by educating our church members about Islam and helping them to reach out to their neighbors who face discrimination and stereotyping; by standing up to governmental actions or policies that are anti-Muslim in character; by working for justice at home and abroad; and by proclaiming through our words and actions an important message to society: that Muslims are our neighbors, made in God's image. Getting to know our neighbors and sharing our perspectives and ideas, our hopes and fears, doesn't always come easily, perhaps especially these days, when there are so many demands on our time and there are public forces that would erect walls between us. We cannot love our neighbors unless we take the time and are intentional about getting to know them. This is our desire, yes; but it is also *God's* desire for us.

CHAPTER 9

Christian–Muslim "Communion" in Indonesia

Challenges and Opportunities

FERNANDO SIHOTANG

I WILL ALWAYS REMEMBER the day back on October 13, 2015, when witnessing the crowds—an estimate of eight thousand out of the total fifteen thousand local Christian residents—who fled their homes to find refuge in the neighbouring province of North Sumatra (the province in which I currently live). Mobs had attacked churches in the Singkil District, Aceh Province, in which Sharia law is the source of law and the core legitimacy for public moral standards within the whole province. On that day, one of the churches of the *Huria Kristen Indonesia* (HKI, the Indonesia Christian Church), a member of the Lutheran World Federation, was burnt down by mob attackers who acted on behalf of *Pemuda Peduli Islam* (PPI, the Islamic Youth Movement of Aceh Singkil). A few days later, ten churches were demolished by the Singkil local government to satisfy the Muslims' demands to close down all "illegal" churches in the district. Eight of the churches were of the *Gereja Kristen Protestan Pakpak Dairi* (GKPPD, the Pakpak Dairi Christian Protestant [Lutheran] Church), with one Catholic and one Pentecostal church (GMII).[1]

For a long time after the incident, Christians in Aceh Singkil lived in fear of being attacked in retaliation for the death of a young Muslim man named Syamsul, who was a member of the mob that had attacked the churches. The

1. Singkil, "Island in Focus."

incident occurred between the church members and a mob who wanted to burn another targeted church of the GKPPD.[2] Wahid (not his real name), a member of the GKPPD, which was targeted in an attack, was accused of the young man's death and sentenced to six years for acting as the key provocator. The attackers themselves were never sent to jail, though. As of today, members of these churches still organize their worship in tents. In an estimated 2,185 square kilometers (843 square miles) of the Singkil district, Christians are allowed to have only one church and four *undung-undung* (equivalent to a smaller mosque called a *mushalla*, or chapel).

Indonesia has been one of many countries on the global watchlist for its human rights violations of freedom of religion or belief. Members of religious minority groups and unrecognized convictions feel worried when publicly manifesting their religion or beliefs. An expression or opinion that can be considered as blasphemy against the religious orthodoxy is a criminal offense. The anti-blasphemy provisions mostly target members of religious or minority groups, and the rise of identity politics consequently shrinks the public space that is, in theory, to be shared equally. This chapter will briefly elaborate on human rights circumstances and social hostilities involving religions in our pluralistic Indonesian society.

Given the fact that many churches or other houses of worship are burnt, sealed off, and demolished in some areas throughout the country due to the involvement of some Islamic groups,[3] some people started making accusations that Muslims deserve to be blamed for the lack of freedom of religious minority groups. According to Human Rights Watch (HRW), over one thousand churches in Indonesia have been shuttered during the time of democratic regimes, ironically after the "religious harmony" decree was enacted in 2006.[4]

Back in Singkil, I found out in my observations and talks with both Christian and Muslim communities that the perpetrators were not locals, and that the incident had nothing to do with religious or theological differences, but more with religiopolitical sentiments. The 2015 incident was the second time I was involved in advocating for freedom of religion or

2. Simanjuntak and Gunawan, "Thousands Leave Aceh."

3. A number of attacks and demolition of houses of worship and private property belonging to religious minorities in Indonesia have occurred during different governmental regimes. Since Indonesia became a democracy in 1998, the Islamic hardliners have made life difficult for Christians and Muslim minority groups such as the Shi'a and Ahmadiyyah communities.

4. Soloway, "Islamist Hard-Liners."

belief in Singkil after 2012. Both incidents happened prior to local district political elections.

Are there always such negative experiences when addressing interfaith coexistence in this nation? This chapter is also dedicated to revealing some of the peacemaking stories which I have collected through literature and interviews with both Muslims and Christians in different areas. There are many stories to tell of positive interfaith relations in the Indonesian context, of consolidated work and mutual interactions for peace, to turn back "common enemies" that include extremism in the name of religion, inequality, poverty, corruption, and so forth. What is it then that allows Christian institutions and ideas to be established in Muslim majority societies and vice versa? Despite the nationwide slogan *bhinneka tunggal ika* ("unity in diversity"), Indonesian plurality has always prompted challenges within the society and at the official state level in the management of religious affairs. Yet, plurality also undeniably creates potential opportunities for both sides to join hands to tackle socio-political matters that indiscriminately affect all believers, regardless of the religion to which they belong.

Bhinneka Tunggal Ika

It was a long journey for the just-mentioned Sanskrit phrase *bhinneka tunggal ika* to become an accepted slogan of the nation, and it is still debatable today whether unity is the original nature of Indonesian society despite societal differences in religion or belief. Formally used for the first time in 1950, the slogan was developed to accompany the official policy of *Pancasila* ("Five Principles"), the country's *philosophische grondslag* ("basic philosophy," if not an ideology), after a long and deliberative debate regarding the country's religion and state relations. There was a debate about whether to accept a secular framework or to follow the rule of Islamic law. The principles were adopted just one day after Indonesia's declaration of independence, August 17, 1945.

Indonesia is made up of many religions and indigenous beliefs, where Islam is the largest religious group (87 %), followed by Christianity (10 %), Hinduism (1.6 %), Buddhism (0.7%), and Confucianism (0.5 %). The remainder is made up of hundreds of smaller groups who hold indigenous religious beliefs. Although, in general, Islam is the largest religion over all, other religions are also dominant in various places of the country. The country's founding parents debated up to the last hours before independence whether to create equal space for all religions to participate in the establishment of the new modern nation. The reality of religious pluralism did challenge the founding parents to publicly recognize their religious traditions in the midst of other different religious perspectives.[5]

However, an Islamic law proposal called for "*dengan kewajiban menjalankan syariat Islam bagi pemeluk-pemeluknya*" ("the obligation for adherents of Islam to implement the Sharia"), now known as the "seven words" in the Jakarta Charter, the *Piagam Jakarta*. An Islamist faction rejected the Western-envisaged separation of church and state, driven by the belief that Islam should never be separated from politics. In contrast, the secularists and multi-cultural nationalists believed that the state should be neutral on religious issues.

The Islamist point of view arose because of the experience of Dutch colonial rule, when Islam was severely marginalized and oppressed. Therefore, after the Dutch were removed, it was believed that Islam should be politically privileged in the independent nation of Indonesia. An opponent to this idea was Soepomo, a Muslim and one of the constitution drafters, who argued for rejecting the idea of forming an Islamic state, that it would be incapable of uniting the archipelago inhabited not only by Muslims but many other religions, and therefore, consequently, it would create factions based on religion.[6]

Eventually, a neutral point of view was adopted. Instead of the "seven words," as a compromise, so that neither secularism nor Islam would take the definition of the country's state-religion relations, the "belief in Almighty God" was chosen to be the neutral form enshrined as the first principle of *Pancasila*. These Five Principles were proposed by the first Indonesian president Soekarno in 1945 and subsequently included in the constitution. They are: 1) belief in Almighty God; 2) a just and civilized humanism; 3) the unity of Indonesia; 4) deliberative democracy; and 5) social justice for all. It was believed that the first principle was the most acceptable way to accommodate the unique composition of religions and beliefs that already existed in the society. To put it differently, Indonesian Protestant theologian Eka Darmaputera explains: ". . . it tried to satisfy both parties, while at the same time, it could not accept any of those ideas in their entirety. That is why the first principle was formulated in the neutral form."[7]

5. Menoh, "Religiusitas Bangsa Sebagai," 83.

6. Latif, *Negara Paripurna*, 71.

7. Darmaputera, *Pancasila*, 153.

Indonesian societies are made up of 360 different indigenous religions. These were in existence before Indonesia's officially recognized religions—Hinduism, Buddhism, Confucianism, Christianity, and Islam—were "blown" at the direction of Indonesian archipelago. Eliza Griswold fascinatingly uses the term "trade winds" in her book *The Tenth Parallel* in order to describe that winds blew the traders in the same direction towards the equator. The trade winds from both the Northern and Southern hemispheres consistently blew towards the equator, allowing the early explorers and merchants to travel vast distances on predictable winds. In this sense, both Christianity and Islam were blown together to reach the Indonesian archipelago.[8]

Buddhism and Hinduism, just like Christianity and Islam after them, came to Southeast Asia over the ocean. Hinduism and Buddhism came to Indonesia in the late fourth centuriy and grew their empires very expansively. Islam was brought to the archipelago in the thirteenth century by Indian Gujarat traders, and was cordially welcomed by the Hindus and Buddhists. Christianity came in the 1500s with the Catholic Portuguese, and later on, Protestantism came with Dutch colonialization. According to Griswold, Indonesian official religions were brought through "the sails of traders and missionaries from Yemen, China, India, Portugal, Spain, and the Netherland."[9] Later German missionaries had influence in the expansion of Lutheranism.

For many centuries, the religions, particularly Christianity and Islam, went through periods of peaceful coexistence. Morever, there was ongoing competition between Christians, whose expansion was much influenced by Dutch colonialism. This resulted in Islam becoming dominant in many islands or territories. There are many stories of how the Christians were opposed by locals, not necessarily only by Muslims, but by other indigenous communities as well. This is because Christianity was perceived as the oppressors' religion.

The *Pancasila* have continued to be threatened and contested in every government since 1945. During President Soekarno's time (1949–66), Indonesia's politics were considered to be inclusive even of atheism (that is, Communism) and mystical beliefs. After that, for thirty-two years under the authoritarian President Soeharto (1966–98), the *Pancasila* were politically used to restrict freedom by keeping the religions firmly under

8. Griswold, *Tenth Parallel*, 178.
9. Griswold, *Tenth Parallel*, 178.

the control of state-sponsored religious institutions. Because of this, Muslims felt marginalized and were forced to accept the ideology of the *Pancasila*. In 1983, the government enacted a law that ordered both mass organizations and political parties to adopt the *Pancasila* as their only ideology, no matter if it was opposed to their religious or philosophical views. The law was accused by Islamic scholars of being the Soeharto regime's "de-Islamization" project.

In post-Soeharto democracy today (1998–present), the official space for religious freedom has become more open than ever before. Yet, at the same time, the new open democracy poses new threats: on one hand, the shrinking of democratic public space within the confines of a majority hegemony, and on the other, the rise of extremism in the name of religious orthodoxy. The *Pancasila* within the confines of a majority hegemony are now widely interpreted to justify the illegitimate actions and vigilantism against religious worships of minority groups, free speech, "deviant" religious groups, and new religious movements.

A prominent Indonesian thinker, Yudi Latif, analogizes the Indonesian religious diversity to mathematical fractions. The *Pancasila* are presupposed to be a denominator for all the fractions that exist in this nation. He emphasizes that, logically, fractions cannot be summed up if there is no single denominator beneath them. It does not matter how many fractions exist, as long as there is one common denominator.[10] Latif's analogy of the denominator is in line with the core definition of the *Pancasila* as described by Soekarno, as the unifying soul of the Indonesian people, the manifestation of unity and territories, and the *weltanschauung* ("worldview") towards national and international friendships. This worldview is the original spirit that recognizes inherent dignity and equal human rights as the foundation of freedom, justice, and peace as found in the 1945 preamble of the Indonesian constitution (*UUD*) and within the 1948 United Nations' *Universal Declaration of Human Rights* (*UDHR*).

Freedom and Human Rights Violations

In democratic Indonesia today, academics, politicians, activists for religious freedom, and scholars keep challenging the commitment of the state to ensure freedom of religion or belief for everyone, regardless of their chosen religion or beliefs. To what extent do state actors understand the signed

10. Latif, "Kewarganegaraan Masyarakat."

and ratified international human rights standards, legally binding the state to promote peace through human rights and to guarantee freedom? This is an especially important question as Indonesia has been signatory to the International Covenant on Civil and Political Rights (ICCPR), which legally binds it to undertake necessary measures to protect the rights of everyone, including the freedom of religion or belief.

Such a question is certainly now frequently raised. It is raised with the memory, the history, and the original nature of the diversity that *bhinneka tunggal ika* needs to be preserved in order for the full meaning of the Five Principles to be fulfilled. How can the *Pancasila* be understood as the *weltanschauung* of Indonesians if a lack of freedom is still dominant in the political sphere and, as a consequence, the government is powerless to bring about justice for everyone? The fact is that the government plays a very strong role by interfering in freedoms that are related to religious matters. For instance, notwithstanding the guarantee of freedom to adopt and manifest a chosen religion or belief freely, the Indonesian government does regulate bans against several religious communities that are considered to be "deviant" from Sunni Islamic orthodoxy in Indonesia, namely Shi'a, Ahmadiyya, Gafatar, and Lia Eden. Their religious activities are frequently labeled as sources of disharmony, namely, the flaming anger of Muslims. This is a potential political resource for elites who play identity politics as democracy is contested.

The compromise between the secularists and Islamists provides space for the government to regulate restrictions on religious matters. In many cases, these restrictions are considered necessary and legitimate in the name of public harmony between religiously diverse societies and in consideration of protecting religious values, which is provided for in the limitation clause of the constitution. For example, the Pew Research Center in its decade-long research (2007–17) found equivalent correlation between government restrictions on religion and social hostilities involving religions. The more the government imposes restrictions, the higher the social hostilities will be.[11] According to Pew, Indonesia consistently scored "high" or "very high" levels of restrictions on religion from 2007 through 2017. These are in the same levels as China and Russia.

Let us review what Pew noted in the following three indicators to measure the level of restriction on religious matters in the country: government favoritism of religious groups (9.3 out of 10); government

11. Pew Research Center, "Closer Look."

harassment of religious groups (8.7); and government limitations on religious activities (7.9).

Firstly, although Indonesia does not consistently posit Islam as the state religion, it recognizes only six religions to be practiced. The orthodoxization of these six religions is never formalized in the constitution. However, it is mentioned in the elucidation of the blasphemy law and in the judges' statement before the Constitutional Court in rejecting the application submitted by civil society communities to revoke that blasphemy law in 2009. The blasphemy law initially was enacted in 1965 to prevent the misuse of religions mostly adhered to in Indonesia, aiming particularly at preventing the "mystical" (indigenous) beliefs to thrive. In practice, however, the law goes further to criminalize individuals for insulting official religions (mostly Islam) and for carrying out their "deviant" religious manifestation.

As the Jakarta-based Setara Institute notes, out of ninety-seven blasphemy convictions since the law was enacted in 1965, nine were issued during the authoritarian regime of Soeharto (from 1966 to 1998), while eighty-eight cases were successfully prosecuted from 1998 through 2017 during the time of democratic regime.[12] Those criminalized include an atheist, "deviant" Muslim clerics, members and leaders of new religious movements such as Gafatar and Lia Eden, and members of religious minority groups.

In 2017, an ethnic Chinese Buddhist woman named Meliana was sentenced to eighteen months in prison for blasphemy against Islam. In 2016, she had privately asked the caretaker of the mosque nearby her house to lower the loudspeaker volume during the *adzan* (call to prayer). Rumors eventually spread, saying that she had asked the mosques in her hometown Tanjung Balai to stop the calls to prayer. A number of provoked Muslims protested and destroyed at least fourteen local Buddhist temples. Like other blasphemy cases, Meliana's court case involved mass pressure outside the courtroom, through which verdicts are made in consideration of maintaining public tranquility.

Secondly, in 2008, the government issued a joint ministerial decree that recognized the Ahmadiyya faith as "deviant" from the teaching of Islam and banned any activities or proselytization carried out by this group with the aim, ironically, of preventing physical violence and vigilantism against them. The regulation was enacted to satisfy the demands

---

12. Setara Institute, "Calls in Indonesia."

decreed by the Majelis Ulama Islam (MUI, the Islamic Clerics Council) in 1980 and 2005, stating that Ahmadiyya is deviant from Islam. As soon as the regulation was issued, a high degree of intolerance rose against the Ahmadis. There were killings and attacks on Ahmadiyah mosques. Discrimination and incitement to hatred and violence have escalated in many regions. This regulation is regarded as legitimate by the MUI and Islamic hardliner groups, because it was passed by the government, which has determined that Ahmadiyah doctrine deviates from the teaching of Islam, and therefore admittedly provokes physical vigilantism. While victims are always disadvantaged by such acts, most of the violent perpetrators have enjoyed a climate of impunity.

Thirdly, another state-sponsored limit on religious freedom was enacted through a regulation issued jointly by the ministers of Religious and Interior Affairs on the restriction of the construction of houses of worship in 2006—the so-called "religious harmony" decree. The decree is frequently applied to minority groups and encourages local governments to regulate pubic tranquility, at the expense of the rights of minority groups to conduct free and safe worship. The regulation has increased the difficulty for churches to apply for building permits from the local governments, due to a restrictive requirement that each permit application needs to get sixty signatures from local residents outside the church. For example, the 4.5 million member Lutheran *Huria Kristen Batak Protestan* (HKBP, the Batak Christian Protestant Church) currently has sixty-one church buildings banned from worship use, mostly because they cannot obtain official permits.

Freedom restrictions by the government have been the cause of social hostilities and physical violence by the majority on the minority who simply want to practice their faith, freely, and safe from danger. This situation has become exacerbated with the encouragement of primal sentiments, which rose after the open democratic regime came into power after 1998. During this period, religious sentiments have been frequently used to drive national and local policies, creating social conflicts between the diverse communities.[13]

In many cases, the terms "peace" or "tranquility" were used to promote freedom, on the one hand, and to protect the interests of the majority exclusively, on the other.

13. Nyman, "Civil Society," 259.

The concept of tranquility should not always be considered the best definition for aspirations of peace. Gray Cox, in his book *The Ways of Peace: A Philosophy of Peace as Action*, notes that the notion of peace as tranquility and concord may end up a hollow peace, like a grave in which the dead are placed to rest. This kind of empty peace often lacks morally acceptable forms of peace, that is, freedom from structural forms of violence. Cox suggests that it is best not to blindly prefer peace at any price, especially if peace accepts injustice simply in order to avoid conflict and disorder.[14]

Peace in the service of human rights is definitely different from the concept of the peace of the "grave." The preamble of the *UDHR* proclaims that "recognition of the inherent dignity and of the equal and inalienable rights of members of the human family is the foundation of freedom, justice and peace in the world."[15] Peace and justice in the context of freedom of religion or belief emphasize the absence of structural violence and intimidation of everyone's freedom to express their religious opinion and practice.

In rejecting the notion of the peace of the "grave," I always remember lectures delivered by my professor Heiner Bielefeldt at the University of Erlangen-Nürnberg. This kind of peace simply aspires to seek for a solution in the mere silence of the minorities, with a consequential rise of religio-political tension in society.[16] As Norwegian philosopher Tore Lindholm reminds us, the failure to understand the universally-acceptable safeguard of religious freedom may trigger threats and hazards for societal peace and stability in a religiously pluralistic society.[17] This is a truism, that if the enforcement of "religious harmony" fails to understand freedom and equality as central to human dignity, we will see only a continued rise in social hostilities in our diverse society.

Identity Politics as a New Challenge

In 2017, the Jakarta governor Basuki Tjahaja Purnama, nicknamed Ahok, a Chinese Christian, was jailed for two-years for blasphemy against Islam. Prior to his blasphemy case, political turmoil was driven by the rejection of the Muslim extremists, that as a Christian he could not lead Jakarta, which

14. Cox, *Ways of Peace*, 15.

15. United Nations, *Universal Declaration of Human Rights*.

16. Bielefeldt, "Contribution of Freedom." See also Bielefeldt, "Freedom of Religion," 28–35.

17. Lindholm, "Philosophical and Religious Justifications."

is 85% Muslim, despite the fact that 75% of Jakartans were satisfied with the achievements he made during his leadership.[18] Ahok's blasphemy case caused him to lose both his gubernatorial position and a potential second term. In addition, this case exacerbated the use of negative propaganda against the *kafir* (infidel, or the non-Muslim candidate). His case and the 2017 Jakarta election were not the first pragmatic marriage of Islam and politics, yet his case began floating the seeds of identity politics that have flourished in the post-authoritarian democracy.

Long before Ahok's case, the trend of emerging identity politics was nurtured in the aftermath of the 1998 reformation movement that opened up spaces for all, including an agenda of religious radicalization. Because of the decentralization of politics in the reformation period, religious sentimentalism and fanaticism have been neatly merged by local politicians to mobilize greater electoral support through their own residential authority. As of 2013, there were 443 religiously-motivated regulations issued by the local authorities, including the ones which regulate the bans on "deviant" religious groups and the restricted activities of religious minorities.[19] These trends toward identity politics generate a fragility in the long-lived social cohesiveness of the pluralistic Indonesian society. This is clearly indicated by the rise of intolerance and human rights violations against minority groups. Religious practice, which is supposed to be a private decision, has now been transformed, somehow, to hegemonize the public sphere at the expense of "equal freedom for all."

The recent 2019 Indonesian presidential election was a tangible example of how the rise of identity politics not only has become a dangerous precedent for the future of any democratic agenda, but also threatens Indonesia's proud tradition of religious pluralism. The 2019 election was reportedly the most divisive one ever in the history of Indonesia's democratic election, dividing the nationalists who longed to keep the *Pancasila* as the ultimate denominator of Indonesia's pluralism and the Islamists who advocated religious sentiments in honor of Islam, to establish an Islamist-friendly political system. Some have even openly declared support for a caliphate against the current system of democracy. Election campaigns triggered intolerance and hate speech, and the spread of false information via social media created a fear or physical violence against moderate Muslims and other religious adherents who were in favour of democracy.

18. "Kinerja Berperan."

19. Siregar, "Mengapa Perda Syariah."

Anti-Christian sentiment and hatred against democracy supporters rose among many conservative Muslim voters as an effect of the polarization by religious fundamentalism.[20]

A Cultural Instead of a Legal Approach

When dealing with violations of religious freedom, I, as a human rights advocate, have always prefered looking for legal solutions when dealing with the infringement on human rights. What struck me and interested me as well, was to hear the experiences of a faithful Muslim man, Kang Wawan, who has devoted the last twenty years of his life to accompany minorities in being heard. He has been a bridge for cultural dialogue between the Muslim majority and minority groups in order to help them learn from each other equally.[21]

To overcome the lack of freedom that has resulted from intolerance and ignorance of interreligious differences, Kang Wawan believes that using a cultural approach works better than looking for legal answers. He adopted this path by learning from his small daughter, who has a good relationship with a child whose father is a pastor. He witnessed the children's fruitful dialogue of their differences, based on the premise that they share a common joy. For Kang Wawan, creating spaces for meeting is the strategic way to let one learn the differences of others, so that we do not simply impose "sameness" on each other.

Kang Wawan told me some success stories from his time accompanying Christian communities, which underlines the original nature of Indonesia's unity and pluralism. The Arca Manik congregation of the *Gereja Kristen Indonesia* (GKI, the Indonesian Christian Church), a Presbyterian denomination located in Sumedang, West Java, purposely allocated some space in the church compound to become an office for the village administration and a sports field for free public use. At one point, a number of Muslim extremists and outsiders came to protest the presence of the church in that Muslim majority community. However, the local Muslims stood in the front line to defend the church and reject the presence of those extremists.

Another story he told comes from a congregation of the *Gereja Kristen Pasundan* (GKP, the Pasundan Christian Church), another Reformed denomination, whose land was granted to the church by a Muslim man

---

20. See "Christian Solidarity Worldwide."

21. Interview with the author, November 2019.

many years ago. Out of respect for the man, the congregation is named after the man's well-known nickname of *pak haji*—meaning a Muslim man who has gone on *hajj*, or the pilgrimage to the Islamic holy land of Mecca. His name was adopted by the church out of appreciation for his kindness and as a reminder of the religious tolerance exemplified by this Muslim *haji*. Kang Wawan has no doubt that the majority of Indonesian communities do not have an intolerance gene to hate others who are different. Yet, dialogue must always be preserved as a way to foster friendships and to find commonalities for issues that need to be addressed collectively.

Myengkyo Seo, who teaches Southeast Asian studies in Malaysia, in his research on church growth, analyzed the example of church growth in Javanese Muslim communities by addressing the sociological patterns that make the position of the church strong amid the "unfavourable" circumstances of Christian-Muslim violence in many places in the region.[22] Seo observed that the 220,000-member *Gereja Kristen Jawa* (GKJ, the Java Christian Church) was one of the fastest growing and most contextualized churches among the Muslims communities across Java island, because they incorporated traditional Javanese customs, such as the prayers for the dead (*bidston*) and the Muslim practice of child circumcision (*sunat*), in church practices, even though the practices are controversial among the members to this day. Seo sees that the fruit of this contextualization resulted from the church's efforts to combine its theological views with the existing religiopolitical reality. Seo also references the example of the Joyodiningrat congregation of the GKJ, which not only shares the same street number address but also the fifteen hundred square meters of land with Al-Hikmah mosque. The church land was purchased from a *haji* in 1927 with the agreement to leave a parcel of 200 square meters of land for the construction of a mosque in the future. Both church and mosque buildings were constructed adjoiningly in 1939 and 1947, respectively. To maintain their relationship and find a way out of issues that result in potential frictions between members, the church pastor, Rev. Widiatmo, and the mosque committee hold regular informal meetings. On several occasions in 1995, the church decided to cancel their four normal Sunday morning services, if they were in conflict with an Islamic holiday, such as on *Idul Fitri* (Eid) or *Idul Adha* (Sacrifice Day). The cancellation of services was done out of respect for the Muslims' holiday celebrations. This was also done because there had been sensitivity concerns by some Muslims, due to some Christian women

22. Seo, "Missions Without Missionaries."

wearing miniskirts on the property. This was believed to be inappropriate by Muslim leaders, especially during the Islamic holiday celebrations. The pastor believed that the decision to not irritate their Muslim neighbours was controversial, but he claimed that Christ knows their situation and that the decision would not be held against them.

This cultural approach was later reciprocated for the church. On the day when the church had the ordination of a new pastor in 2008, Pastor Widiatmo requested the mosque *ulama* (Islamic clerics) to reduce the loudspeaker volume of the *adzan* (call to prayer). He would have understood if the *ulama* had refused to do so, as he knows how important the *adzan* is to the mosquegoers. To his pleasant surprise, the *ulama* decided to turn off the loudspeaker, based on the reasons that the mosquegoers could hear the *adzan* from other mosques in the area and for the sake of a good celebration for the church on that day. It is also important to note that recently, during a riot, the church was protected by the youth of Al-Hikmah from the extremist attacks.

I would definitely need a longer chapter to write down all the good stories created by interreligious relationships in the country, to share how interfaith tolerance is still a prominent value in our pluralistic society. Given the reality that plenty of churches have been sealed off, attacked, and burnt in the pro-democracy era, cultural ties between Christian and Muslim communities constitute a basic foundation for peacemaking wherever post-conflict reconciliation is initiated through the scheme of interfaith relations. This is what we found among the Pakpak people after the attacks on Singkil churches in the Aceh Province back in 2015.

Living in the Aceh Province for many generations, the current Pakpak people still practice their cultural rituals of weddings, funerals, harvest festivals, home blessings, and so forth. Cultural traditions are the only reason for all of the people to join together for feasting, dancing, and singing, no matter what religion each person holds. Islam and Christianity are two religions mostly adhered to by the Pakpak people scattered in Singkil as part of Aceh Province and Pakpak Bharat, part of North Sumatra Province. These cultural-ties have encouraged the GKPPD church to advocate for peace by using an anthropological approach, instead of relying only on legal responses. That is, the Pakpak all share the same blood, regardless of their religious tradition.

We must keep intiating and encouraging cultural dialogues with Pakpak Muslims and Christians as part of their public roles within a conflicted society like Singkil. Such a dialogue is the best way to overcome misunderstandings and to help both sides become well informed, so that the perpretrators of conflict are not the Pakpak locals but those outsider radicals. Dialogue is a form of self-reflection for all religious communities to become aware that violent conflict only destroys their own culture and local economy.

Interfaith Communion for the Sake of Peace and Justice

In March 2019, I invited various church representatives and prominent people from the largest Islamic organization in Indonesia, *Nahdlatul Ulama* (NU), to speak in two conferences to counter messages of hate speech, including the inflammatory words *kafir* (infidel), "fake Muslim" (meaning moderate Muslim), and "non-Muslim." This invitation was a follow-up to the NU's *keputusan Muktamar* (religious decree) issued a few weeks earlier to prohibit its Muslim members in Indonesia from using the word *kafir*. The decree included an Islamic theological justification that such language would irritate others and disrupt public order. NU's decision, I believe, was the product of mutual respect for the sake of interfaith peace against the rise of religiously-motivated hate speech that may harmfully incite people to be intolerant and discriminatory and to act physically violent toward others who are of different faiths. As Adama Dieng put it, ". . . big massacres start always with small actions and language."[23]

"No one is born to hate. Intolerance can be prevented and unlearned," underscored U.N. Secretary General Mr. António Guterres, addressing anti-Semitism, racism, and other forms of hatred in 2019. For Guterres, intolerance and hate speech can only be countered with messages of peace, investment in social cohesion, embracing diversity as wealth, and promoting human rights. Such harmful actions are surely toxic to the democracy and religious diversity that our society has held for many centuries. I am encouraged by the data about Indonesian society today, that religions in the public space still hold important roles in maintaining interfaith communion in the name of peace and justice. A recent report notes that 84.8% of Indonesians surveyed confirm their public support of democracy for a just, clean, and prosperous society. This is an opportunity for religions to bring the message of equality to the democracy adopted by a nation where

23. "Interview with Special Advisor."

religion is deeply embedded in people's everyday life. To create peace and justice in this religious society, religious literacy needs to be promoted as a foundation toward full understanding of diversity. As Martin Lukito Sinaga wrote, religious literacy is not merely a way to strengthen knowledge of texts, but most importantly to strengthen the living contexts.[24] Our living contexts include religious diversity, socio-economic injustices, humanitarian concerns, human rights issues, and so forth. In a pluralistic Indonesian society, interfaith communion is an undeniable way of helping all religions (both institutionally and individually) to think of themselves not as separate, but as one body. In Michael Kinnamon's 2014 book *Can a Renewal Movement Be Renewed?,* communion is the last of five steps that include competition, coexistence, cooperation, commitment, and communion, for building relationships between churches or between religions. Interfaith communion, if applied correctly, is the way to build relationships that recognize the validity of each other and that mutually respect the issues which concern us all. These issues are not merely Christian or Muslim problems. We are living in a context where events may indiscriminately affect all religions.

In May 2012, I was with several church deacons visiting a small HKBP church, the Sikhem congregation in Sopokomil village in North Sumatra, that was about to be relocated due to the planned construction of a multinational mining company. The church authorities were divided by the company's relocation request. The church members and other villagers were overwhelmingly against both the relocation of the church and the company itself, for its unsustainable activities that would adversely harm the environment and human beings. With the uncertainty among church authorities about how to respond, a Muslim man, Mr. Boangmanalu, spoke up against the relocation and organized Christian villagers (who make up about 98% of the village population) to reject the planning and the company exploration activities. When I asked him why he did so, Boangmanalu said:

> The church does not only belong to Christians, but also to me and my family, though we are Muslims. If the church is relocated, that means the company is allowed to exploit our nature and therefore affects me and my family first because we live next to the church.[25]

24. Sinaga, "Literasi Teologis."
25. Interview with the author, May 2012.

Another example of an interfaith communion story comes from Java. Pastor Aris Widodo is currently serving a congregation of the GKJ in Kulon Progo in a strong Javanese Muslim societal context. Apart from his routine work as a parish pastor, already for some years he has been promoting community development programs for the poor, who find it difficult to escape from their economic constraints. Most of them used to migrate to the big cities, looking for jobs and wishing to find better economic resources. Furthermore, none of these lower economic Javanese are Christians.

Pastor Aris called them home and looked for financial assistance through his Christian community to fund community development projects, such as *Javanese batik* canting. The canters, Muslim individuals who never learned the Christian Bible, produce images in hot wax and dye on cloth, based on the stories told in the Bible, incorporating depictions common in Javanese culture. For example, the one I bought from the canter is the story of Jesus' baptism (Matt 3:13–17) that shows the images of both Jesus and John the Baptist in a Javanese setting, wearing *blangkon* and *sarong* (the traditional Javanese headdress and wrap around the waist). The Muslim canters and Pastor Aris have a joint mission to contextualize Christianity and the church there to express Javanese culture. They are also concerned to teach that socio-economic injustices, like poverty, are a common concern for all people of different faiths.[26]

Kinnamon, author of the aforementioned *Can a Renewal Movement Be Renewed?*, explores the fruits of having all religions join together at a common table. His ideas can be summarized through the concept of communion:

- Communion recognizes that we are no longer simply separate entities, but that we fully accept and recognize our neighbours;

- Communion causes us to act as one in sharing our sacred things;

- Communion challenges us to manifest a unity, common mission, and service;

- Communion turns our understanding from "they (them)" to "we (us)";

- Communion compels us toward full participation, meaning that we are to strive for equal levels of participation.[27]

---

26. Interview with the author, November 2019.

27. Kinnamon, *Can a Renewal Movement*, 35–43..

The communion model particularly elucidates what makes a church strong and inclusive of others, signifying the intimacy of God through Christ and with one another in Christ. Likewise, by extending this concept to interfaith communion, intimacy between Christians and the majority of Muslims in Indonesia is established in the name of sharing the sacred equally. Sharing the sacred equally means that we are on the way toward understanding our responsibilities to humanity and the preservation of creation. Religious communities face many challenges, like corruption, environmental destruction, poverty, hunger, unemployment, human trafficking, pandemic disease, etc. We cannot deal with such things alone. We truly need other people. This is the ideal path for our churches, especially for those Christians in majority contexts. The public space should not be treated as a place for revenge, given the reality that, even though Christians are discriminated against as a minority community in particular areas, this should not be taken as justification to discriminate against Muslims in the Christian majority places.

I will conclude this chapter with the story of Wahid, the story with which I opened the chapter. After Wahid was found guilty of the death of a young Muslim man and sentenced to prison, a crime he never committed, he was released, having spent three and a half years in jail, two-thirds of his six-year sentence. He had lost his job and had no option except to leave for Malaysia to become a migrant worker for a fishing pond owner, in order to get away from some Muslims in Singkil who were motivated to take revenge on the one who had killed Syamsul.

With the help of the Evangelical Lutheran Church in America (ELCA), Wahid enrolled as a theological student at a seminary. When he was still in jail, he had prayed that one day he would become a pastor and serve a mission to Muslim and Christian communities to help them unlearn intolerance and to help build peace. For him, Christians and Muslims in Singkil must create a common platform that will work for peace, repudiate any form of violence, and work against injustices. In other words, he looks at past conflict as an opportunity. Instead of looking for a moment for revenge, both Christians and Muslims can become united and walk through the light of peace together.

CHAPTER 10

Senegal

Land of Hospitality, Peace,
and Mutual Understanding

PETER HANSON

IN A COUNTRY WHERE Islam is the predominant religion, Lutherans have long cooperated with their Muslim neighbors for the good of their shared community. A prime example of this has been the work of the Senegal Lutheran Development Services (SLDS).

SLDS: A Day in the Life

On a typical Wednesday afternoon in Yeumbeul, a crowded, fast-growing community that is part of the sprawling *banlieue* (suburb) surrounding Dakar, Senegal, hundreds of young people line up in front of Community Center *Galle Nanondiral* (CCGN), a multifaceted education and training program of the SLDS. Most youth are waiting for a seat in the library, where they are certain to find both the schoolbooks and the quiet space they need to do their homework. Others will be taking part in vocational training programs in computers and office systems, restaurant services, and commercial sewing. Still others come for recreation, either informally to pass the time playing ping-pong, foosball, or Scrabble, or else to participate in one of the center's basketball leagues or formal karate instruction.

Meanwhile, in the neighborhoods surrounding CCGN, groups of women gather for weekly literacy classes or to participate in economic activity groups, supported by microloans administered through CCGN's credit union. Neighborhood groups of adolescent girls discuss questions of self-esteem, positive peer pressure, family planning, and reproductive health. And although there is officially no school after the lunch break on Wednesdays, scores of elementary students come back to *École Primaire Nanondiral* anyway, to review their lessons, talk with their teachers, or just play with their classmates in a clean, safe, and friendly environment.

Three hundred kilometers away, in the dry, dusty provincial town of Linguère, a group of people living with HIV and AIDS gather discreetly at the SLDS health office for a nutritious meal, to receive their prescription medications, and above all, to offer moral support to one another. Later in the day, community health workers from neighboring villages will converge upon the office to check in with the SLDS health coordinator, re-stock their village pharmacies, or share information about critical cases seen at one of a dozen village "health huts." The coordinator, in turn, will revise and share her schedule for visits to each of these health huts, conduct pre-natal screenings and well-baby care, lead in-service training for community health workers or community oversight committees, or perhaps intervene in difficult cases, providing an additional level of care or even evacuation to a larger medical facility.

Finally, as the heat of the Sahel sun begins to give way late in the afternoon, the proverbial cows come home to the SLDS's *Fedannde Jolof* farm, where they will be milked and their contributions carefully marked in a notebook and credited to their owners. At the end of the month, the herders may use their credit for assistance offered by the farm—veterinary services, additional feed, and crossbreeding with Holstein and Jersey bulls in order to increase future milk production. Conversely, they may choose to take their payment in cash, profiting directly from the milk. Once collected and pasteurized, a portion of the milk is transformed into *fedannde*, a light, drinkable yoghurt; the rest is packaged as fresh whole milk. Later, many will enjoy this local milk, thanks in part to this project, which provides dairy products in safe and hygienic conditions, while also providing economic benefits to primarily Fulani herders and their families.

These geographically distant and programmatically different activities are held together by an interfaith community development organization of which they are all a part, and to which the Evangelical Lutheran Church in America (ELCA) and its predecessors have been relating for forty years. Officially registered in 1980 by missionaries of the American Lutheran Church

(ALC), the organization now known as the SLDS provides a platform and opportunity for Muslim-Lutheran relationships on an everyday basis. A good deal of the success of this organization over the years is due to the widely held Senegalese cultural values of hospitality and peace, as well as willingness on the part of the ALC and its successors to intentionally engage in mission in a particular way in Muslim West Africa, placing mutual understanding across religious differences at the very heart of its work.

Shared Festivals, Shared Life, Shared Values

According to the 2013 census, Senegal's population of approximately fifteen million people is estimated to be about 95% Muslim, 4% Christian (99% of whom are Roman Catholic), and 1% followers of traditional religions. Lutherans make up the second largest Christian denomination, accounting for nearly half of those affiliated with the various Protestant and evangelical faith communities. The result is that Lutherans are a double minority in their national context. They are first Christians in a predominantly Muslim country, and secondly Protestants in an overwhelmingly Catholic minority. In addition, since the Lutheran Church of Senegal draws primarily from the Serer ethnic group, Fulani Christians (with whom the ALC/ELCA has most closely worked over the years) are in fact a triple minority: Fulani among Serer, Protestants among Catholics, and Christians among Muslims. Fortunately, the context of religious life in Senegal means that even such minorities have been able to flourish, benefiting from a culture whose central value is that of hospitality shown to all, and whose elaborate greeting rituals in most of the national languages revolve around the idea of being at peace with God and others.

While we may not often hear such a positive narrative in our U.S. context, Senegal is a striking example of a country where Muslims and Christians truly live together in harmony, where both a widely held understanding of and deeply shared respect for another's religion are overwhelmingly the norm. There are a number of historical reasons why this is the case. Rather than following the sort of hierarchical structure of religious leadership found in Islamic republics like Mauritania or Iran, the practice of Islam in Senegal is largely organized around a number of Sufi *confrèries,* or brotherhoods. This diverse and decentralized arrangement allows for healthy acceptance of differences within the faith, as well as a heightened sense of tolerance offered those from other faith traditions. In addition, thanks to the strong influence by its French colonizers, Senegal was constituted as a secular republic, politically stable since independence in 1960. There is a prohibition on any political party being organized along religious lines, nor can such a movement be based on ethnicity, language, or regional strength. The French also instituted a number of Christian festivals as public holidays, alongside major Muslim observances and more secular national and international celebrations. Because of the long reach of the national media, it is as fairly common for Senegalese Muslims to know that Christians commemorate Jesus' resurrection on Easter, as it is for Senegalese Christians to appreciate that Eid al-Adha (known locally as *Tabaski)* celebrates God's faithfulness to Abraham.

Beyond these historic and institutional reasons, however, such a tendency for religious tolerance, understanding, and respect can be credited to the shared value of unity deeply embedded in the identity of the Senegalese people. This value, reflected in their national motto, "one people, one goal, one faith," tends to outweigh any tendency toward the separation of identities along ethnic, linguistic, or religious lines. "Nearly every Christian I know, myself included, has many Muslim relatives," says Pastor Pierre Adama Faye, president of the Lutheran Church of Senegal. "And so we grow up together, celebrating holidays and festivals together, despite the differences in our own affiliation or practice."[1]

Indeed, not only are Senegalese people likely to have some understanding of one another's religious festivals and observances, it is quite possible that they have shared frequently in these celebrations, or at least in the events surrounding them. Christian neighbors are regularly invited to Muslim weddings, naming ceremonies, and funerals, and then especially to the meals which follow each event. Similarly, Muslims are often guests at weddings and funerals, as well as at the receptions that follow baptisms and first communions. Meat from the family sheep butchered for *Tabaski* is typically shared with Christian households, and Christians offer their Muslim neighbors bowls of *ngalaax* (a sweet dessert made from peanuts and baobab fruit) during Easter weekend. Given the shifting dates of these festivals, there is often some good-natured teasing about which neighbor owes the other whenever these foods are shared!

However, celebrating each other's holidays is not limited to food, nor is such mutual respect and understanding reserved for the high holy days.

1. Interviews with author, October 2010 and May 2020.

"We look forward to receiving greetings, blessings, and offers of forgiveness from our Muslim neighbors during their festivals, even as we are sure to remember them in our prayers and offer them blessings during our own," says Pastor Faye. "But this is just as common in our everyday life, too. If my Muslim neighbor sees me heading to church on a Sunday morning, he will ask that I pray for him, and I do the same when I see him walking to the mosque on Fridays. Despite our differences, we have always known that we serve the same God, the God of peace."

It is no wonder that Senegal is often referred to as the "Land of *Teranga*," a word meaning hospitality in Wolof, the most widely spoken of Senegal's national languages. While *Teranga* has certainly been well marketed for the growing tourist trade, even the most cynical of visitors quickly learns that this is simply a recent promotion of a long-held value. *Teranga* is a central feeling sensed in open markets and restaurants. It shines through offers of shared meals and invitations to visit someone's home. Even the national soccer team is known as the Lions of Teranga, preferring to describe themselves as hospitable, unlike other African teams, who prefer such descriptors as wild, super, indomitable, or unbeatable.

The Exceptional Work of the Senegal Mission

It was into this context of the shared values of peace and hospitality that the ALC embarked on a new era of mission work, sending their first missionaries to Senegal in the mid-1970s. From the beginning, this undertaking was to be different from most previous global engagements made by U.S.-based Lutheran church bodies. Coming rather late to the missionary venture, the Senegal mission and the larger "Fulani Project," launched by the ALC in response to the Sahel drought, had the opportunity to chart a new course for engaging in the concept of global mission.[2] At the heart of this new ministry opportunity were several elements that were to characterize ALC and later ELCA involvement in Senegal for the next four decades and beyond: a deliberate focus on the Fulani ethnic group, a conscious prioritizing of holistic humanitarian and development work, and an intentional engagement with Islam.

---

2 Traditionally a nomadic people, the Fulani (also known as Peul, Fula, or Fulbe) live in more than a dozen countries ranging from Senegal to Sudan, often crossing borders as they lead their cattle to pastures. Numbering thirty million by some estimates, the Fulani were the ethnic group most affected by the drought in the Sahel in the early 1970s.

From the beginning, this work was seen as being exceptional, one of the only places in Africa where ALC personnel did not serve directly within the context of a Lutheran church which had been established as a result of earlier mission initiatives. Missionaries from the earliest years in Senegal often spoke about their call to be "faithful, not successful," to provide a Christian witness of presence in a place with little Christian presence and to minister intentionally to the whole person, prioritizing humanitarian work and community development in their encounter with Senegalese people. At times, these first missionaries found themselves questioning what they were doing there, as there did not seem to be much hope of ever establishing a Lutheran church among the Fulani, an ethnic group overwhelmingly Muslim in both identity and practice.

As the years went by, and as the ALC merged into the ELCA in 1988, many of the missionaries called to work in Senegal continued to be attracted to the ministry precisely because of its exceptional nature. For some, it was a chance to serve the neighbor in need without any other agenda—hidden or otherwise—such as winning converts or planting a church. For others, it was a way to reconcile some of what had gone before in previous missional or colonial contexts, moving beyond many of the troublingly paternalistic tendencies that were unfortunately often part of the missionary venture. But by and large, most people called to ministry with the ELCA in Senegal understood this to be an unmatched opportunity to be engaged in interfaith relationships and efforts on an everyday basis.

We can see this emphasis on interfaith relationships woven into the work that was established. From the very beginning, many of the various projects and programs contained some form of the word *Nanondiral* in their name. In Pulaar (the language of the Fulani), *Nanondiral* literally means "to hear one another," but more accurately, it describes the concept of mutual understanding. Community centers in both Yeumbeul and Linguère were called *Galle Nanondiral*, "the house of mutual understanding." The program which provided literacy resources along with translation and publishing services was known as *Editions Nanondiral*. The preschool, elementary, and secondary schools created by the SLDS are collectively referred to as *Complexe Scolaire Nanondiral*.

While this central focus on mutual understanding may have been put in place initially by mission personnel and further affirmed through the ELCA's "Focus on Islam" initiative, this core value has continued through various iterations of the ELCA's mission work in Senegal. The concept of

Nanondiral offered a key sense of identity to those delivering programs of health care, education, and community development, particularly as more Senegalese became involved in the work and took over the positions of leadership. Today, local leaders—Senegalese Christians and Senegalese Muslims—are sharing visions, making decisions, overseeing activities, and working to improve the lives of the people in their own communities. Whether or not they would articulate it this way themselves, the people who have actively transformed this foreign mission association into a truly Senegalese organization are now involved in living out a permanent Christian-Muslim dialogue, as they work together to bring about God's reconciliation in their own communities.

Fostering Christian–Muslim Relationships at the Grassroots Level

While the ELCA continues to be a major funding source, the SLDS now functions as an autonomous Senegalese non-governmental organization (NGO). The preamble of the constitution for the SLDS states that this organization is intentionally made up of Christians and Muslims alike who, in response to a calling from God, commit to common work based on broadly shared (if differently articulated) religious values. These values include the presumption of the dignity of all people, love of neighbor, service to the poor and vulnerable, and care for creation, as matters of both divine privilege and religious responsibility.

Though its activities are neither overtly evangelistic nor self-consciously religious, most employees of the SLDS—the vast majority of whom are practicing Muslims—tend to characterize their involvement in the SLDS's work as a calling from God, a way to be about God's will in the community. At the time of its transformation into a Senegalese NGO, SLDS leadership embodied the interfaith relationship inherent in its existence at its highest level. Co-directors Philipe Badji and Aly Ndione, Christian and Muslim respectively, had both been employed by the ELCA Senegal mission from its earliest days. Baptized in the Lutheran Church of Senegal and educated at two ELCA colleges, Badji often spoke of his work as "vocation," citing Jesus' words about loving God and neighbor (Matt 22:25–40) as a major motivation. Ndione, a lifelong member of the Mouride *confrèrie,* also spoke of work in general as a form of devotion to God and described his specific involvement in the community development as one of his "highest spiritual commitments." Their shared witness, embodying an intentional and constant example of Christian-Muslim cooperation, set the tone throughout the SLDS organization that only Senegalese could do. This has been both admired and appreciated in the larger community.

As SLDS programs took hold within both urban and rural communities, this sense of intentional interfaith cooperation proved vital to their expansion. Along with local governments, neighborhood religious leaders were consulted about the placement of neighborhood literacy groups, some of which ended up meeting in the home of a local imam or on the terrace of the Catholic school. Meeting with faith leaders early in the process of developing programs for adolescent reproductive health or support for people living with HIV proved to be invaluable to their success. On multiple occasions, the clergy of all confessions reassured their communities that SLDS programs were founded on deeply held and widely shared interfaith commitments, which in turn empowered these religious leaders to become strong and vocal advocates for the programs. This, in turn, further enhanced the credibility of the SLDS as an authentically interfaith organization, as well as a valuable presence in the community.

Opportunities for More Formal Interfaith Dialogue

Over time, the reputation for being a genuinely interfaith NGO (with no proselytizing agenda) caught the attention of civil and religious leaders at the national level. Not only was there a growing recognition that the work the SLDS was doing in education, health care, and economic empowerment was both important and largely successful, there was an appreciation for the deeply engrained sense of mutual understanding at almost every level of the programs provided. In particular, SLDS programs were recognized for leveraging their intentional interfaith make-up in order to bring together various segments of the community around issues of health, education, and community development. As a result, members of the SLDS leadership have been called upon to participate in more formal settings of Christian-Muslim dialogue, specifically concerning the spiritual or religious motivations held by individuals working for the SLDS, or of the organization as a whole for its shared action on behalf of the community.

Other, more formal avenues for Christian-Muslim dialogue and understanding have been embraced by one of the ELCA's companions in

Senegal, the Lutheran Church of Senegal (*Église Luthérienne du Sénégal*, or ELS). Through such international and ecumenical associations as the Programme for Christian-Muslim Relations in Africa (PROCMURA), the ELS has been involved in theological and academic discussions for many years. Pastor Joseph Diouf, who played a pivotal role in both ecumenical and interfaith partnerships thanks to his long tenure as pastor of the ELS Dakar Parish, has directed the ELS's involvement with PROCMURA. Since Pastor Diouf's retirement, Pastor Faye has taken more of the lead on ecumenical and interfaith dialogue. With a master's degree in Christian-Muslim relations from St. Paul's University in Nairobi, Kenya, and currently serving as the president of the ELS, Pastor Faye has been able to build on the foundation of Pastor Diouf's well-established dialogue with Christian and Muslim leaders, while effectively moving such work much closer to the institutional center of the ELS.

Like many Christian church bodies, however, the ELS struggles at times with how best to engage in interfaith dialogue and cooperation. On the one hand, as Pastor Faye pointed out above, practically all Senegalese Christians interact daily with Muslim relatives, co-workers, neighbors, classmates, and friends. Given both the pervasiveness and the seeming effortlessness of such relationships for most Senegalese, it often does not occur to folks to engage in a level of official religious dialogue beyond the everyday exchange of curious and respectful companions. On the other hand, there is pressure, both from within the ELS and from some of the more evangelical Christian denominations with which it interacts, for interfaith engagement to be a precursor to more formalized evangelistic efforts, with the goal of winning converts to Christianity from among their Muslim neighbors.

Paradoxically, this makes the work and witness of the SLDS as an interfaith organization, with which the ELS is increasingly involved through its governing board, all the more crucial for developing positive Christian-Muslim relationships. Having a legally separate entity through which the church can engage in intentional interfaith activities, while still maintaining a healthy evangelistic program within the church proper, has allowed for both to flourish without significant confusion as to their overall direction or preferred outcomes. Put another way, even as the ELS engages in reaching out to their Muslim neighbors with the proclamation of the good news of Jesus, the SLDS can simultaneously embody respect, reconciliation, and mutuality between the religions, as they work together for the common good.

Educating ELCA Members through Interfaith Immersions

The shared values of hospitality, peace, and mutual understanding are so deeply embedded in Senegalese culture, so tightly woven into both the identity and work of the SLDS, that they can seem obvious, even unremarkable, to many of the Senegalese involved. This does not tend to be the experience, however, for many in the U.S. in general, or even some members of the ELCA in particular. For this reason, the ELCA's work of accompaniment in Senegal provides a unique opportunity for ELCA members to experience firsthand such everyday interfaith relationships. Particularly after the events of September 11, 2001, Senegal became a place to highlight the realities of Christian-Muslim understanding and interfaith cooperation for visitors from the ELCA.

Since 2003, groups from various expressions of the ELCA have traveled to Senegal to take part in a number of interfaith immersion programs. These guests have included adults from the churchwide task force on nonviolence, youth and young adults from the Grand Canyon Synod (Senegal's official ELCA companion synod), and groups led by former ELCA missionaries to Senegal, as well as students from Wartburg College, Lutheran School of Theology in Chicago, and Luther Seminary. In addition to visiting the programs of the SLDS and parishes of the ELS, immersion participants receive an overview of Senegalese history and culture, a crash course in West African Islam (including a discussion of the network of *confrèries* active in Senegal), and visits to sites beyond the normal scope of the ELCA companion work. A highlight for many of these visitors is the brief homestays that are arranged with both Christian and Muslim families connected to ELCA companions. Even in the course of a couple of weeks, their firsthand experience of life in the continuing context of peaceful and respectful Christian-Muslim realities has been described as life changing. The visitors return to the U.S carrying the profound impact of such mutual understanding and share it in many different contexts across the ELCA.

Young Adults Continue the Work of Mutual Understanding

In the past few years, ELCA accompaniment in Senegal has been increasingly undertaken by Young Adults in Global Mission (YAGM). YAGM volunteers currently work with the SLDS as classroom aids, facilitating HIV/AIDS support groups, working at a dairy processing program, assisting in literacy and health education groups, and supporting maternal-child health care. Volunteers also work with the ELS, assisting in faith formation in parishes or supporting community-based work with the national church. In almost every case, they are deeply immersed in interfaith relationships and work alongside Muslims on a daily basis, learning what it means to be a religious minority and how interfaith leaders in Senegal are working together to serve their shared community. Some of the YAGMs, especially those serving with SLDS, also have the opportunity to live with Muslim host families, allowing them to experience firsthand the faith practices of that household. This experience provides young adults from the ELCA a rare opportunity to continue to benefit from Lutheran-Muslim relationships where they have most frequently happened in Senegal, in everyday life.

Hospitality, Peace, and Mutual Understanding

There is little doubt that the work of ELCA accompaniment in Senegal was significantly influenced both by the ALC's "Fulani Project" and the ELCA's "Focus on Islam" initiatives. Indeed, the very nature of this new and exceptional venture in global mission was a direct result of these initiatives, reflecting new ways of thinking about evangelism, dialogue, and partnership for the common good with our global Muslim neighbors. Building on the vision of the denominational leaders who sent them, as well as the solid foundation in ministry instituted by the ALC missionaries who preceded them, recent ELCA mission personnel have benefited greatly from the ways these initiatives intersected with the values of tolerance, respect, and mutual understanding rooted within Senegalese culture.

The ELCA can be proud of what it helped to establish, proud that our instincts for charting a new course in interfaith engagement and cooperation were welcomed with such grace. Our companions in Senegal, especially the SLDS, provide important ministry to the people of Senegal, drawing on shared religious and national values to work for the common good of their communities. In the last decade or so, the work once carried out by ELCA missionaries has become largely localized; that is, the vision, direction, and implementation of the programs and projects of the SLDS are now provided almost exclusively by Senegalese in an authentically Senegalese organization. As this transformative shift has taken place, there are new opportunities for Senegalese partners to become our teachers, guides, and mentors. Our Christian and Muslim siblings in Senegal can, in fact, be missionaries to us in the ELCA, providing us with a vivid example of how to live together in harmony across religions, how to find and nurture commonly held values, and how to work together for the common good of our community. We have much to learn from the Senegalese values of hospitality, peace, and mutual understanding, all of which hold the potential to transform the way we see our neighbors, across the street and around the world.

CHAPTER 11

"There Is No God Save Allah"

Reflections on Theological Phobias and
Habits of Hostility

J. Paul Rajashekar

THE FIRST BOOK I read on Islam as a seminarian was at the United
Theological College, Bangalore, India: *The Call of the Minaret,* by
Kenneth Cragg. It was a book prescribed for a course on Islam taught
by Cragg himself, a world-renowned Christian scholar on Islam. Taking
the Muslim call to prayer as the focus, the book is an introduction to
Islam and explores the summons of the *muezzin* as transcending religious
boundaries, summoning *all* to prayer.

I, of course, heard that call every morning when I was growing up
in a small town in South India, long before I read Cragg's book. I could
even partially recite it aloud without knowing or understanding what it
meant then. I also observed the *muezzin* chanting the call to prayer on top
of a minaret in a melodious voice in Arabic, from a local mosque near my
home. Now and then, I have pondered about the significance of the call
to prayer and its theological implications for non-Islamic religious communities and for interreligious relations in society. I will address this issue
towards the end of these reflections.

In abbreviated English translation, the Muslim call to prayer (*adhan*)
reads:

God is Greater! God is Greater! God is Greater! God is Greater!

I bear witness that there is no god except the One God.

I bear witness that Muhammad is the messenger of God.

Hurry to the prayer. Hurry to the prayer.

Hurry to salvation. Hurry to salvation.

God is Greater! God is Greater!

There is no god except the One God.

Hearing this call to prayer melodiously blasted over loudspeakers, every morning at dawn, was my wake-up alarm. It was so loud that it literally woke up everybody in the neighborhood. But no one complained about it, because in a multireligious society, respect for one another's faith and worship practices was a grudgingly accepted social norm and we were careful not to question each other's faith or religious practices. After all, Muslims were our neighbors with whom we interacted daily.

My Hindu neighbors, too, had their own morning rituals. Hindu temples, not to be outdone, had their own liturgical songs (*Suprabatham*, morning greetings to the divinity) and other mantras blaring over loudspeakers every morning. At times, it seemed, as if the Hindus and Muslims were in competition with one another as to whose religious chanting/music was the loudest and reached the farthest part of the town! Lutheran and other churches, of course, were far more subdued and tolled the church bells only prior to Sunday worship or to announce a death in the Christian community.

Divine Surveillance

As I recall, the religious atmosphere in my hometown was somewhat chaotic. Each religious community had its own ways of announcing its presence and its commitments to the public. And yet, we were not only aware of our religious differences and commitments but also accepted those differences as a fact of life. If there were religious prejudices (and I'm sure there were), they were not conspicuous, were seldom voiced in public, or were suppressed for the sake of communal harmony. Anyone who has visited or lived in India knows that religion is everywhere. It hangs in the air, and one can literally breathe spirituality all around. There are temples, shrines, mosques, and churches everywhere you turn, especially in cities and urban areas. Ride a three-wheeled auto-rickshaw, taxi, public bus, or visit a bar, restaurant or shop; garlanded portraits of Hindu deities, Jesus or Mary, and pictures of Muslim saints or the Kaaba in Mecca, are all prominently displayed on the dashboard or on the mantel. In India, it is an inescapable fact: gods are everywhere, in a multitude of manifestations, as if gods are watching over you, and you are under some sort of divine surveillance.

In the environment where I grew up, I got used to waking up every morning to the Muslim call to prayer. That call to prayer, five times a day, had an impact on me. I often wondered whether it was directed only to Muslims or to all people in the neighborhood. Like our Muslim neighbors, my parents too observed our Christian devotions every morning and night, reading the Bible and kneeling to pray to God. In this regard, Muslims and Christians shared a mutual adoration of God as an important element in daily life.

My more orthodox Hindu friends, too, began their morning at dawn with the ritual of bathing and chanting the *Gayatri Mantra*, a universal prayer in Sanskrit addressed to the creator God. Adoration of God was not something that only Muslims or Christians did, but also my Hindu friends. Most Hindu homes have a special altar for the worship of their favorite deities, but *Gayatri Mantra* is a prayer universal among Hindus. Here is a succinct summary of that prayer: "We meditate on that most adored Supreme Lord, the creator, whose effulgence (divine light) illumines all realms (physical, mental and spiritual). May this divine light illumine our intellect."

Although this prayer is drawn from the Hindu Vedas, acknowledging the divine source of life is something Christians, Hindus, and Muslims share and confess. Though we all worshipped in our segregated sanctuaries, churches, mosques, temples, and shrines, I always felt that there were significant elements among people of all faiths that bound us together, especially our allegiance to God (however understood or defined). And yet, when we are farther into our segregated sanctuaries—Christian in the church, Hindu in the temple, Muslim in the mosque, Jew in the synagogue, Sikh in the gurdwara, and so forth—we tend to be farthest from one another. While our religious yearnings are the same or similar when it comes to our shared social, cultural, and political space, we tread gingerly as not to offend others. There are certain etiquettes that one must follow in a religiously pluralistic society, and any claims of religious superiority are to be confined to one's places of worship and community. This was an important element of my early formation as a Christian growing up in a multireligious India.

At the time when I grew-up, there were no overt hostilities between religious communities in my hometown or in my home state, as there are now in the twenty-first century India. My parents were schoolteachers and therefore had healthy relationships with people of all different faiths, especially Muslims and Hindus. As a matter of fact, in the state of Mysore (today, Karnataka), Muslims were viewed positively, because the state had been ruled by both Hindus and Muslims. In my middle and high school years, I mingled with Hindus, Muslims, and others as we studied together, played together, watched Bollywood movies together, and often visited one another's homes. There were a couple of things that we seldom did together or carefully avoided. That is, we seldom ate or prayed together. I never thought of this fact until later, that religious differences were not merely about faith convictions, differing histories, and religious doctrines, but extended to dietary and worship practices.

The friendship and comraderie I enjoyed with my fellow students of different faiths, as noted above, displayed no overt sense of antipathy, animosity, discrimination, or hatred among religious communities. We accepted our religious differences as something given or inherited and not to be argued about. Sure, we lived in segregated communities, Christians living in the Christian street, Muslims in the Muslim street, Brahmins in the Brahmin street, Harijans in the Harijan street, etc. In a religiously stratified society, religious boundaries were often demarcated or dictated by tradition and history. I often thought that those boundaries were sacred and must be respected, lest we trespass on each other's territories, beliefs, and commitments.

As a member of the Boy Scouts, I was taught to respect that animals, too, have different boundaries and live in their own communal habitats. So, I grew up recognizing that plurality in the biological world was and is a fact of life; just as individuals differ from one another, so communities differ from one another, in their faith, traditions, beliefs, practices, and values. Yes, some ate meat, and others were vegetarians; some worshipped in a mosque, and others worshipped in a temple or a church. I often wondered, What difference does that make? Should we all be the same and worship and pray together in unison? Though my friends and I never prayed or worshipped together, did our prayers uttered in a Muslim mosque, Hindu temple, or

Christian church differ in our existential needs, anxieties, and longings? Does God hear only Christian prayers and not those of others?

The Emergence of Religious Hostility

A lot of things have changed since my early school experiences. My family and I left India over thirty-five years ago to work in Switzerland, where I served as the first executive secretary for Church and People of Other Faiths at the Lutheran World Federation in Geneva. A few years later, I landed in Philadelphia to teach at the Lutheran Seminary in Philadelphia. Soon after I left India, things began to change—should I say, unravel? In the intervening years, the rise of a political movement based on the ideology of "Hindutva" claimed India to be the homeland of Hindus, while other minority religious groups were viewed as not sufficiently loyal to "Mother India." When this Hindu fundamentalist movement gained political power, the atmosphere was vitiated with frequent interreligious conflicts, at times violent, directed against Muslims, Sikhs, and sometimes Christians, by fanatic Hindus.

It may be recalled, the roots of the Hindu-Muslim conflict go back to the period of British colonialism that led to the partition of India into Hindu India and Muslim Pakistan in 1947. Since then, there have been continued tensions and occasional wars, conflicts, and boundary disputes between the two countries over the past seven-plus decades of independence from Britain. The secular India with a majority Hindu population retained a significant Muslim population (10–12%) and had managed to coexist with Muslims and other religious minorities until recently. Certain events disrupted this, especially the destruction of the Babri Masjid, the site of an existing mosque founded by the Moghul emperor in 1528, by a Hindu fundamentalist group in 1990. The Hindu nationalists claimed that the site was the original birthplace of the Hindu deity Rama and had once been a Hindu temple. It was argued by this group, Vishwa Hindu Parishad, that the remains of the mosque should be removed and a new Hindu temple be built in its place. This incident had a profound impact upon existing communal harmony between Hindus and Muslims and led to protests, riots, and bloodshed. Occasionally, the hostilities and violence directed against Muslims spilled over into other religious minorities, especially Christians, who are a minority of less than 3% of the Indian population.

Anti-conversion laws, the persecution of Christians in some areas, and the banning of cow slaughter are some ways Hindus have exercised their antipathy toward religious minorities in India in recent years. With the rise of religious nationalism or Hindu fundamentalism, and the control of the national government by a Hindu nationalist party (BJP), contemporary India seems to have made a decisive turn away from being a secular state to increasingly a Hindu-dominated nation. For example, after twenty long years of court cases, the Supreme Court of India in 2019 ruled that the claim of Hindus is legitimate and allowed the construction of Rama's temple at the site of the destroyed Babri Masjid. This issue, coupled with the Kashmir issue, which is the revoking of the special status accorded to the majority Muslim state since Indian independence, have further exacerbated ongoing tensions between Hindus and Muslims.

As I began to write these reflections in December 2019, I was shocked to read the news that the Indian Parliament had passed legislation called the "Citizenship Amendment Bill," which uses religion as a criterion for determining whether illegal migrants from neighboring countries can be fast-tracked for citizenship. The bill favors members of all South Asia's major religions except Islam, and leaders of India's two hundred-million-strong Muslim community have called it a blatant discrimination. Opponents of the legislation in India and international rights groups have called the bill a major blow to India's long-held commitment to a secular democracy and have organized nationwide protests.[1]

As reported in the media, the citizenship bill would allow Hindus, Christians, Sikhs, Buddhists, Parsees, or Jains who have immigrated from Bangladesh, Pakistan, or Afghanistan a clear path to naturalization in India. Immigrants who are Muslim—which might include people who lived in India for generations but were unable to produce an old property deed or a birth certificate to prove it—would not be afforded the same protection. The bill excludes Muslim members of ethnic minorities from neighboring countries, such as the Rohingya, who have been persecuted ruthlessly in neighboring Myanmar. The big question many Muslims in India are now asking is, Who will be considered an Indian citizen, and who will be considered an illegal foreigner? Many of the Muslim people who failed to pass the citizenship test in the state of Assam had lived in India all their lives, felt deeply Indian, and were despondent to be stricken from the citizenship rolls.

1. "Citizenship Amendment Bill."

What is happening to "Mother India" where I grew up decades ago, where religious tolerance and acceptance of different faiths was part of its history and legacy? Has contemporary India succumbed to the wave of "Islamophobia" (whatever that means) that is sweeping across the globe, especially in the West in recent years? Is it based on the fear of the "religious other" that is threatening our religious identity? Living in the United States for over thirty years, I am also appalled about recent governmental restrictions imposed upon travelers from certain Muslim countries by banning or restricting their entrance into the U.S.

It hardly needs to be mentioned that, ever since 9/11, the American public has expressed a deep distrust, resentment, or phobia of Muslims and their religion as potential terrorists. As religious pluralism has become more and more pronounced in North America in recent decades, there seems to be an increased fear and blame directed towards newly arrived immigrants and religious minorities. As an immigrant and a naturalized Indian American, I see certain parallels between the United States and India regarding attitudes toward Islam and Muslims. The rise of religious hostility in recent years between Muslims and Hindus in India, and Christians and Muslims in some contexts or communities in the United States—both multireligious societies, not to mention two of the world's largest democracies, where religious pluralism has been an established fact—is deeply disturbing. What has happened to India in my lifetime is something that I have pondered a lot, and as a Christian, I deeply worry about similar trends in Christian responses to growing religious diversity and pluralism in the United States.

Muslim and Christian Presence in India

A few miles from the city of Mysore in South India, there is a stone marker at the site where a Muslim ruler, Tipu Sultan, died in a battle against the British army. Tipu was a much-celebrated hero in the then state of Mysore (today, Karnataka), where I grew up. He had succeeded his father, Hyder Ali, and earned the title "Tiger of Mysore," by defeating the British forces in 1782. But his peace treaty with the British ended when, at the Fourth Anglo-Mysore war, Tipu's army was defeated by the British, and he was killed on the battlefield in 1799.

Tipu is still fondly remembered for his heroic and defiant resistance against the British occupation of India. He was an able administrator and the inventor of the world's first rocket technology, which was deployed against the British army. He also developed the Mysore silk industry, minted new coinage, and created a new revenue structure in the region he ruled. Tipu's military, economic, and agricultural contributions were no doubt admirable, but his religious legacy is mixed. On the one hand, he patronized some Hindu temples by endowing them with land and financial grants; on the other hand, as a devout Shia Muslim, he also suppressed Hindus and Christians through forced conversion to Islam. He even suppressed other Muslim communities for political and religious reasons.

Studying the history of Muslim rule in India has always evoked mixed emotions in me. The early Muslim invasions resulted in enormous destruction of historic Hindu and Buddhist temples in North India. Later, during the Mogul rule of India 1526–1720, there were some great Muslim rulers, such as Akbar (1542–1605), who practiced religious tolerance, as well as some fanatic rulers, like Aurangzeb (1618–1707), who engaged in wanton plundering and destruction of Hindu and Buddhist religious and cultural heritages. The majority of Indian Muslims were forcefully converted from Hinduism to Islam during the Mogul era.

The expansion of Christianity in India occurred primarily during the British and European colonization, although Christian presence in India dates back centuries. While there were forceful attempts by Portuguese Roman Catholic missions to reconvert indigenous Syrian Orthodox Christians to Catholicism, and later attempts by British missionaries to convert them to Anglicanism, Western Protestant missionaries did not generally engage in forceful conversion of Hindus to Christianity. (There were, however, mass conversions among indigenous people through the offering of benevolence and other inducements.) Muslim rulers of India, though, were at times ruthless and acted differently. Their military and political conquest of the Indian subcontinent entailed a religious conquest as well. Political and military control of conquered lands often involved coercion and conversion.

Given this history, the deep-seated Hindu hostility toward Muslims and sometimes toward Christians continues to play out in contemporary India. While Muslims seem to have borne the brunt of Hindu hostility in recent years, Christians too have been subject to Hindu hostility in some parts of India. The once celebrated Muslim rulers, like Tipu Sultan in Karnataka, are no longer seen by Hindus as freedom fighters against the British, but as villains and anti-Hindu zealots! How soon perceptions of the religious other have undergone change, due to changing political climate in the wake of resurgent Hindu nationalism. Unfortunately, a revisionist history of Muslim contributions to India (good or bad) is now promoted by the Hindu nationalists who govern India today.

The Islamic *Shahada* in the Context of Religious Pluralism

My personal reflections thus far have been descriptive of complex histories of interreligious encounters in India. I now want to return to my opening focus on the Islamic *shahada*, "There is no God save Allah," and its theological significance for both Muslims and non-Muslims.

Confessing the greatness of God (*takbir*) is undeniably the foundation of Muslim life, theology, and liturgy, a theme that both Christians and Jews also share. The profound affirmation of theocentrism or absolute monotheism that governs Muslim spirituality is unsurpassed by other theistic or monotheistic faiths. But how this confession is transposed in the contexts of religious plurality in society has been the burden of faiths that share the Abrahamic heritage.

Both Christians and Muslims have often used their acknowledgment of divine authority, sovereignty, and greatness in forms that have led to widespread negation and denial of the religious claims of other faiths, not to mention the desecration of houses of worship, vandalism of monuments, and iconoclasm in human history. While instances of iconoclasm are found in virtually all cultures, civilizations, and religions, for political, religious, or social reasons, Christianity and Islam, as the most aggressively proselytizing religions, have been the worst perpetrators of theologically inspired vandalism of rthe eligious histories and heritages of others.

The roots of this iconoclasm, of course, are found in the Hebrew Scriptures. Nevertheless, more than the ancient Israelites, their Abrahamic siblings, Christians and Muslims have used and abused their creedal commitments in an ideology of conquest and subjugation of other nations and civilizations. Christians are as guilty as Muslims in this regard. Christians may be prone to forget that much of the Christian zeal for evangelism, until relatively recent times, was based not on Matthew 28: 18–20, the "great commission," but on Luke 14:23, "compel them to come in." This obscure verse inspired the Roman Catholic missions in the era of Christian colonialism to engage in a violent evangelism and genocide in Latin America. How easily the zeal for the Lord can degenerate into zealotry against people of other cultures and civilizations! Killing people in the name of God is an ugly facet of the Christian evangelization of indigenous cultures in Latin America.

In the case of Islam, it is a well-known fact that in backdrop of the pre-Islamic Arab society of a pagan plurality of deities may have led the Prophet Muhammad to repudiate what he deemed to be "false worship" (*shirk*) as a necessary precondition for the establishment of a Muslim society. The Muslim sense of the divine greatness and the duty to affirm it resolutely became the mission and vocation of Islam, undoubtedly influenced by Jewish and Christian monotheisms. Nonetheless, to ban the evil of *shirk* became the unifying creed implied in the *shahada*, that "there is no God save Allah." Islam is adamant in its affirmation of the singularity of God, and therefore God cannot be understood as or made plural. Belief in absolute monotheism implied absolute rejection of a plurality of gods or divinities. The existence of the plurality of Hindu deities and gods in society was considered intolerable and therefore must be suppressed or treated as an enemy of the unity of God. Thus Islam in the course of its history has exhibited a profound "iconophobia" or hostility toward idols that is unsurpassed among all other religious faiths.

Stated differently, confessing the "oneness of God" or "divine unity," in an Islamic perspective, necessarily demanded dethronement of pagan deities or destruction of idols wherever they were found. (A recent example is the destruction of Buddhist sculptures and statues by the Taliban in Bamiyan, Afghanistan, in 2001.) To acknowledge the existence of deities or idols is a denial or negation of the Islamic *shahada*. Pagan deities or non-Muslim deities are deemed as Satanic substitutes and thus the Islamic creed, "There is no God save Allah" was understood and proclaimed as an ideological or iconoclastic creed: "That you shall have no other gods." Islamic iconophobia, in the context of the Muslim conquest of nations and civilizations in Asia, was expressed as a mandated duty in defense of God's sovereignty and vindication of God's name. The loyalty and reverence to God that Islam seeks to affirm often was distorted when the divine will was subordinated by a misplaced human will to subjugate others. The Muslim view of apostasy, blasphemy, *hudud* laws, and characterization of non-Muslims as infidels in some Muslim societies are some consequences of an ideological interpretation of the Islamic creed.[2] That God and coercion

2. *Hudud* crimes are those where the full extent of punishment which may be applied. They are specified in the Qur'an or sayings of Muhammad and include unlawful

do not belong together is something Muslims have often ignored in their history and that some extremist Muslim groups still haven't grasped. Unfortunately, killing in the name of God or dying for God has come to define extreme forms of Islam in our world.

It is also unfortunate that Muslims, unlike Hindus, did not develop an articulated theology of idol worship, an appreciation for arts and imagery without idolatrous reproach, and an understanding of the importance of symbols in worship, notwithstanding the fact that some sectarian Muslim traditions, like the Sufis and Ismailis, have retained images and the veneration of Muslim saints. Nonetheless, the Islamic hostility to visual representation and its iconoclastic history in defense of God's honor has often missed the point of its own rich and impressive calligraphic tradition. Islamic calligraphy is an art form that Muslims often fail to recognize.

These brief observations on Muslim views of God, seen from the perspective of religious pluralism, has made me rethink the Muslim call to prayer that I once admired while growing up. What seemed like an innocuous invitation to prayer then, today makes me wonder how it translates in the hearing of others. Understandably, in Hindu hearing, especially in the context of Hindu nationalism today, its thrust comes across as offensive and an affront to their religious sensitivities and convictions. The memory of Muslim atrocities of the past provokes a continued sense of threat and leads Hindus to recoil in anger and resentment. The *muezzin's* call to prayer of the "oneness of God," five times a day, is heard over manifold manifestations of religious beliefs, avatars, claims, and commitments of people of other faiths. The zeal to publicly confess one's faith may be warranted by the Muslim faith, but implicitly or explicitly it seeks to negate and undermine the religious identities of Muslim neighbors and thus invites hostility and reactionary responses. This, and the experience of the Muslim subjugation of Hindu India, explains contemporary Hindu reactions and antipathy toward Muslims in India.

Martin Luther and the "Enemies of God"

My critique of the theological implications of the Islamic creed in pluralistic societies is not intended to single out or indict the Muslim faith. I have earlier pointed out similar tendencies in Christian traditions. As a

intercourse (*zina*) or false accusation of unlawful intercourse, drinking wine, some forms of theft, highway robber, and apostasy.

Lutheran pastor and theologian, I am acutely aware that my own theological tradition has in the past subscribed to the vilification or demonization of other religious traditions in the name of God. I am particularly referring to the writings of Martin Luther, the most prominent reformer of the church in the sixteenth century.[3]

It is all too well-known that Luther penned treatises against Jews, Turks, "papists" (that is, medieval Roman Catholics), and other Christian reformers of his day. But the most chilling aspect of Luther's writings, especially in his sermons towards the end of his life, is the characterization of his opponents as "enemies of God." In some of his sermons preached weeks before his death, Luther *first* aimed to reaffirm the essentials of evangelical faith. *Second*, he exhorted his hearers to be vigilant against the errors of the enemies of God. *Third*, he encouraged magistrates to expel enemy populations, especially Jews, who persisted in "open blasphemy." In his final sermons, and his writing entitled "Warning" (1546), Luther used vivid depictions of the enemies of God not only to inspire official action against enemies, but also to clarify what made evangelical Christians—in his view, the only true Christians—distinct in faith and life from every other religion. Directed against the Jews who lived in his birthplace, Eisleben, Luther wrote, "I want to say this to you as a native son, as a final word, to warn you not to participate in the others' sins." Luther's warning was heeded by the magistrates, and Jews were expelled from Eisleben in 1547.

I have lifted up a small snippet of Luther's writings to illustrate that the characterization of other faiths as enemies of God led to certain consequences. If one were to scan Luther's voluminous writings, one would find ample evidence of a "theology of hostility" toward those who differed from his Christian theological convictions. It is not surprising that Luther often attacked enemies both present and absent, living and dead—Jews, Turks, heathens of the Greco-Roman world, fanatics (that is, Radical Reformers), and, of course, papists.

Any attempt to absolve Luther or to explain away his hostile posture toward others who differed from his theological views, as part of the rhetoric of his age or results based on his theological readings of Christian scriptures, seems problematic today. Undeniably, Luther lived in an age of polemics rather than pluralism, disputations rather than dialogue, condemnation rather than concord, anathemas rather than acceptance. But the fundamental error of Luther's theology is the characterization of religious

3. Rajashekar, "Luther and Islam."

convictions of people other faiths as "unbelief," falsehood, and blasphemy against God. His notions of truth and certitude, seen from the perspective of the twenty-first century, is a form of Christian self-righteousness that his entire theology was directed against.[4] The consequences of Luther's theological legacy, whether acknowledged or not, implicitly or explicitly, may have contributed to one of the greatest tragedies of human history: the Holocaust. Lutherans today, however, have publicly disassociated themselves from Luther's anti-Semitic remarks, but have not yet formally or publicly disassociated themselves from his anti-Muslim views. The Lutheran-Muslim panel of the ELCA hopes to issue such a statement with a commentary on Luther's views on Islam in the near future.[5]

Concluding Thoughts

Before I entered the seminary to become a pastor, I had the privilege of assisting a group of Lutheran pastors in India who were engaged in evangelism among Muslims. There is long history of Lutheran efforts to evangelize Muslims in India. One of the pioneering efforts in this regard was a Muslim mission founded in the early twentieth century by the Lutheran Church Missouri Synod in South India. I served as an intern in this mission for a few months.

During my brief stint as an evangelist among Muslims, we did biblical and qur'anic studies every day before we set out to propagate our faith by distributing tracts that explained Muslim misunderstandings of the Christian faith and handed out portions of the gospels in a predominantly Muslim village. The pastors engaged in the Muslim mission were at it for several years. One day, after our daily study, I ventured to ask, "How many Muslims have you converted?" There was total silence for a minute. Finally, the senior pastor of the group, said in a soft voice, "None." I was taken aback by this response, for these pastors were evangelizing among Muslims at this village for years, but they had nothing to show for it!

The pastor's response was a conversion experience for me that led me to become a pastor and later to work for the Lutheran World Federation in Geneva promoting interfaith relations around the world. That experience equipped me to engage in meaningful dialogue with Muslim neighbors and friends and to revise my views on Christian mission and evangelism. After

4. Rajashekar, "Luther as a Resource."

5. See ELCA Church Council, *Declaration of ELCA to the Jewish Community.*

years of involvement with people of other faiths and dialogue with them, I have come to recognize that the reality of religious plurality in our world cannot be wished away, banished, or baptized. If anything, it will become more pronounced, especially in Western societies.

However, the recognition of religious plurality in our midst does not necessarily warrant that faiths confine themselves to their chosen ghettos or segregated sanctuaries, but rather provides us a splendid opportunity to confess what we believe in relation to and not over against others, without denying, denigrating, or negating the validity of all other faith claims. Religious pluralism in our midst, especially in Western societies, does not call for abandoning our faith claims, their integrity, or identity, but, for the same reason, it also demands respect and understanding of counter-claims by others. Christians may need to remind ourselves that we don't need to uphold Christ at the expense of other faiths or their gods and divinities.

That said, in pluralistic societies, all faiths are subject to some form of public accountability in the presence of others. When theological claims, creeds, and confessions are absolutized, without public accountability, religious communities are in danger of practicing a conceptual and creedal idolatry that they seek to condemn. The divine ultimacy that monotheistic faiths seek to affirm and preserve can easily be distorted by falsely locating it in themselves by their extension or self-promotion. Claims of religious superiority or exclusive possession of truth often serve to promote self-righteous attitudes that vilify counterclaims. Our notions of religious truth and falsehood, faith and unbelief, our religious uniqueness over against others, our cultural, religious, or racial superiority, are some issues that are radically challenged by our context of religious plurality. Christians in Western societies and Muslims in predominantly Muslim societies have to come to terms with these issues with a sense of urgency.

My reflections on the implications of Islamic *shahada* and *adhan* in religiously pluralistic societies and my exposition of Martin Luther's rhetoric and vitriol against the enemies of God in the sixteenth century serve to illustrate and remind us that all creedal claims and theological assertions, unless properly understood, interpreted, and moderated, have the potential to engender hostilities among religious communities. Religious claims that faiths make are not necessarily confined to the privacy of their sanctuaries or communities, but they are often overheard by others on the outside and thereby provoke hostilities between religious communities. Memories of past atrocities are seldom forgotten and are often invoked to legitimize current social and political conflicts in our world. How we overcome habits of hostility and inherited phobias is a challenge to all faiths.[6]

One last point: it appears that the era of aggressive proselytism is over, although it will continue to persist in some communities. Nonetheless, it is obvious that the contemporary ethos of pluralism will invariably and inevitably come into conflict with the ethics and propriety of proselytism, whether scripturally mandated or theologically legitimated by adherents of religious faiths. Proselytism has been viewed by some as a spiritual malpractice. Whether one agrees with such characterization or not, it is self-evident that claims to exclusive truth or absolute truth today are indeed contested claims in pluralistic societies that one can neither ignore nor wish away. Objectifying others as enemies or threats to our culture, beliefs, and ways of life, whether Muslims, Hindus, Buddhists, or other immigrants to the United States, only serves to promote intolerance of neighbors of other faiths. Awareness of pluralism, paradoxically, may make us all turn inward, that is, to become "fundamentalists," seeking to preserve and protect our particular identity, beliefs, ways of life, claims of superiority, etc., and blame others, especially immigrants, Muslims, and those whom we perceive as strangers in our midst. It is the nature of prejudice, like bad breath, that we recognize it in others but not in ourselves.

Religious intolerance is a form of self-righteousness, that denies or negates other expressions and articulations of the unity and sovereignty of God. Christians and Muslims—for that matter, any other faith—do not have a monopoly on God's revelation or God's offer of grace and mercy. This is a challenge to both Christians and Muslims that they must somehow come to terms with divine oneness and the reality of pluralism in our world. If there is a failure to do so, as is already evident in many societies, our inherited habits of hostility and theological phobias may overpower us into mutually assured destruction. However, while it may be obvious to most of us that the reality of religious pluralism in our midst demands that we create a hospitable social, cultural, religious, and political space for people of all faiths to coexist, it also implies that we strive to create a theological space for all to flourish. This is a burden and challenge to all religious faiths, particularly Christians and Muslims.

6. Rajashekar, "Our God and Their God," 105–16.

Further Resources on Islam and Muslims in North America and Christian–Muslim Relations

Introduction to Islam

Islam: What Non-Muslims Should Know, John Kaltner (2003)

> A good overview written for North American Christians.

Muhammad: A Biography of the Prophet, Karen Armstrong (1992)

> Still one of the most readable introductions to the life of the Prophet Muhammad.

Memories of Muhammad: Why the Prophet Matters, Omid Safi (2010)

> A progressive American Muslim view of the Prophet.

No God but God, Reza Aslan (2011)

> Very readable history of Islam.

The Story of the Qur'an: Its History and Place in Muslim Life, Ingrid Mattson (2013)

> A college-level overview of the spiritual importance of the Qur'an for Muslims.

North American Islam

Acts of Faith: The Story of an American Muslim, the Struggle for the Soul of a Generation, Eboo Patel (2008)

> The inspiring autobiography of the founder of Interfaith Youth Core.

A History of Islam in America, Kambiz GhaneaBassiri (2010)

> A short history of Islam in the United States.

Islam and the Blackamerican: Looking toward the Third Resurrection, Sherman Jackson (2011)

> One of the most important overviews of Islam in the African-American community.

Mecca and Main Street: Muslim Life in America after 9/11, Geneive Abdo (2007).

> Extremely well-researched study of the variety of Muslim communities in the United States.

Muslims and the Making of America, Amir Hussain (2017)

> Excellent overview of the diversity of American Muslim cultures.

Out of Many Faiths: Religious Diversity and the American Promise, Eboo Patel (2018)

> Guides readers through the possibilities of a positive multifaith society.

Servants of Allah: African Muslims Enslaved in the Americas, Sylviane A. Diouf (2013)

> A ground-breaking study on the stories of enslaved African Muslims brought to North America.

Christian–Muslim Relations

Allah: A Christian Response, Miroslav Volf (2011)

> Good for group discussions on the topic of "Do Christians and Muslims worship the same God?"

Christian Century articles:

"Yes, Christians Can Love Jesus and Their Muslim Neighbors Honorably," (June 1, 2017)

"Who is Jesus for Muslims?" (May 23, 2017)

> Two helpful reflections in a popular Christian magazine.

Engaging Others, Knowing Ourselves: A Lutheran Calling in a Multi-Religious World, Carol Schersten LaHurd, Darrell Jodock, and Kathryn Mary Lohre, eds. (2016)

> A resource for congregations considering interfaith education or partnerships.

Neightbors: Christians and Muslims Building Community, Deanna Ferree Womack (2020)

> An excellent resource for congregations and groups who want to learn more and become active in interfaith relationships.

Oil and Water: Two Faiths: One God, Amir Hussain (2006)

> Includes an overview of the basics of Islam, as well as points and issues for dialogue.

Sacred Ground: Pluralism, Prejudice, and the Promise of America, Eboo Patel (2012)

> Places the issue of prejudice against Muslims within the broader experience of other religious minorities and the highest ideals of American inclusion.

"Variations on a Theme: Lutheran Accompaniment and God's Mission In Senegal," Peter Hanson (2010).

> DMin thesis based on the ELCA model of accompaniment at the Episcopal Divinity School, Cambridge, MA.

Extremism

The Great Theft: Wrestling Islam from the Extremists, Khaled M. Abou el Fadl (2005)

Still one of the most readable and important views of extremists from within the Islamic faith.

Presumed Guilty: Why We Shouldn't Ask Muslims to Condemn Terrorism, Todd H. Green (2018)

Focuses on non-Muslim responsibilities to fight Islamophobia.

This Muslim American Life: Dispatches from the War on Terror, Moustafa Bayoumi (2015)

An excellent account of American Muslim life under suspicion and duress.

Who Speaks for Islam: What a Billion Muslims Really Think, John L. Esposito and Dalia Mogahed (2008)

The results of an international Gallup poll of Muslim views on violence and international issues.

Gender Issues

American Muslim Women, Jamilliah Karim (2009)

An ethnographic university-style book that covers a variety of ethnicities and economic levels.

Do Muslim Women Need Saving? Lila Abu-Lughod (2011).

An excellent study of Arab women's perspectives.

I Speak for Myself: American Women on Being Muslim, Maria M. Ebrahimi (2011)

Readable, with multiple perspectives of young American Muslim women

Islamophobia

American Islamophobia: Understanding the Roots and Rise of Fear, Khaled Beydoun (2018).

Well written exposé of the legal history of exclusion of Muslims from American civil life.

The Fear of Islam: An Introduction to Islamophobia in the West, Todd H. Green (2015)

One of the most important introductions to the topic.

Islamophobia and Anti-Muslim Sentiment, 2nd ed., Peter Gottschalk (2018)

An engaging resource laid out in graphic novel form.

The Islamophobia Industry: How the Right Manufactures Fear of Muslims, Nathan Lean (2017).

Provides an overview of general views of Muslims in the media from 9/11 to the first year of the Trump presidency.

Film Resources

Discover Islam [six-part DVD series with ELCA intro study guide] (2010)

Fordson: Faith, Fasting, Football (2011)

The Jesus Fatwa (2015)

Little Mosque on the Prairie (2007–2012)

Malcolm X (1992)

The Message (1976; twenty-fifth anniversary edition, 2005)

Mooz-lum (2010)

The Mosque and Me (2005)

The Prince Among Slaves (2007)

Soft Walk in a Distant Place, Mosiac Video 1:1 (1988)

Taqwacores (2010)

Veiled Voices (2009)

Website Resources

Building Bridges Seminar, Georgetown University, https://berkleycenter.georgetown.edu/projects/the-building-bridges-seminar

A Center of Christian-Muslim Engagement for Peace and Justice, The Lutheran School of Theology at Chicago, https://www.lstc.edu/academics/ccme

Christian-Muslim Talking Points, Evangelical Lutheran Church in America, https://download.elca.org/ELCA%20Resource%20Repository/TP1_The_Bible_And_The_Quran.pdf

ELCA Consultative Panel on Lutheran-Muslim Relations, https://www.elca.org/Faith/Ecumenical-and-Inter-Religious-Relations/Inter-Religious-Relations/Muslim-Relations

Lutheran Social Service of MN, *My Neighbor Is Muslim Study,* https://www.lssmn.org/services/refugees/my-neighbor-is-muslim

National Council of Churches, Interfaith Relations and the Church Study Guide, http://nationalcouncilofchurches.us/shared-ministry/interfaith/resources.php

The Pluralism Project at Harvard University, https://pluralism.org/

Presbyterian (U.S.A.) Principles for Interfaith Dialogue, Witness and Evangelism, https://www.presbyterianmission.org/wp-content/uploads/principlesfordialogue1.pdf

Prince Alwaleed Bin Talal Center for Christian-Muslim Understanding, Georgetown University, https://acmcu.georgetown.edu/

Shoulder to Shoulder Campaign, https://www.shouldertoshouldercampaign.org/

Seeing God in Little Mogadishu Blog, http://www.seeinggodinlittlemogadishu.com/

Standing Together: Christians and Muslims Creating Good. www.standingtogethernow.org.

The United States Conference of Catholic Bishops General Resources on Islam, http://www.usccb.org/beliefs-and-teachings/ecumenical-and-interreligious/interreligious/interreligious-documents-and-news-releases.cfm

Windows for Understanding: Jewish—Muslim—Lutheran Relations, Evangelical Lutheran Church in America, http://download.elca.org/ELCA%20 Resource%20Repository/Windows_For_Understanding.pdf

Muslim Websites

AltMuslim, https://acmcu.georgetown.edu/

AltMuslmiah, http://www.altmuslimah.com/

The Amman Message, http://ammanmessage.com/

A Common Word, https://www.acommonword.com/

The Community of Imam Warith Deen Muhammad, https://www.iwdmcommunity.com/

The Council for American-Islamic Relations, https://www.cair.com/

Muslim Public Affairs Council, https://www.mpac.org/

Search the web or Facebook for the mosques or Islamic centers near you.

Sociological Studies of Muslim Communities

Institute for Social Policy and Understanding, https://www.ispu.org/

- *American Muslim Poll* (2019)
- *Born in the U.S.A.* (2018)
- *To Have and To Hold* (2018)

Pew Research Center, https://www.pewresearch.org/

- *Muslims in America* (2007, 2011, 2017)
- *Mapping the Global Muslim Population* (2009)

U.S. Mosque Survey 2011, http://www.hartfordinstitute.org/

- *Activities, Administration, and Vitality of the American Mosque*
- *Basic Characteristics of the American Mosque*
- *Women and the American Mosque*

Bibliography

American Civil Liberties Union. "Timeline of the Muslim Ban." February 10, 2020. https://www.aclu-wa.org/pages/timeline-muslim-ban.

American Lutheran Church, Division for World Mission and Inter-Church Cooperation. *God and Jesus : Theological Reflections for Christian-Muslim Dialog.* Minneapolis: DWMIC, ALC, 1986.

Anti-Defamation League. "Murder and Extremism in the United States in 2018: A Report from the Center on Extremism." January 2019. https://tinyurl.com/yxna9glm.

Bail, Christopher. *Terrified: How Anti-Muslim Fringe Organizations Became Mainstream.* Princeton, NJ: Princeton University Press, 2015.

Bailey, Sarah Pulliam. "Jerry Falwell Jr.: 'If More Good People Had Concealed-Carry Permits, Then We Could End Those' Islamist Terrorists." *Washington Post,* December 5, 2015. https://www.washingtonpost.com/news/acts-of-faith/wp/2015/12/05/liberty-university-president-if-more-good-people-had-concealed-guns-we-could-end-those-muslims/.

Bash, Dana. "Peter King: The Man Behind Muslim Hearings." *CNN,* March 10, 2011. https://www.cnn.com/2011/POLITICS/03/09/king.profile/index.html. Site discontinued.

Beinart, Peter. "The Denationalization of American Muslims." *The Atlantic,* March 19, 2017. https://tinyurl.com/leeygyc.

Beydoun, Khaled A. *American Islamophobia: Understanding the Roots and Rise of Fear.* Oakland, CA: University of California Press, 2018.

Bielefeldt, Heiner. "The Contribution of Freedom of Religion or Belief to the Societal Peace." Religious Freedom Project, organized by the Norwegian Centre for Human Rights. Unpublished paper, 2018.

———. "Freedom of Religion or Belief: A Human Right under Pressure." *Oxford Journal of Law and Religion* 1, no. 1 (April 2012) 15–35.

Bijlefeld, Willem A. "A Prophet and More than a Prophet?: Some Observations on the Qur'anic Use of the Terms 'Prophet' and 'Apostle.'" *The Muslim World* 59, no. 1 (January 1969) 1–28.

Böttcher, Reinard, ed. *Prophetic Diakonia: "For the Healing of the World."* Geneva: Lutheran World Federation, 2002. https://www.episcopaldeacons.org/uploads/2/6/7/3/26739998/prophtcdiak_lutho2.pdf.

A Center of Christian-Muslim Engagement for Peace and Justice (website). Accessed November 21, 2019. http://ccme.lstc.edu/.

Christian Solidarity Worldwide. *Indonesia: Visit Report.* London: CSW, 2019.

"Citizenship Amendment Bill: India's New 'Anti-Muslim' Law Explained." *BBC News,* December 11, 2019. https://www.bbc.com/news/world-asia-india-50670393.

Clarfield, A. Mark, Shimon M. Glick, and Rivke Carm. "American Funding Cutback to East Jerusalem Hospitals: A Blow to the Health of the City." *American Journal of Public Health* 108, no. 12 (December 2018) 1624-25. https://ajph.aphapublications.org/doi/full/10.2105/AJPH.2018.304792.

A Common Word (website). Accessed November 22, 2019. https://www.acommonword.com/.

Council on American-Islamic Relations (CAIR). "Hijacked by Hate: American Philanthropy and the Islamophobia Network." 2019. https://tinyurl.com/yyzmgadl.

Cox, J. Gray. *The Ways of Peace: A Philosophy of Peace as Action.* New York: Paulist, 1986.

"Dallas Pastor's Broad-Brush Criticism of Islam Goes Way Too Far." *The Dallas Morning News,* September 5, 2010. https://www.dallasnews.com/news/2010/09/05/dallas-pastor-s-broad-brush-criticism-of-islam-goes-way-too-far/. Site discontinued.

Darmaputera, Eka. *Pancasila and the Search for Identiy and Modernity in Indonesian Society.* Leiden, Neth.: E. J. Brill, 1988.

Davidson, Joe. "State of the Nation: Alleged White-Supremacist Killer Finds Inspiration in Trump." *Washington Post,* March 18, 2019. https://www.washingtonpost.com/politics/2019/03/18/state-nation-alleged-white-supremacist-killer-finds-inspiration-trump/.

Discover Islam (website). Accessed November 21, 2019. https://www.discoverislam.com/elca.

Eaton, Elizabeth A. "An Open Letter to the Muslim American Community." *Evangelical Lutheran Church of America,* December 11, 2015. https://tinyurl.com/y6nl2lfd.

————. "Trump's Travel Ban Is 'Deeply Upsetting.'" *Houston Chronicle,* June 26, 2018. https://www.houstonchronicle.com/local/gray-matters/article/trump-travel-ban-religious-bigotry-13027245.php.

Evangelical Lutheran Church in America (ELCA). *Constitutions, Bylaws, and Continuing Resolutions of the Evangelical Lutheran Church in America.* 1987, revised 2020. https://download.elca.org/ELCA%20Resource%20Repository/Constitutions_Bylaws_and_Continuing_Resolutions_of_the_ELCA.pdf?_ga=2.46439651.517356569.1617289138-874421208.1614872120.

————. *A Declaration of Ecumenical Commitment: A Policy Statement of the Evangelical Lutheran Church in America.* 1991. http://download.elca.org/ELCA%20Resource%20Repository/The_Vision_Of_The_ELCA.pdf?_ga=2.40055782.517356569.1617289138-874421208.1614872120.

————. *A Declaration of Inter-Religious Commitment: A Policy Statement of the Evangelical Lutheran Church in America.* In *The Vision of the Evangelical Lutheran Church in America,* 5–9. https://download.elca.org/ELCA%20Resource%20Repository/Inter-Religious_Policy_Statement.pdf?_ga=2.162780668.1597882298.1596824847-1250384125.1580939281.

———. *Ecumenical and Inter-Religious Relations: Online Resources* (website). Accessed July 31, 2020. https://www.elca.org/Faith/Ecumenical-and-Inter-Religious-Relations/Inter-Religious-Relations/Online-Resources.

———. "ELCA Presiding Bishop Issues Letter to Muslim-American Community." December 11, 2015. https://www.elca.org/News-and-Events/7803.

———. *Global Mission in the Twenty-First Century: A Vision of Evangelical Faithfulness in God's Mission.* Chicago: Evangelical Lutheran Church in America, 1999.

———. *Litany of Confession: Based on the 1994 'Declaration of the ELCA to the Jewish Community.'* Accessed November 21, 2019. https://download.elca.org/ELCA%20Resource%20Repository/Litany_of_Confession.pdf.

———. "October Thirty-One Commemoration." https://www.elca500.org/resources/october-31-commemoration/.

———. "Peace Not Walls." Accessed December 1, 2019. https://www.elca.org/Our-Work/Publicly-Engaged-Church/Peace-Not-Walls.

———. *Pre-Assembly Report: Report of the Memorials Committee,* 25–39. 2019.

ELCA Church Council. *Declaration of ELCA to the Jewish Community.* https://download.elca.org/ELCA%20Resource%20Repository/Declaration_Of_The_ELCA_To_The_Jewish_Community.pdf.

———. *Declaration of the ELCA to People of African Descent.* https://download.elca.org/ELCA%20Resource%20Repository/Slavery_Apology_Explanation.pdf.

ELCA Consultative Panel on Lutheran-Jewish Relations. *Guidelines for Lutheran-Jewish Relations.* Accessed July 31, 2019. https://download.elca.org/ELCA%20Resource%20Repository/Guidelines_For_Lutheran_Jewish_Relations_1998.pdf?_ga=2.142410930.1024152220.1616546033-1776519076.1616546033.

———. *Luther and Contemporary Inter-Religious Relations.* http://download.elca.org/ELCA%20Resource%20Repository/Why_Follow_Luther_Past_2017.pdf.

ELCA Consultative Panel on Lutheran-Muslim Relations. *Guidelines for Christian-Muslim Relations.* https://download.elca.org/ELCA%20Resource%20Repository/ELCA%20Muslim-Christian%20Guidelines%20March%202018%202004%20draft.pdf?_ga=2.234006488.790565402.1595621279-529607599.1592513499.

Evangelical Lutheran Church of Jordan and the Holy Land. *Our Schools.* Accessed December 19, 2019. http://www.elcjhl.org/department-of-education/schools/. Site discontinued.

Falatūri, Abdoldjavad. "Experience of Time and History in Islam." In *We Believe in One God: The Experience of God in Christianity and Islam,* edited by Annemarie Schimmel and Abdoldjavad Falatūri, 63–76. New York: Seabury, 1979.

Federal Bureau of Investigation (FBI). *Hate Crime Statistics, 2015* (website). *Uniform Crime Reports.* https://ucr.fbi.gov/hate-crime/2015.

———. *Hate Crime Statistics, 2016* (website). *Uniform Crime Reports.* https://ucr.fbi.gov/hate-crime/2016.

Fornek, Kimberly and Steve Schering. "Sikh Man Who Was Attacked in Darien Returns Home from Hospital." *Chicago Tribune,* September 10, 2015. https://www.chicagotribune.com/suburbs/burr-ridge/ct-police-investigate-after-sikh-man-called-terrorist-beaten-in-darien-20150910-story.html.

Fransisco, Adam. "Luther's Knowledge of and Attitude Toward Islam." In *The Routledge Reader in Christian-Muslim Relations,* edited by Mona Siddiqui, 129-153. New York: Routledge, 2013.

Fretheim, Terence E. *The Suffering of God: An Old Testament Perspective*. Philadelphia: Fortress, 1984.

"Full Transcript of Bin Laden's Speech." *Al Jazeera*, November 1, 2004. https://tinyurl.com/y8xxvlrg.

Gardner, Gary. *Inspiring Progress: Religions' Contributions to Sustainable Development*. New York: W. W. Norton & Co., 2006.

Graf, Georg. *Geschichte der christlichen arabischen Literatur*. 5 vols. Vatican City: Biblioteca Apostolica Vaticana, 1944–53.

Grafton, David D. *Piety, Politics, and Power: Lutherans Encountering Islam in the Middle East*. Eugene, OR: Wipf & Stock, 2009.

Grafton, David D., ed. *Mark W. Thomsen: Remembering the Missiologist and the Man*. Currents in Theology and Mission 42, no. 1 (January/February 2015). http://currentsjournal.org/index.php/currents/issue/view/8.

Grafton, David D., Joseph F. Duggan, and Jason Craige Harris. *Christian-Muslim Relations in the Anglican and Lutheran Communions*. New York: Palgrave Pivot, 2013.

Green, Todd H. *The Fear of Islam: An Introduction to Islamophobia in the West*. Minneapolis: Fortress, 2019.

———. *Presumed Guilty: Why We Shouldn't Ask Muslims to Condemn Terrorism*. Minneapolis: Fortress, 2018.

Griswold, Eliza. *The Tenth Parallel: Dispatches from the Fault Line between Christianity and Islam*. New York: Farrar, Straus and Giroux, 2010.

Hanson, Mark S. "Response from Bishop Rev. Mark S. Hanson." October 12, 2007. https://www.acommonword.com/response-from-bishop-rev-mark-s-hanson/.

Hanson, Peter. "Variations on a Theme: Lutheran Accompaniment and God's Mission in Senegal." DMin thesis, Episcopal Divinity School, 2010.

Hasan, Mehdi. "Mike Pompeo Has Extreme Views on Muslims—and Liberals Don't Seem to Care." *The Intercept*, August 20, 2019. https://tinyurl.com/y26a56az.

Hathout, Maher, et al. *In Pursuit of Justice: The Jurisprudence of Human Rights in Islam*. Washington, D.C.: Muslim Public Affairs Council, 2006.

Hawkins, Larycia, Michael Mangis, and Patti Mangis. *Same God*. Austin, TX: Tugg Educational, 2018. Video.

Henry Martyn Institute (website). Accessed February 2, 2020. http://hmiindia.org/.

Husain, Atiya. "Moving Beyond (and Back to) the Black-White Binary: A Study of Black and White Muslims' Racial Positioning in the United States." *Ethnic and Racial Studies* 42, no. 4 (2019) 589–606.

———. "Retrieving the Religion in Racialization: A Critical Review." *Sociology Compass* 11, no. 9 (September 2017). https://doi.org/10.1111/soc4.12507.

"Interview with Special Advisor on Genocide Adama Dieng on Hate Speech." *Office of the High Commissioner for Human Rights* (website). Accessed April 21, 2020. https://www.ohchr.org/EN/NewsEvents/Pages/InterviewSpecialAdvisoronGenocideAdamaDiengonHateSpeech.aspx.

Jenkins, Will and Jennifer McBride, eds. *Bonhoeffer and King: Their Legacies and Import for Christian Social Thought*. Minneapolis: Fortress, 2010.

"Join in the Journey at Interfailth [*sic*] Walk for Peace." *The Claremont Courier*, October 12, 2018. https://www.claremont-courier.com/articles/opinion/t29607-interfaith.

Kendi, Ibram X. *Stamped from the Beginning: The Definitive History of Racist Ideas in America*. New York: Nation Books, 2016.

Kessler, Glenn. "Ben Carson's Claim That 'Taqiyya' Encourages Muslims 'to Lie to Achieve Your Goals." *Washington Post*, September 22, 2015. https://tinyurl.com/gkq2j9f.

"Kinerja Berperan Besar dalam Pilihan Warga DKI." *Saifulmujani Research and Consulting* (website). October 20, 2016. https://saifulmujani.com/kinerja-berperan-besar-dalam-pilihan-warga-dki/.

Kurzman, Charles. "Islamic Statements against Terrorism." *Charles Kurzman* (website). Accessed October 12, 2019. https://kurzman.unc.edu/islamic-statements-against-terrorism/.

Kinnamon, Michael. *Can a Renewal Movement Be Renewed?: Questions for the Future of Ecumenism*. Grand Rapids: William B. Eerdmans, 2014.

LaHurd, Carol Schersten, Darrell Jodock, and Kathryn Mary Lohre, eds. *Engaging Others, Knowing Ourselves: A Lutheran Calling in a Multi-Religious World*. Minneapolis: Lutheran University Press, 2016.

Latif, Yudi. "Kewarganegaraan Masyarakat Adat dalam Filsafat Pancasila." Forum of the Second Symposium of Indigenous Peoples at Pancasila University, Jakarta, Indonesia, 2016. Video. https://www.youtube.com/watch?v=EMgyhUJW2Ho&t=1065s.

————. *Negara Paripurna: Historisitas, Rasionalitas, dan Aktualitas Pancasila*. Jakarta, Indonesia: Gramedia, 2015.

Lean, Nathan. *The Islamophobia Industry: How the Right Manufactures Fear of Muslims*. London: Pluto, 2017.

Lindholm, Tore. "Philosophical and Religious Justifications of Freedom of Religion or Belief." In *Facilitating Freedom of Religion or Belief: A Deskbook*, edited by Tore Lindholm et al., 22–4. Leiden, Neth.: Springer, 2004.

Lohre, Kathryn Mary. "A Prayerful Place: Trinity Evangelical Lutheran Church in Wexford." In *Engaging Others, Knowing Ourselves: A Lutheran Calling in a Multi-Religious World*, edited by Carol Schersten LaHurd, Darrell Jodock, and Kathryn Mary Lohre. Minneapolis: Lutheran University Press, 2016.

Lutheran School of Theology at Chicago. "Public Church." https://www.lstc.edu/academics/public-church.

————. "Year of Re-Envisioning for A Center of Christian-Muslim Engagement for Peace and Justice." June 6, 2018. https://www.lstc.edu/news-events/news/article-505.

Lutheran Social Service of Minnesota. *My Neighbor Is Muslim: Exploring the Muslim Faith*. 2015. https://www.lssmn.org/sites/default/files/2021-03/LSS%20My%20Neighbor%20is%20Muslim%20Study-2021.pdf.

MacAskill, Ewen, Richard Adams, and Kate Connolly. "Pastor Terry Jones Calls Off Qur'an Burning." *The Guardian* (UK), September 10, 2010. https://www.theguardian.com/world/2010/sep/10/pastor-terry-jones-quran-burning.

Mahdawi, Arwa. "The 712-Page Google Doc That Proves Muslims Do Condemn Terrorism." *The Guardian* (UK), March 26, 2017. https://tinyurl.com/k7hdbnk.

Mathias, Christopher. "A Pastor Who Said Islam Is 'Evil' Is Speaking at Trump's Inauguration." *Huffington Post*, January 18, 2017. https://www.huffpost.com/entry/franklin-graham-islamophobia-trump-inauguration_n_587e3ea5e4b0aaa369429373.

McCormack, Bruce L. "In Memoriam: Robert Jenson (1930-2017)." *International Journal of Systematic Theology* 20, no. 1 (January 2018) 3–7.

McCrummen, Stephanie. "Love Thy Neighbor?" *Washington Post*, July 1, 2017. https://www.washingtonpost.com/national/in-a-midwestern-town-that-went-for-trump-a-muslim-doctor-tries-to-understand-his-neighbors/2017/07/01/0ada50c4-5c48-11e7-9fc6-c7ef4bc58d13_story.html.

Meer, Nasar and Tariq Modood. "The Racialisation of Muslims." In *Thinking through Islamophobia: Global Perspectives*, edited by. S. Sayyid and AbdoolKarim Vakil, 69–84. New York: Columbia University Press, 2011.

Menoh, Gusti A.B. "Religiusitas Bangsa Sebagai Hasil Penalaran Publik Agama-Agama di Indonesia: Diteropong dari Perspektif Filsafat Politik Jurgen Habermas." *Waskita Jurnal Studi Agama dan Masyarakat* II, no. 1 (April 2014) 82–104.

Minneapolis Area Synod of the ELCA. *Engaging in Solidarity with Our Muslim Neighbors.* http://www.mpls-synod.org/files/Resolution-on-Solidarity-with-Muslims-with-background-information.pdf.

———. *Allies and Friends Workshop.* https://mpls-synod.org/event/allies-friends-workshop/.

Mogahed Dalia, and Azka Mahmood. "American Muslim Poll 2019: Predicting and Preventing Islamophobia." *Institute for Social and Policy Understanding* (website). May 1, 2019. https://www.ispu.org/american-muslim-poll-2019-predicting-and-preventing-islamophobia/.

Moran, Lee. "The RNC Asked Tweeters to Tell Donald Trump Their Priorities. They Didn't Hold Back." *Huffington Post*, February 24, 2018. https://tinyurl.com/y4hvhckw.

Mosher, Lucinda Allen. *Toward Our Mutual Flourishing: The Episcopal Church, Interreligious Relations, and Theologies of Religious Manyness.* New York: Peter Lang, 2012.

Mosher, Lucinda and David Marshall, eds. *Sin, Forgiveness, and Reconciliation: Christian and Muslim Perspectives.* Washington, D.C.: Georgetown University Press, 2016.

Neighbors in Faith (website). Accessed November 21, 2019. https://www.neighborsinfaith.org/. Now called *Paths to Understanding*, https://pathstounderstanding.org.

"NYT Columnist: Moderate Muslims Held Responsible Too." *CNN*, January 9, 2015. Video. https://tinyurl.com/y7upgaa5.

Nyman, Mikaela. "Civil Society and the Challenges of the Post-Suharto Era." In *Democratization in Post-Suharto Indonesia*, edited by Marco Bünte and Andreas Ufen. London: Routledge, 2009.

Pannenberg, Wolfhart. *Basic Questions in Theology.* 2 vols. Philadelphia: Fortress, 1971.

Pape, Robert. *Dying to Win: The Strategic Logic of Suicide Terrorism.* New York: Random House, 2005.

Papenfuss, Mary. "Trump Promotes Far-Right Commentator Who Blames Jews for Deadly U.S. Synagogue Attack." *Huffington Post*, July 21, 2019. https://www.huffpost.com/entry/katie-hopkins-trump-anti-semitic-ocasio-cortez-omar-tlaib-pressley_n_5d34f9ece4b02ocd99453a4f.

Pashman, Manya Brachear. "Wheaton College, Professor at Impasse after Her Suspension." *Chicago Tribune*, December 24, 2015. https://www.chicagotribune.com/news/breaking/ct-wheaton-college-hijab-larycia-hawkins-1223-met-20151222-story.html.

Paul VI. *Declaration on the Relation of the Church to Non-Christian Religions: Nostra Aetate.* October 28, 1965. https://www.vatican.va/archive/hist_councils/ii_vatican_council/documents/vat-ii_decl_19651028_nostra-aetate_en.html.

Peace Not Walls (blog). "ELCA Churchwide Assembly Passes Assembly Actions Related to Israel and Palestine." *ELCA*, August 7, 2019. https://blogs.elca.org/peacenotwalls/elca-churchwide-assembly-passes-assembly-actions-related-to-israel-and-palestine/.

Peters, Shawn Francis. "'Courting Anarchy'?: Religious Pluralism and the Law." In *Gods in America: Religious Pluralism in the United States*, edited by Charles L. Cohen and Ronald L. Numbers. New York: Oxford University Press, 2013.

Pew Research Center. "A Closer Look at How Religious Restrictions Have Risen Around the World." July 15, 2019. https://www.pewforum.org/2019/07/15/a-closer-look-at-how-religious-restrictions-have-risen-around-the-world/.

———. "What Americans Know about Religion." July 23, 2019. https://www.pewforum.org/2019/07/23/what-americans-know-about-religion/.

———. "U.S. Muslims Concerned about Their Place in Society, but Continue to Believe in the American Dream." July 26, 2017. http://www.pewforum.org/2017/07/26/how-the-u-s-general-public-views-muslims-and-islam/.

Pontifical Council for Inter-Religious Dialogue. "Dialogue and Proclamation: Reflection and Orientations on Interreligious Dialogue and the Proclamation of the Gospel of Jesus Christ." http://www.vatican.va/roman_curia/pontifical_councils/interelg/documents/rc_pc_interelg_doc_19051991_dialogue-and-proclamatio_en.html.

Puchalski, Christina and Betty Ferrell. *Making Health Care Whole: Integrating Spirituality into Patient Care*. West Conshohocken, PA: Templeton, 2010.

Rajashekar, J. Paul. "Luther and Islam." In *Lutherjahrbuch* 57 (1990): 174–91.

———. "Luther as a Resource for Christian Dialogue with Other World Religions." In *Oxford Handbook of Martin Luther's Theology*, edited by Robert Kolb et al., 435–42. London: Oxford University Press, 2014.

———. "Our God and Their God: A Relational Theology of Religious Plurality." In *Engaging Others, Knowing Ourselves: A Lutheran Calling in a Multi-Religious World*, edited by Carol Schersten LaHurd, Darrell Jodock, and Kathryn Mary Lohre, 121–58. Minneapolis: Lutheran University Press, 2016.

———. "Rethinking Lutheran Engagement with Religious Plurality." In *Transforming Theological Perspectives*, edited by Karen Bloomquist, 105–16. Minneapolis: Lutheran University Press, 2009.

Ramadan, Tariq. *Western Muslims and the Future of Islam*. New York: Oxford University Press, 2004.

Sahas, Daniel. "*Holosphyros*? A Byzantine Perception of the 'God of Muhammad.'" In *Christian-Muslim Encounters*, edited by Yvonne Y. Haddad and W.Z. Haddad, 109–25. Gainesville, FL: University of Florida Press, 1995.

Sampathkumar, Mythili. "US National Security Adviser John Bolton Was Chairman of 'Anti-Muslim Think Tank,'" *The Independent* (UK), April 24, 2018. https://tinyurl.com/y3fnnef8.

Sandmeyer, Ellie and Michelle Leung. "Muslim Leaders Have Roundly Denounced Islamic State, but Conservative Media Won't Tell You That." *Media Matters for America*. (website). August 21, 2014. https:/tinyurl.com/y7zygmep.

Selod, Saher and David G. Embrick. "Racialization and Muslims: Situating the Muslim Experience in Race Scholarship." *Sociology Compass* 7, no. 8 (August 2013) 644–55.

Semati, Mehdi. "Islamophobia, Culture and Race in the Age of Empire." *Cultural Studies* 24, no. 2 (2012) 256–75.

Seo, Myengkyo. "Missions Without Missionaries: The Social Dimension of Church Growth in Muslim Java, Indonesia." *Islam and Christian-Muslim Relations* 24, no. 1 (January 2013) 71-89. http://dx.doi.org/10.1080/09596410.2013.745300.

Setara Institute for Democracy and Peace. "Calls in Indonesia for Repeal of Blasphemy Law." May 12, 2017. http://setara-institute.org/en/english-calls-in-indonesia-for-repeal-of-blasphemy-law/.

Sevig, Julie B. "CCME Leads the Way in Christian-Muslim Relations." *A Center of Christian-Muslim Engagement for Peace and Justice.* https://www.lstc.edu/assets/pdf/CCME.pdf .

Siegel, Benjamin. "President Trump Falsely Claims Rep. Omar Praised al Qaeda." *ABC News,* July 15, 2019. https://abcnews.go.com/Politics/president-trump-falsely-claims-rep-omar-praised-al/story?id=64349788.

Simanjuntak, Hotli, and Apriadi Gunawan. "Thousands Leave Aceh after Church Burning." *The Jakarta Post.* October 15, 2015. https://www.thejakartapost.com/news/2015/10/15/thousands-leave-aceh-after-church-burning.html.

Sinaga, Martin Lukito. "Literasi Teologis: Agar umat Beragama Tidak Merasa Dinista." *Satu Harapan,* September 4, 2019. http://www.satuharapan.com/read-detail/read/literasi-teologis-agar-umat-beriman-tidak-merasa-dinista.

Singkil, Aceh. "Island in Focus: Aceh Starts Demolition of Ten Churches." *The Jakarta Post,* October 20, 2015. https://www.thejakartapost.com/news/2015/10/20/island-focus-aceh-starts-demolition-10-churches.html.

Siregar, Liston P. "Mengapa Perda Syariah bermunculan di Indonesia sejak 1998?" *BBC News Indonesia,* February 21, 2017. https://www.bbc.com/indonesia/indonesia-39033231.

Smith, Jane Idleman. *Muslims, Christians, and the Challenge of Interfaith Dialogue.* New York: Oxford University Press, 2007.

Soloway, Benjamin. "Islamist Hard-Liners Attack Indonesian Churches." *Foreign Policy,* October 20, 2015. https://foreignpolicy.com/2015/10/20/islamist-hardliners-attack-indonesian-churches/.

Standing Together: Christians and Muslims Creating Good (website). Accessed October 1, 2019. www.standingtogethernow.org.

Statistical Atlas. "Household Income in the Minneapolis Area (Metro Area)." Accessed May 2, 2020. https://statisticalatlas.com/metro-area/Minnesota/Minneapolis/Household-Income.

Tappert, Theodore G. *The Book of Concord*: *The Confessions of the Evangelical Lutheran Church.* Philadelphia: Fortress, 1959.

Thomas, David, ed. *Christian-Muslim Relations: A Bibliographical History.* 16 vols. Leiden and Boston: Brill, 2009–20.

Thomsen, Mark W. *Christ Crucified: A Twenty-First-Century Missiology of the Cross.* Minneapolis: Lutheran University Press, 2004.

"US Is 'Battling Satan' Says General." *BBC,* October 17, 2003. http://news.bbc.co.uk/2/hi/americas/3199212.stm.

Tracy, Abigail. "'They're As Different As People Come': The Complex Truth about the 'Squad,' Trump's Favorite Foil." *Vanity Fair.* August 16, 2019. https://www.vanityfair.com/news/2019/08/the-squad-donald-trump.

Trice, Michael. "Lutheran and Muslim Relations: An Encounter." In *Christian-Muslim Relations in the Anglican and Lutheran Communions,* edited by David D. Grafton, Joseph F. Duggan, and Jason Craige Harris, 111–26. New York: Palgrave Pivot, 2013.

"UMC Stands Against Islamophobia." *United Methodist Insight,* December 11, 2015. https://um-insight.net/in-the-church/practicing-faith/umc-stands-against-islamophobia/.

United Church of Christ. *On Actions of Hostility against Islam and the Muslim Community.* UCC General Synod Resolution, 2011. http://uccfiles.com/synod/resolutions/Resolution-On-Actions-of-Hostility-Against-Islam.pdf.

United Nations. *Universal Declaration of Human Rights.* 2015. https://www.un.org/en/udhrbook/pdf/udhr_booklet_en_web.pdf.

Virji, Ayaz. *Love Thy Neighbor: A Muslim Doctor's Struggle for Home in Rural America.* New York: Convergent Books, 2019.

Vogelaar, Harold S. "Twenty-Five Years of Christian-Muslim Work at LSTC: 1985–2010." *Currents in Theology and Mission* 37, no. 5 (October 2010) 400–10.

Volf, Miroslav. *Allah: A Christian Response.* New York: HarperOne, 2011.

Index

accompaniment, 33, 80, 81, 82, 89, 90
ACT! for America, 75. *See also*
    Islamophobia
adhan, 87, 94, 153, 166
Ahmadiyyah, 124n3
American Lutheran Church (ALC), 9,
    13, 14n4, 22, 26, 29, 143, 145,
    146, 151
Anti-Defamation League, 73
Anti-sharia laws, 5, 63, 68, 75. *See also*
    Islamophobia
Arab Educational Institute, 120. *See also*
    Lutheran Schools in Palestine
Augsburg University, 81–3, 85, 86
Augusta Victoria Hospital (AVH),
    112–17

bigotry, 38n8, 47, 51–5, 61, 63, 65, 67, 73,
    76, 121. *See also* racism
Bijlefeld, Willem A., 22, 23, 25n24, 26–30
Bonhoeffer, Deitrich, 91, 99–100

Cedar-Riverside, 80–90
A Center for Christian-Muslim
    Engagement for Justice and Peace
    (CCME), 103–10, 174
Christian Muslim Consultant Group
    (CMCG), 92–4, 97

Churchwide Assembly, ELCA, 44, 48n2,
    49, 51, 54, 55, 57, 58, 60, 97, 102
Claremont School of Theology (CST), 91,
    96, 99, 100
"Copernican Revolution," 17
A Common Word, 40, 52, 175
communion, 32, 35, 37, 38, 48n2, 49,
    137–40
Confrèriers, 143, 150
Consultative Panel on Lutheran-Jewish
    Relations, 34–9, 50–1, 56, 57, 58,
    61, 174
Consultative Panel on Lutheran-Muslim
    Relations, 38, 42–6, 52, 56

Dar al-Kalima, 119
    See Lutheran Schools in Palestine
Dar al-Hijrah, 84–6
A Declaration of Ecumenical
    Commitment, 45, 49, 58
A Declaration of Inter-Religious
    Commitment, 7, 15, 45, 50, 58,
    60, 65, 102
A Declaration of the ELCA to People of
    African Descent, 39, 60
A Declaration of the ELCA to the Jewish
    Community, 35, 38, 50, 52, 58,
    61. *See also* Consultative Panel on
    Lutheran-Jewish Relations

diakonia, 115
Division for World Mission and Inter-Church Cooperation (DWMIC), 3, 13, 14, 16, 22, 32

Eaton, Elizabeth, Presiding Bishop, vii–ix, 53, 55–7, 65
ecumenism, 35–6, 46, 49–50
Eid al-Adha, 135, 144
Eid al-Fitr, 135
East Jerusalem, 115, 116, 117
Evangelical Lutheran Church in America (ELCA), vii–xix, 3, 4, 6–8, 13, 15, 18, 29, 31–46, 47–62, 64, 65, 81, 89, 95, 97, 102, 103, 106, 140, 142, 145–47, 150–52, 152–54
Evangelical Lutheran Church in Jordan and the Holy Land (ELCJHL), 117–21
Engaging Others—Knowing Ourselves, 42, 56, 65, 97

"Focus on Islam," 3, 4, 8, 29n28, 146, 151
"full communion," 38, 49, 138–41

God and Jesus: Theological Reflections for Christian-Muslim Dialog, 3, 5, 8, 13–30, 64
Guibord Center, 60, 92

Haddad, Charlie D., 121. See Lutheran Schools in Palestine
Hanson, Mark, Presiding Bishop, 35, 40, 52
Hart-Celler Immigration Act, 15
Hindu Nationalist Party (BJP), 158
Hindus, 60, 127 154–59, 160, 163, 167
Henry Martyn Institute (HMI), xxii, 102
Holy Land, 97, 117. See Evangelical Lutheran Church of Jordan and the Holy Land
human rights, xv, 9, 113, 115, 120, 124, 128, 129, 132, 133, 134, 137, 138
Human Rights Watch, 124
hudud, 162

iconophobia, 162

iftar, 4, 85–7, 94, 97, 98, 104, 113, 121
Indonesian Churches
    Gereja Kristen Indonesia (GKI), 134
    Gereja Kristen Jawa (GKJ), 135, 139
    Gereja Kristen Protestan Pakpak Dairi (GKPPD), 123–36
    Huria Kristen Batak Protestan (HKBP), 131, 138
    Huria Kristen Indonesia (HKI), 123
Inner City Muslim Netork (IMAN), 106, 107
Islamophobia, xv–xvii, 4, 5, 8, 38, 53, 54, 63–76, 90, 106, 121, 154
Islamic Society of North America (ISNA), xii, xiii, 41, 47, 48, 54–6, 58
Institute for Social and Policy Understanding (ISPU), 66, 67

Jerusalem, 3, 9, 111, 112, 114–21
Jesus, viii, 8, 14, 16–22, 28, 36, 37n5, 92, 101, 139, 144, 149, 155

Kaaba, 155
Karnataka, 156, 159, 160
khutbah, 94

LaHurd, Carol Schersten, 34, 105, 109
Lutheran Church in America (LCA), 9n9, 14n4, 22, 26
Lutheran School of Theology at Chicago (LSTC), 32, 55, 103–10. See also CCME
Lutheran Schools in Palestine, 117–21
Lutheran World Federation (LWF), 51, 61, 112–15, 117, 121
Lutheran-Jewish Relations. See Consultative Panel on Lutheran-Jewish Relations

Minneapolis Area Synod, 89, 90
Mediation Program, 119. See also Lutheran Schools in Palestine
mosque, viii, 4, 53, 56, 64. 79, 84–7, 95, 96, 98, 124, 130, 135, 136, 145, 153, 155–7
Majelis Ulama Islam (MUI), 131

nabi, 22
Nahdlatul Ulama (NU), 137
Nanondiral, 141, 142, 146, 147

Oak Creek gurdwara, 59

Palestinians, 97, 112, 113, 115, 116, 118,
    120, 121
Pancasila, 125–29, 133
Park, 51, 75
Public Church Fellows (PCF), 107
Pew Research Center, 5, 129
Program for Christian-Muslim Relations
    in Africa (PROCMURA), 149
Prophet Muhammad, xii, xiii, 1, 8, 23,
    25n24, 105, 154, 162n2

Qur'an, xv, 22, 23, 24, 27, 29, 53, 66, 96,
    105, 162n2, 165

racism, 5, 32, 33, 52, 60, 61, 66, 68, 69,
    70, 72, 73, 108, 121, 137
Ramadan, xi, xiii, 83, 85, 87, 88, 94, 104,
    111, 113
rasul, 22
relational ethics, 98, 99
Roof, Dylan, 73

September 11, viii, xiv, 1, 4, 5, 32–34, 40,
    51, 52, 54, 64, 67, 69, 72, 74, 150,
    159, 161
Shahada, 161, 162, 166
Shelly, Michael, 34, 105
Shi'a, 124n3, 129
shirk, 23, 24, 29, 162

Shoulder to Shoulder, xvi, 38, 41, 53–55,
    58, 105, 108
Senegal Lutheran Development Services
    (SLDS), 141–43, 146–52
Sikh, 57, 59, 60, 69, 108, 155. *See* racism
Singkil, Indonesia, 123–24, 136, 137, 140
Soekarno, 126–28. *See also* Pancasila
Southern California Islamic Center, 92
Standing Together, 92, 93, 178

takbir, 161
Talking Points, 50n7, 52. *See also*
    Consultative Panel on Lutheran
    Muslim Relations
Thomsen, Mark W., 3, 5, 13–18, 29n29,
    32, 34, 103n2
Trinity Lutheran congregation, 80, 86, 89

ulama, 131, 132, 136
Universal Declaration of Human Rights
    (UDHR), 128, 132
United Nations Relief and Works Agency
    (UNRWA), 112, 117
The Urban Hub, 86–88

Vatican II, vii, xii, 2, 36, 37, 44
Vogelaar, Harold S., 22, 34, 103

Walk for Peace, 96–97. *See also*
    Claremont School of Theology
West Bank, 112, 114–16, 119
World Sikh Council, 59

Young Adults in Global Mission
    (YAGM), 150–51